This book examines the relationship between processes of accumulation and aspects of distribution. The analyses of Ricardo and Marx are re-evaluated and redeveloped in the light of advances made by von Neumann, Sraffa and more contemporary theoreticians. Joint production systems are integrated into the analysis which allows the authors to reconsider the problems of choice of technique (in connection with demand analysis), rent theory, the problem of obsolescence of machines and dynamic evolution. New views about standard commodities and blocking goods are also introduced.

Prices, profits and rhythms of accumulation

Prices, profits and rhythms of accumulation

GILBERT ABRAHAM-FROIS
University of Paris X at Nanterre

AND

EDMOND BERREBI
University of Paris X at Nanterre

Translated by
SONIA BEN OUAGRHAM

CAMBRIDGE
UNIVERSITY PRESS

CAMBRIDGE
UNIVERSITY PRESS

University Printing House, Cambridge CB2 8BS, United Kingdom

Cambridge University Press is part of the University of Cambridge.

It furthers the University's mission by disseminating knowledge in the pursuit of education, learning and research at the highest international levels of excellence.

www.cambridge.org
Information on this title: www.cambridge.org/9780521395328

First published 1997

A catalogue record for this publication is available from the British Library

Library of Congress Cataloguing in Publication data

Abraham-Frois, Gilbert.
    [Prix, profits et rythmes d'accumulation.   English]
    Prices, profits and rhythms of accumulation / Gilbert Abraham-Frois and Edmond Berrebi; translated by Sonia Ben Ouagrham.
        p. cm.
    Includes bibliographical references (p.   ) and index.
    ISBN 0 521 39532 1
    1. Prices – Mathematical models.   2. Profit – Mathematical models.
    3. Saving and investment – Mathematical models.   I. Berrebi, Edmond.
    II. Title.
    HB221.A1913   1995
    336.5′2–dc20   94-42383
                                                                CIP

ISBN 978-0-521-39532-8 Hardback

Contents

Preface

How are the prices of reproducible goods determined?

Can the analysis of the distribution of the gross national product and the determination of production prices ignore wants, the level and structure of demand? How does the choice of techniques, a switch in the methods of production, interfere with the accumulation process, the distribution of the gross national product, and therefore with the structure of prices? What kind of relationship is there between market prices and production prices? How should the contemporary analysis contemplate the problem of exploitation and the relation between labour-values and production prices? What is the meaning of the 'standard commodity'? Can the analysis of accumulation limit itself to permanent regimes with constant returns to scale? What is the importance of the 'golden rule' of accumulation? How is the dynamic evolution to be analyzed? . . .

These are the main topics we intend to address in the present book.

We shall more specifically analyse the problems generated by the accumulation and the prices of the so-called 'reproducible' commodities, assuming first that there are constant returns to scale; then we will contemplate the increasing costs of production, the appearance of different kinds of rents, and the determination of natural resources' prices. We shall assume that commodities are reproduced by means of heterogeneous commodities and labour, the supply of which is taken to be unlimited. Production which is, so to speak, pulled by demand, is supposed to be disposed of without any difficulties. At each period, the stocks of the means of production, the available (heterogeneous) commodities that can be used for production, appear to be a constraint, limiting production; this constraint is relaxed as time goes by, owing to accumulation.

The link with the classical approach is thus obvious. the classical school focussed its analysis on 'such commodities only as can be increased in quantity, by the exertion of human industry' (D. Ricardo, 1984, chapter 1) and tended to put aside those for which the quantity could not be increased. Ricardo referred to these as follows.

There are some commodities, the value of which is determined by their scarcity alone. No labour can increase the quantity of such goods, and therefore their value cannot be lowered by an increased supply. Some rare statues and pictures, scarce books and coins, wines of a peculiar quality, which can be made only from grapes grown on a particular soil, of which there is a very limited quantity, are all of this description. Their value is wholly independent of the quantity of labour originally necessary to produce them, and varies with the varying wealth and inclinations of those who are desirous to possess them.

These commodities, however, form a very small part of the mass of commodities daily exchanged in the market. By far the greatest part of those goods which are the objects of desire are procured by labour: and they may be multiplied, not in one country alone, but in many, almost without any assignable limit, if we are disposed to bestow the labour necessary to obtain them.

This approach is not only due to Ricardo; many other classics[1] adopted it and it was approved by Marx (XXXX) in the first pages of *The Poverty of Philosophy*. *Production of Commodities by Means of Commodities* by Sraffa (1960) follows on the same line. However, this considerable work is limited to the price theory while the scope of the classical analysis is much broader, including, among other things, the problems of growth and accumulation of capital which are at the heart of the general equilibrium model due to J. von Neumann (1945–6). The latter introduced the first characteristic of the system he intended to analyse as follows: 'Goods are produced not only from "natural factors of production", but in the first place from each other. These processes of production may be circular, i.e., good G_1 is produced with the aid of good G_2, and G_2 with the aid of G_1.'

In von Neuman's model, consumption is limited to the subsistence level. Such a limitation will be cleared in the very first chapter of the present book. The problems arising from the satisfaction of wants, or demand, are mentioned from the very beginning, and this will allow us to draw a typology of the structures of production and of goods. The accumulation/consumption conflict is indeed quite different, depending on whether joint production prevails and whether it is 'strong' or 'weak'.

The determination of production prices under 'simple' production will be developed in chapter 2; we shall temporarily assume that the choice of the methods of production has been previously made, so that there are as many methods of production as there are commodities to produce.

The analysis of production prices is continued in chapter 3 which deals with peculiar structures of production, the decomposability and irregularity of production systems. Chapter 4 is devoted to a prior study of price systems under joint production; indeed, the decomposability of productive systems brings about some new problems. Joint production cannot be addressed independently of the problems of viability and efficiency of the system, problems that we shall develop in chapter 7.

The meaning and the determination of the invariant standard of value are developed in chapter 5. We shall more particularly emphasise the treatment of decomposable systems where the notion of a blocking sector appears to be relevant. We will show that under joint production there is always a standard of prices. This is to be linked with the existence of a solution to von Neumann's model. Finally, we shall address the standard of activity levels which appears to be the dual of the standard of prices.

Chapter 6 is totally devoted to the analysis of the problems developed by Marx, i.e., the relation between labour values and production prices, as well as between the rate of profit and the rate of exploitation; the reformulation that we shall suggest allows us to maintain a relation between the rate of profit and the rate of exploitation through a specific commodity, or rather, through a combination of activities similar to Sraffa's standard of prices. This will lead us to deal with the problem of luxury goods and the decomposability of productive systems; we shall also examine the difficulties arising from joint production systems where some commodities may have negative labour values; this demonstrates the interest of the notion of separately reproducible goods, defined in chapter 1.

The problem of switch in methods of production or the choice of techniques is dealt with in chapter 7. We shall see that under simple production, the choice among alternative methods of production is made with the view to minimising production costs (von Neumann's rule of profitability). Under joint production, giving up some activities may be the optimal solution, which, in some circumstances, may entail the appearance of free goods available at zero price. The life span of fixed capital, the depreciation of old machines, is analysed under the same principles. Finally, we shall compare the theory of production prices and linear programming.

The last chapter deals with some problems related to the dynamic evolution, where the hypothesis of constant returns to scale is relaxed. Indeed, provided there are no technical improvements leading to new methods of production, the development of accumulation entails increasing difficulties in production, leading to the appearance of differential rents and possibly surplus profits. We shall also analyse the problems due to an intensified use of scarce natural resources. Even if the problems of instability, cycles, and economic crisis are not developed here, this chapter is no doubt at variance with some analyses holding that the theory of production prices can only take into account permanent regimes; change is at the heart of this chapter.

This book builds on previous works.[2] The problems related to demand, the level of activity and the rhythm of accumulation have been developed on the basis of suggestions due to D. Lacaze and Ph. de Lavergne and more recently on those due to Ph. Saucier. We may say that the aim of this book is to link Sraffa's and von Neumann's analyses using at best M. Morishima's, B. Schefold's, I. Steedman's, and N. Salvadori's works. It is certainly to Ch. Bidard that this book owes the most, through his papers, the friendly discussions we had and at the seminars he organised in Paris-X University at Nanterre. On these latter occasions, we had the great pleasure and the great chance to have sometimes passionate but always fruitful discussions with N. Salvadori and P. Garegnani. We certainly will not forget in these acknowlegements A. d'Autume whose numerous contributions allowed us to specify and sometimes correct some of our propositions. We are grateful to G. Dumenil, D. Levy and F. Larbre, for their apposite suggestions. The present book is an English update of our previous work *Prix, profits et rythmes d'accumulation*, published by Economica in 1987.

1   The golden rule of accumulation and prices

Within a simplified model with two goods and two activities (or methods of production), we will graphically analyse some problems related to accumulation, assuming a steady accumulation of means of production at a uniform rate $g \geq 0$ and a rate of profit $r \geq 0$ that is identical in all industries. The golden rule hypothesis, i.e., $r = g$, is not only convenient for drawing figures, but, as we shall see in chapter 7, it is also a sufficient condition allowing to choose efficiently among different methods of production. We will use it extensively in the following pages.

We shall start with a brief typology of the different activities. The obvious difference between 'simple' production and 'joint' production needs to be addressed within a more general context, emphasising the contrast between 'weak' and 'strong' joint production. But situations may vary with the rhythm of accumulation; which explains the notion of joint g-production, that is either weak or strong according to the situation. Through simple diagrams, we will analyse the meaning of the non-substitution theorem and the problem caused by the satisfaction of demand in the different systems we contemplate. We shall also see that the golden rule hypothesis allows to show very simply on the same diagram the evolution of relative prices with the rate of profit.

Then, we will analyse the relationship between the level of consumption (the structure of which is taken to be fixed) and the rhythm of accumulation, though it appears clearly that the relation between both variables is decreasing (which explains the use of the term 'conflict'), the problem has to be dealt with differently according to the kind of model contemplated. Finally we shall emphasise the importance of a peculiar category of goods, i.e., seperately reproducible goods, under joint production. In the simple production case this issue is not relevant since every good is seperately reproducible.

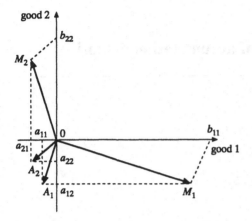

Figure 1.1

1.1 Typology of activities

Before dealing with the issue of accumulation let us first contemplate a stationary economy ($g = 0$) with each activity (i) using a certain quantity of both goods ($x_{i1} \geq 0$, $x_{i2} \geq 0$) and homogeneous labour l_i. As a normalisation hypothesis, we assume that all activities use the same quantity of labour (it may be one hour of work, a man-year, or any labour force available in the economy), taken to be equal to 1. Consequently, we write $a_{i1} = x_{i1}/l_i$ and $a_{i2} = x_{i2}/l_i$ which respectively represent the quantities of each good used in the ith activity when the latter uses one unit of labour. The final consumption structure of both goods is fixed and known; we have $0 < d_1/d_2 < +\infty$.

The hypothesis of a stationary economy ($g = 0$) allows to draw a first typology of activities or methods of production.

The *activity* can be *specialized*, in the sense that it produces only one of both goods exclusively; this is *simple production*.

When both activities are specialised, we have

$$A = \begin{bmatrix} a_{11} & a_{12} \\ a_{21} & a_{22} \end{bmatrix} \qquad B = \begin{bmatrix} b_{11} & 0 \\ 0 & b_{22} \end{bmatrix}$$

For activity 1 which produces only good 1, the quantity produced b_{11} is thus obtained using quantities a_{11} and a_{12} of both goods. Hence figure 1.1 where the quantities of goods 1 and 2 are respectively shown on the vertical and horizontal axes.

The quantities a_{11} and a_{12} of both goods used as inputs are written negatively, which allows to define $\overrightarrow{0A_1}$ as the vector of used inputs.

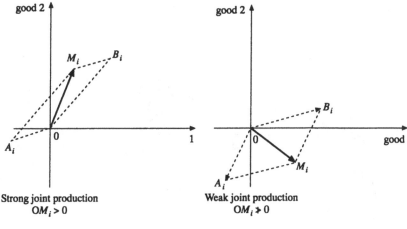

Strong joint production
$OM_i > 0$

Figure 1.2a

Weak joint production
$OM_i \not> 0$

Figure 1.2b

We finally define $\overrightarrow{0M_1} = \overrightarrow{0A_1} + \overrightarrow{0b_{11}}$ as the net product of the considered activity, which is devoted to the production of good 1.

Similarly, if activity 2 is specialised in the production of good 2, $\overrightarrow{0M_2}$ denotes the net product of the considered activity which produces b_{22} by using respectively a_{21} and a_{22} of both goods (plus one unit of labour).

Note that only one of $\overrightarrow{0M_1}$'s and $\overrightarrow{0M_2}$'s components is positive; since each activity is specialised, it produces only one of the two goods.

If the activity is not specialised, it produces both goods simultaneously: this is joint production. If both activities have joint productions:

$$A = \begin{bmatrix} a_{11} & a_{12} \\ a_{21} & a_{22} \end{bmatrix} \qquad B = \begin{bmatrix} b_{11} & b_{12} \\ b_{21} & b_{22} \end{bmatrix}$$

The considered activity produces vector B_i, the components of which, b_{i1} and b_{i2}, are strictly positive. *Joint production is said to be strong* when both components of the net production vector are positive, and *it is said to be weak* in the opposite case (figure 1.2). It is worth noting that weak joint production includes simple production, thus we only need to distinguish between both cases of joint production.

When the economy is not at a stationary state and the rhythm of accumulation g becomes positive, point B_i, representing the gross production of the considered activity, does not move since by assumption we are dealing with the level of production springing from the use of a given quantity of labour equal to unity; however, all the means of production increase at a rate g since we respectively use $(1+g)a_{11}$ and $(1+g)a_{12}$ of each

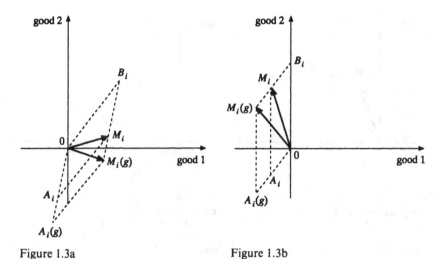

Figure 1.3a   Figure 1.3b

good; thus $A_1(g)$ moves along $\overrightarrow{0A_1}$ with, by construction $0A_1(g)/0A_1$ $= 1+g$; similarly, $M_1(g)$ moves along B_1M_1 with $B_1M_1(g)/B_1M_1 = 1+g$ (figure 1.3).

Thus, we can show the evolution of the activity's net product as a function of the means of production growth rate or rhythm of accumulation; to simplify we shall speak of net g-product.

1.2 Choice of methods of production and satisfaction of demand

In what follows, we shall assume that the economy in question includes several activities[1] or methods of production $1,2,3,\ldots,n$; the growth rate g is given and identical in the whole economy. The structure of demand d_1/d_2 is also given; the methods of production retained are those allowing to maximise the level of consumption (at a given g), i.e., to produce the highest number of consumption baskets. Here, we shall use the terms weak or strong *joint g-production* to remind us that g is given.

1.2.1 Context of weak g-production

In this context which includes simple production, let us first contemplate the case with two methods of production represented by the net g-products M_1 and M_2. In this case, the use of only one of the two methods would not allow the self-replacement of the system, since M_1 and M_2 have negative components: each method is a net user of one or both goods.

However, by using both methods of production, we may in some

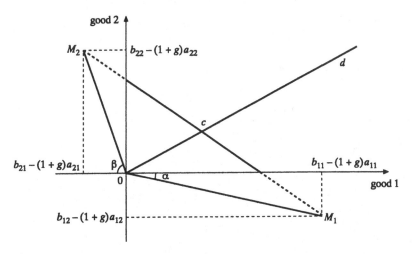

Figure 1.4

conditions obtain a net positive product of each good. These conditions are those underlined by Hawkins and Simon under simple production:

The first requirement is that at the considered growth rate g of the means of production, a net surplus of the first good emerges, that is
$$b_{11} - (1+g)a_{11} > 0$$

The second requirement is shown on figure 1.4. In order to have a positive surplus of both goods, line $M_1 M_2$ must cross the space of goods in the positive quadrant.

Let $|tg\beta| > |tg\alpha|$ and thus $\dfrac{b_{22} - (1+g)a_{22}}{b_{21} - (1+g)a_{21}} > \dfrac{b_{12} - (1+g)a_{12}}{b_{11} - (1+g)a_{11}}$

or also $\begin{vmatrix} b_{11} - (1+g)a_{11} & b_{12} - (1+g)a_{12} \\ b_{21} - (1+g)a_{21} & b_{22} - (1+g)a_{22} \end{vmatrix} > 0$

Hence, $b_{22} - (1+g)a_{22} > 0$, since we are in a context of weak joint production, and thus $b_{12} - (1+g)a_{12} < 0$ and $b_{21} - (1+g)a_{21} < 0$.

On the other hand (see figure 1.5), $b_{11} - (1+g)a_{11} > 0$ and $b_{22} - (1+g)a_{22} > 0$ are necessary but not sufficient conditions to obtain a net positive product of both goods.

If the previous conditions are satisfied, the intersection between segment $M_1 M_2$ and the positive quadrant of the diagram shows the set of consumption possibilities. Indeed, each point on segment $M_1 M_2$ represents a linear combination of two activities using the same quantity of labour (remember that for simplicity's sake we assume it is equal to 1).

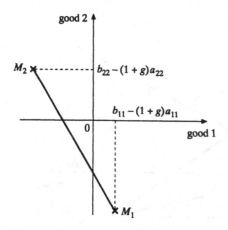

Figure 1.5

Example

Let $M_1 = (-2, +3)$ and $M_2 = (+4, -1)$. Any convex combination of M_1 and M_2 is given by $M = hM_1 + (1-h)M_2$ with $0 \leq h \leq 1$. We can see that $M \geq 0 \Leftrightarrow 1/4 \leq h \leq 2/3$.

Intersection C between M_1M_2 and the line bearing vector d is equal to a number c of baskets $d = (d_1, d_2)$. (Remember that the structure of demand is taken to be fixed.) The ratio CM_1/CM_2 gives the relative importance of employment in both activities. Finally, we note that the simultaneous use of both methods M_1 and M_2 allows us to satisfy any structure of demand: suffice to give line d any slope between 0 and infinity on the diagram.

If a large number of methods of production are available, all of them will not be used. We shall show that, except in the case of collinearity which we will return to in chapter 7, we will use two methods of production to produce two goods (more generally, this means that there are as many methods of production as there are goods to produce and therefore that the system is square).

Among the ten methods of production shown on figure 1.6, it appears clearly that methods M_2 and M_8 are those which, for a given quantity of used labour, allows us to maximise the level of consumption (at a given g). The intersection between M_2M_8 and the positive quadrant (bold on the figure) defines the *efficiency frontier* of the considered economic system. The choice of methods of production defining the efficiency frontier is independent of the structure of consumption, and thus of the direction of line d. We find here the conclusion of the *non-substitution theorem*.

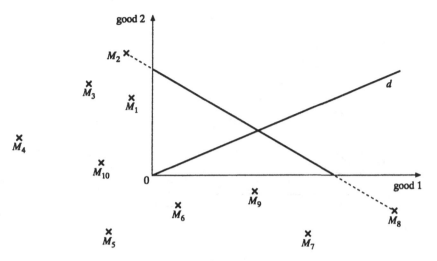

Figure 1.6

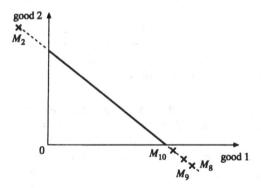

Figure 1.7

Remark

In some cases of collinearity (figure 1.7), the number of activities used can be greater than the number of goods produced. Thus, if activities M_9 and M_{10} are located on segment M_2M_8, in addition to activities 9 and 10 we will be able to use activities 2 and 8.

1.2.2 Context of strong joint g-production

Let us first suppose that to produce both goods, we have at our disposal two methods of production such that their respective net g-productions are

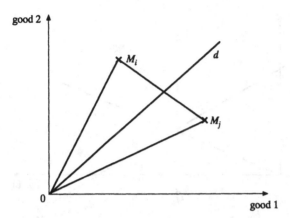

good 2

M_i

d

M_j

0

good 1

Figure 1.8

represented by the coordinates of M_i and M_j. Let f_i and f_j be the slopes of $0M_i$ and $0M_j$ respectively. Then several cases have to be distinguished as a function of what was assumed about the structure of demand (i.e., the slope f of d).

(a) If $f_j < f < f_i$ (see figure 1.8) the demand line is within the cone formed by the net g-production vectors. We have here a case similar to the one contemplated under weak joint production: demand can be perfectly satisfied by using both methods of production simultaneously; both goods are economic goods.

(b) If $0 < f < f_j$, as shown on figure 1.9, demand cannot be perfectly satisfied because it is located outside cone $M_i 0 M_j$. However, it is better to use exclusively activity M_j, whose production structure is closer to d; thus, the supply of good 2 exceeds demand, as line $M_j K$ shows, which is perpendicular to the horizontal axis. Good 2 is thus considered a *free good* or *non-economic* good; it is available at zero price, under the assumption of free disposal. Good 1 is the only economic good. Activity j is the only activity used and keeps on producing two goods, only one of them being considered as an economic good. Consequently, there are *as many economic goods as there are activities* (except in the peculiar cases already contemplated).

(c) If $f_i < f < +\infty$ as shown in figure 1.10, the treatement is symmetrical to b; since demand, whose structure is d, is located outside cone $M_i 0 M_j$, it cannot be perfectly satisfied. However, using exclusively activity $0M_i$ allows us to get closer to the desired structure; as a result, the supply of good 1 exceeds demand (see line $M_i L$, perpendicular to the vertical axis). Thus, good 2 is the only economic good produced by activity (i),

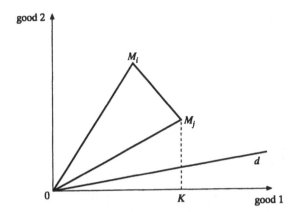

Figure 1.9

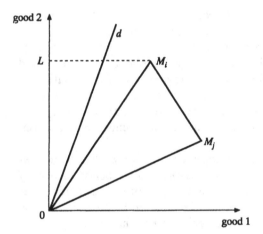

Figure 1.10

which, however, keeps on producing good 1. The latter is a free good
and thus is available at zero price.

Thus, within cone $M_i 0 M_j$, demand can be perfectly satisfied and both
goods are economic goods (we will see later on how their prices are
determined). Outside the cone, demand cannot be perfectly satisfied. Only
one of the goods is an economic good; the good produced in excess is
available at zero price. And there always is an equal number of economic
goods and activities (except in the case of collinearity, contemplated
earlier).

It is also worth studying the case when the structure of demand, the set of

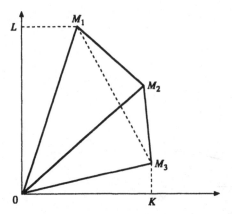

Figure 1.11

desired goods, merges with one of the edges of the cone and thus intersects one apex of the efficiency frontier. Assume for instance that d merges with $0M_j$; then demand would be perfecly satisfied; only one activity would be used to produce two economic goods; and the number of activities would no longer be equal to the number of economic goods. In such a situation we cannot endogenously determine the price system: one price must be considered as fixed exogeneously (we can set it equal to 0 as if it were a free good); the other would be set as a function of the first (under the usual non-negativity constraints).

Thus, except in peculiar cases, this simple example shows that *the systems of production prices are square: i.e., there is an equal number of methods of production and of economic goods* – 'the assumption previously made of the existence of a "second process" can now be replaced by the more general assumption that the number of processes should be equal to the number of commodities' (Sraffa, 1960, para. 50). As a matter of fact, we may also ponder on the relationship between such a statement and the assumption of a fixed structure of wants. The latter is a traditional assumption in classical economics and it is no doubt justified in the first stage of development (Sraffa is very brief on this issue and only talks about 'the proportions in which [the commodities] are required for use' (para. 50, footnote 2). But what happens when consumers are able to substitute one good for another? Then, it is quite possible that, in some cases of joint production, production systems are not square, which generates some problems which we will address in chapter 8.

Under strong g-production, we have up to now limited ourselves to a context with only two methods of production. Let us now relax such a simplified assumption and turn to figure 1.11.

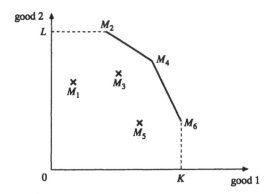

Figure 1.12

In the situation contemplated in figure 1.11, there are three methods of production M_1, M_2, M_3 and demand can be perfectly satisfied whenever the demand line d is located within cone $M_1 0 M_3$. Thus, we have here to consider the outside edges of the cone.

However, within the cone, the choice of methods of production depends on the structure of demand. This is a very different situation from the one prevailing under weak joint production; the non-substitution theorem is not satisfied any more. Indeed, if d is located between $0 M_1$ and $0 M_2$, it is the pair of methods $M_1 M_2$ that will be used; if d is located between $0 M_2$ and $0 M_3$, then we will use the combination $M_2 M_3$. Finally, as indicated earlier, if d is located outside the cone, we shall use only one method, either M_1 or M_3 depending on the situation and one of the goods will become a non-economic good. Therefore, here the efficiency frontier is $L M_1 M_2 M_3 K$. The broken line shows that demand is not perfectly satisfied and that only one activity is used. It is worth noting that combination $M_1 M_3$ (broken line) is no doubt possible for some structures of demand, but it will never be used. Indeed, we can always obtain a greater net product by using either $M_1 M_2$ or $M_2 M_3$. Thus, frontier $L M_1 M_2 M_3 K$ is actually an efficiency frontier in the sense that at given g and d it is not possible to obtain a greater net product by using a different combination of activities.

The same reasoning can be applied to figure 1.12, which shows clearly that activities M_1, M_3 and M_5 are dominated and that the efficiency frontier is $L M_2 M_4 M_6 K$.

If we can choose between activities M_i and M_j (figure 1.13), it appears clearly that at the considered rhythm of accumulation g, M_i will never be used because it is dominated by M_j, in that it produces more of both goods. Thus, the efficiency frontier is here $L M_j K$: there is only one economic good, the other being available at zero price. In this connection, the direction of

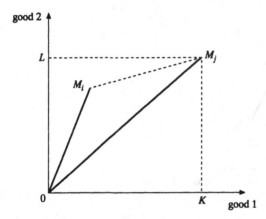

Figure 1.13

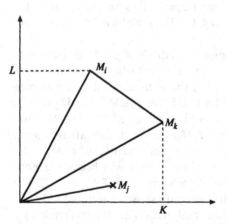

Figure 1.14

the demand line plays a determining role (we have already studied the case where d merges with $0M_j$). This example leads to an important conclusion: the efficiency frontier cannot include increasing segments like M_iM_j in which we can obtain more of both goods simultaneously. Thus, the efficiency frontier is bound to be non-increasing. For example, in figure 1.14, the efficiency frontier is LM_iM_kK and activity M_j is never used (at a given g). The non-increasing aspect of the efficiency frontier refers to the analysis of prices that we will address here very briefly (the system of production prices is dealt with in the following chapters).

1.3 An analysis of the golden rule of prices

Consider an economic system with two activities producing two goods. Remember that we are contemplating the case where for $l_i = 1$ each activity i ($i = 1,2$) produces b_{i1} and b_{i2} quantities of both goods by respectively using a_{i1} and a_{i2} of each of them. Let p_1 and p_2 be the prices of one unit of each good. We assume that all the workers receive the same wage w and that capitalists retrieve a rate of profit r that is uniform for the whole set of the means of production. Thus, the system of (production) prices writes

$$b_{11}p_1 + b_{12}p_2 = (1+r)(a_{11}p_1 + a_{12}p_2) + wl_1$$
$$b_{21}p_1 + b_{22}p_2 = (1+r)(a_{21}p_1 + a_{22}p_2) + wl_2$$

Under the assumption $l_1 = l_2$, by substracting corresponding terms of the previous equations, we have

$$p_1(b_{11} - b_{21}) + p_2(b_{12} - b_{22}) = (1+r)[p_1(a_{11} - a_{21}) + p_2(a_{12} - a_{22})]$$
$$p_1[b_{11} - (1+r)a_{11} - b_{21} + (1+r)a_{21}]$$
$$= p_2[b_{22} - (1+r)a_{22} - b_{12} + (1+r)a_{12}]$$

from which we obtain

$$\frac{p_1}{p_2} = \frac{[b_{22} - (1+r)a_{22}] - [b_{12} - (1+r)a_{12}]}{[b_{11} - (1+r)a_{11}] - [b_{21} - (1+r)a_{21}]}$$

As previously, if we assume that within the same system, growth is the same for all the means of production, the net g-products of each activity are

	good 1	good 2
activity 1	$b_{11} - (1+g)a_{11}$	$b_{12} - (1+g)a_{12}$
activity 2	$b_{21} - (1+g)a_{21}$	$b_{22} - (1+g)a_{22}$

hence figure 1.15.

Then, the slope of the efficiency frontier on segment $M_1 M_2$ can be easily calculated

$$tg\alpha = \frac{b_{22} - (1+g)a_{22} - [b_{12} - (1+g)a_{12}]}{b_{21} - (1+g)a_{21} - [b_{11} - (1+g)a_{11}]}$$

But if this value is compared to the one found earlier for p_1/p_2, we note that

$$r = g \Rightarrow \frac{p_1}{p_2} = -tg\alpha$$

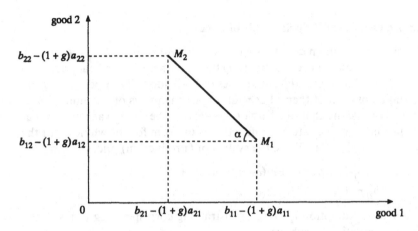

Figure 1.15

Thus, in a golden rule situation, where the rate of profit equals the growth rate, *the price ratio p_1/p_2 is equal to the opposite of the slope of the efficiency frontier*; therefore, it is independent of the structure of demand.

We can see that the non-increasing aspect of the efficiency frontier does not allow negative prices. Negative prices would mean that on a part of the efficiency frontier segment M_iM_j has an increasing slope, which is not possible owing to the requirement set earlier. The efficiency frontier may as well be horizontal ($p_1 = 0$) or vertical ($p_2 = 0$). Then one of the two goods becomes a non-economic good since only one activity is used which no longer allows demand to be perfectly satisfied.

Koopmans (1951, p. 67) notes that on one 'facet', one segment of the efficiency frontier, the price ratio can be interpreted as a marginal rate of substitution. This marginal rate of substitution is constant on each segment of the efficiency frontier. When we shift to another facet, from one segment of the efficiency frontier to another, the marginal rate of substitution cannot be increasing, which rules out a configuration like $M_iM_jM_k$ (figure 1.16): it is indeed obvious that combination M_iM_k dominates combination M_iM_j which cannot belong to the efficiency frontier. Thus, *the marginal rate of substitution is non-increasing.*

Also, it is worth noting that the price ratio p_2/p_1 can be directly represented by the line perpendicular to the efficiency frontier with a slope $-p_1/p_2$ (indeed, the ratio between the slopes of both orthogonal lines is equal to -1). The slope of this perpendicular line directly gives the relative price ratio p_2/p_1 in a golden rule situation.

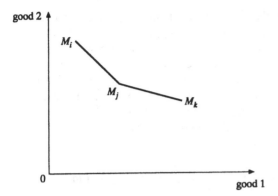

Figure 1.16

1.4 The accumulation–consumption conflict under 'simple' production

Let us first contemplate the case where there are as many methods of production as there are goods; we will relax such a restrictive assumption later on.

1.4.1 An equal number of methods and goods

Let us first contemplate the case where both goods are produced by two activities that are specialised in the production of each of them, in other words we have a context of 'simple production', and there is no choice to make between different techniques; there are two (and only two) activities to produce each good. The system is taken to be productive, i.e., at $g = 0$ there is a net surplus of at least one good. Remember that on a diagram (figure 1.17), this means that $M_1 M_2$ crosses the positive quadrant at $g = 0$. The intersection between $M_1 M_2$ and line d representing the final structure of demand, stands for the maximum level of consumption that can appear in the considered system at a zero rhythm of accumulation.

What happens when the rhythm of accumulation becomes positive and then increases? Note that (refer to Saucier 1984b, p. 170) the coordinates of vectors M_1 and M_2 are decreasing functions of g (more precisely, they are non-increasing functions since one of the goods may not be used as a means of production). If we write M_i^1 and M_i^2 the vectors of net surplus generated by the exclusive allocation of one unit of labour, with growth rates respectively equal to g^1 and g^2 and if $g^1 < g^2$ then $M_i^1 > M_i^2$.

As a result, the set of consumption possibilities pertaining to g^2 ($> g^1$) must be included in the set pertaining to g^1, so that for a higher rhythm of accumulation (g) corresponds a lower level of consumption (c) (whatever the structure of consumption). The relation $c(g)$ is strictly decreasing.

This demonstration can easily be applied to the case with k goods produced (simple production) by k activities. Let A be the matrix ($k \times k$) of inputs, taken to be indecomposable, L be the column vector of labour needs, d the final consumption vector (with $d \geq 0$), c the level of consumption, g the rhythm of accumulation (or the growth rate of the means of production) and y the row vector of the activity levels.

The system of activities then writes

$$yB = (1+g)yA + cd \text{ where } B = \begin{bmatrix} b_{11} & 0 \\ 0 & b_{22} \end{bmatrix} \text{ is a diagonal matrix}$$

It is completed by condition $yL = 1$, expressing the assumption according to which the system uses one unit of labour. (Such an assumption is similar to the one made for the previous simple example, where we used a combination of linear activities so that only one unit of labour was used, the definition of the unit of labour being arbitrary.) The previous system may also write

$$y[B - (1+g)A] = cd$$

Let's first contemplate the following peculiar cases.

If $g = 0$, the surplus is totally consumed; the level of consumption reaches a peak C. The activity level system then writes

$$y[B - A] = Cd \text{ or } y[I - AB^{-1}]B = Cd$$

That is $[I - \bar{A}]CdB^{-1} = C\bar{d}$ with $\bar{A} = AB^{-1} \geq 0$ and $\bar{d} = dB^{-1} > 0$.

Note that multiplying A or d by B^{-1}, is the same as changing units for each of both goods.

Assuming that the system is productive, matrix $(I - \bar{A})$ has an inverse $(I - \bar{A})^{-1}$ which is strictly positive. Thus we have

$$y = C\bar{d}(I - \bar{A})^{-1} > 0$$

Owing to the normalisation hypothesis $yL = 1$ we have

$$1 = yL = C\bar{d}(I - \bar{A})^{-1}L$$

That is

$$C = \frac{1}{\bar{d}(I - \bar{A})^{-1}L}$$

Note: we can define L the vector of direct and indirect labour ('labour values' in the sense of Marx) (see chapter 5) as follows

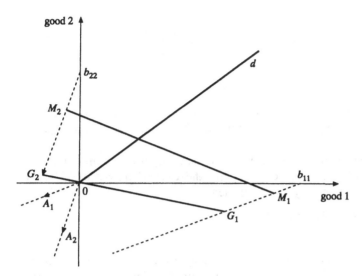

Figure 1.17

$$A = \bar{A}A + L \Rightarrow A = (I - \bar{A})^{-1} L$$

Thus C, the maximum level of consumption of structure d, resulting from the use of one unit of labour in system $(\bar{A}, I, L)$ is such that $Cd\Lambda = 1$: *the labour value of the basket of goods produced with one unit of labour equals unity.*

If $c = 0$, we assume that all the surplus is accumulated, then the growth rate g reaches a peak G, and we have:

$$yB = (1+G)yA \Leftrightarrow \frac{1}{1+G} yB = yA \Leftrightarrow \frac{1}{1+G} y = yAB^{-1} = y\bar{A}$$

The vector of activity levels is then an eigenvector corresponding to the dominant eigenvalue $\alpha = 1/(1+G)$ of the indecomposable matrix $\bar{A} = AB^{-1}$. The Perron-Frobenius theorem ensures that this vector is strictly positive: $y(G) > 0$.

On figure 1.17 representing the case of two goods produced by two activities, this finding shows that for a zero consumption level, both vectors representing the net g-products (written $0G_1$ and $0G_2$) are collinear and points $G_1, 0$ and G_2 are on the same line: line G_1G_2 intersects the origin. Indeed, from $y = (1+G)y\bar{A}$ we obtain

$$y[I - (1+G)\bar{A}] = 0$$

Taking into account the normalisation condition $yL = 1$

$$(y_1, y_2) \begin{bmatrix} 1 - (1+G)\dfrac{a_{11}}{b_{11}} & -(1+G)\dfrac{a_{12}}{b_{22}} \\ -(1+G)\dfrac{a_{21}}{b_{11}} & 1 - (1+G)\dfrac{a_{22}}{b_{22}} \end{bmatrix} = 0$$

Since $y = (y_1, y_2) > 0$, then the determinant of the matrix above is zero: both vectors representing the net G-products of both activities are on the same line.

When $g > G$, there is no net surplus remaining for consumption, that is the reason why we only contemplate the case where $g \in [0\,G[$. The k equations of the activity levels are then

$$yI = (1+g)y\bar{A} + c\bar{d}$$
$$y[I - (1+g)\bar{A}] = c\bar{d}$$

When matrix $\bar{A}$ is indecomposable (as we assume it is here) with the Perron-Frobenius theorem we demonstrate that for all $g \in [0\,G[$ matrix $[I - (1+g)\bar{A}]$ has an inverse; its inverse is positive and an increasing function of g.

Hence

$$y = c\bar{d}[I - (1+g)\bar{A}]^{-1} > 0 \text{ if } c > 0 \text{ and } g \in [0\ G[$$

In view of requirement $yL = 1$, we have $(k+1)$ equations with $k+2$ unknowns (the k levels of activities c and g); if for example g is exogenously determined, then $g \in [0\ G[$, and we can easily determine the consumption level, the activity level vector y and the resulting vector of output yB.

Moreover, from requirement $yL = 1$, we obtain

$$1 = yL = c\bar{d}[I - (1+g)\bar{A}]^{-1}L$$

Hence

$$c = \frac{1}{\bar{d}[I - (1+g)\bar{A}]^{-1}L}$$

As $g \in [0\ G[$, matrix $[I - (1+g)\bar{A}]^{-1}$ is positive and an increasing function of g, then $c(g)$ is a decreasing function of g. On figure 1.18, the intersections between the curve and the axes represent two cases that we have already analysed

$$g = 0 \Rightarrow c(g) = C$$
$$c = 0 \Rightarrow \quad g = G$$

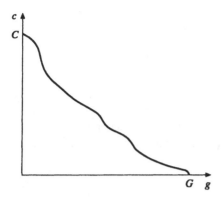

Figure 1.18

Under simple production, the latter case corresponds to von Neumann's model, provided it is assumed that the consumption required by workers is taken into account in the characteristics of matrix A.

Remark

In the case of an economy with two goods and two activities (see G. Abraham-Frois and E. Berrebi, 1980, pp. 12 and 31–3), we can show that the curve $c(g)$ *is convex, linear or concave* depending on whether ratio dAL/dL *is greater than, equal to or less than* the dominant eigenvalue α of the indecomposable matrix A.

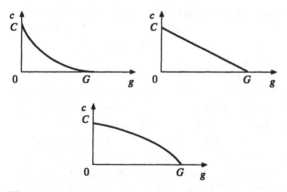

Figure 1.19

Hence, the following three configurations (see figure 1.19):

$$\text{convex curve} \quad \frac{dAL}{dL} > \alpha$$

$$\text{linear curve} \quad \frac{dAL}{dL} = \alpha$$

$$\text{concave curve} \quad \frac{dAL}{dL} < \alpha$$

Further, since we have set $yL = 1$ in the general case of k goods produced by k methods, the relation $c - g$ is linear when L is the eigenvector on the right of the input matrix $\bar{A}$ which corresponds to the case where all the processes have the same organic composition (see chapter 6, section 6.3.2).

1.4.2 More methods than goods

Up to now, we have assumed that there are an equal number of goods and methods of production. This restrictive assumption will be relaxed in the following developments.

Example
Consider an economy with only two goods to produce and where three methods of production are available to meet a demand with a given structure d. We have

$$A = \begin{bmatrix} 5 & 2 \\ \frac{1}{3} & \frac{4}{3} \\ 4 & 3 \end{bmatrix} \quad L = \begin{bmatrix} 1 \\ 1 \\ 1 \end{bmatrix} \quad B = \begin{bmatrix} 10 & 0 \\ 0 & \frac{10}{3} \\ 0 & 10 \end{bmatrix}$$

Now, the problem is to know which method of production to choose in order to produce the second good. The selection criterion is based on the maximisation of the consumption level, that can be obtained per unit of labour (at given g).We will show that *the choice of method varies with the (exogenous) rhythm of accumulation retained.*

We can see on figure 1.20 that, at $g = 0$, the second activity is not used, since segment $M_1^0 M_3^0$ dominates $M_1^0 M_2^0$. When g increases, the net g-products of each activity shift to the directions shown by the arrows. We note that for $G_1 = 25\%$, the three points representing the net g-products of the three activities are on the same line: this is the case we have already mentioned where the number of activities used can be greater than the number of goods produced: for $g_1 = 25\%$, combinations $M_1^1 M_2^1$ and $M_1^1 M_3^1$ allow us to obtain the same level of consumption. At $g > 25\%$, the set of activities 1 and 2 is dominant and remains as such until the maximum rate of profit $R_{12} = 2/3$ is obtained, when points M_1^2 and M_2^2 are lined up with the origin, thus dominating M_3^2 (moreover, note that for $R_{13} = 3/7 < 2/3$ the compound system of activities 1 and 3 is not productive any more).

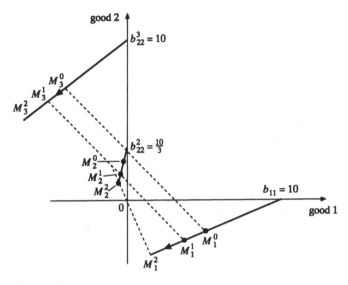

Figure 1.20

$$g=0: M^0 = B-(1+g)A = B-A = \begin{bmatrix} 5 & -2 \\ \frac{-1}{3} & 2 \\ -4 & 7 \end{bmatrix}$$

$$g=\tfrac{1}{4}: M^1 = B-(1+g)A = B-\tfrac{5}{4}A = \begin{bmatrix} \frac{15}{4} & \frac{-5}{2} \\ \frac{-5}{12} & \frac{5}{3} \\ -5 & \frac{25}{4} \end{bmatrix}$$

$$g=\tfrac{2}{3}: M^2 = B-(1+g)A = B-\tfrac{5}{3}A = \begin{bmatrix} \frac{-5}{3} & \frac{-10}{3} \\ \frac{-5}{9} & \frac{10}{9} \\ \frac{-20}{3} & 5 \end{bmatrix}$$

The accumulation growth curve is then represented by the outside envelope of curves $c(g)$ (figure 1.21), each of them plotting one of the systems of activities. As both curves are decreasing, the outside envelope is also decreasing.

For $g \in [0 \; 25$ per cent] it is system (13) which is dominant.

For $g = 25$ per cent both systems allow to obtain the same level of consumption per unit of labour.

For $g \in [25$ percent $3/7]$ it is system (12) which is dominant.

For $g \in [3/7 \; 2/3]$ system (12) is the only productive one.

Thus, under simple production, at a given g, the choice of techniques is independent of the structure of demand. On the figure showing the net g-

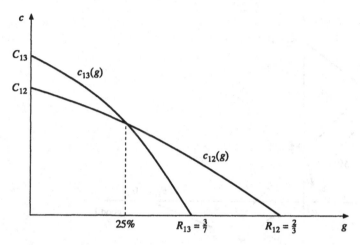

Figure 1.21

products, it appears that one of the two systems of activities dominates the
other (at a given g) whatever the direction *d* chosen. More particularly, if
two systems are compatible at a given growth rate, they are so independently of the structure of demand. This important property stops being
necessarily satisfied under joint production. *But under weak joint production
as under simple production, the choice of techniques depends on g for a given d,
while it is independent of d at a given g.*

1.5 The accumulation–consumption conflict under strong joint production

Weak joint production brings about the same problems as simple production and needs to be analysed in the same way. However, additional
difficulties appear when it comes to analysing strong joint production. For
simplicity's sake, the following developments will be limited to two goods.
They can be applied to a greater number of goods, but this would not allow
a diagrammatic approach.

1.5.1 Joint production can be either weak or strong depending on the rhythm of accumulation

Joint production may be 'strong' for $r = g = 0$, and weak when $r = g = R_0$
(figure 1.22), and remains so until $R = G$. Thus, when $g \in [0 \ R_0[$, demand is
perfectly satisfied only if it is located within the cone formed by vectors $0M_i^g$
and $0M_i^g$, a cone that changes according to g. On the other hand, when
$g \in [R_0 \ R[$ demand is perfectly satisfied whatever its structure. Thus R_0 can

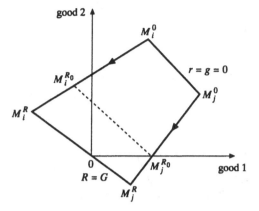

Figure 1.22

be defined as the 'minimum' rate of profit in the sense that in interval $[R_0 \ R[$ all the valid propositions under simple production are satisfied.

Thus it is obvious that the distinction between free and economic goods varies with g (and with d). When $g \in [R_0 \ R[$, the non-substitution theorem is satisfied: both goods are economic goods and their prices are determined by the system of production prices. But for $g \in [0 \ R_0[$ there will necessarily be a free good available at zero price if demand is located outside the cone formed by the net g-product vectors.

It is worth noting that interval $[R_0 \ R[$ does not always exist and that joint production may remain strong all over interval $[0 \ R]$. For instance

$$A = \begin{bmatrix} 1 & 2 \\ 3 & 4 \end{bmatrix} \quad L = \begin{bmatrix} 1 \\ 1 \end{bmatrix} \quad B = \begin{bmatrix} 4 & 4 \\ 1 & 8 \end{bmatrix}$$

for $r = g = 0$, we have

$$M(0) = B - A = \begin{bmatrix} 3 & 2 \\ -2 & 4 \end{bmatrix}$$

The maximum rate of profit is $R = 1$, for which we have

$$M(R) = B - (1 + R)A = \begin{bmatrix} 2 & 0 \\ -5 & 0 \end{bmatrix}$$

When $R = 1$, vectors $0M_1^R$ and $0M_2^R$ are lined up on the horizontal axis. The surplus becomes negative when $r > 1$.

We can see (figure 1.23) that when $r \in [0 \ R[$ joint production remains strong; it stops being so at $r = 1$, the value of the rate of profit (or growth rate) at which the surplus disappears. Thus, there is no interval $[R_0 \ R[$.

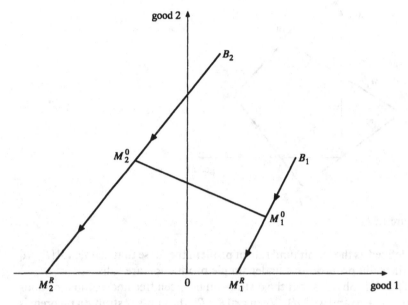

Figure 1.23

Note that this refers to production systems which are at the same time indecomposable and non-basic (vectors A^2 and B^2 are linearly dependent: $A^2 = 2B^2$).

1.5.2 Possibility of reversing the slope of the efficiency frontier

For instance, at $r = 0$ (figure 1.24), the slope of the efficiency frontier is positive: as we have already seen, this corresponds to the case when one activity dominates the other for the considered rates of growth and/or profit; the slope of the frontier becomes null at a rate of profit R_L beyond which both goods can be economic goods provided the structure of demand is located within the cone formed by the net g-products.

It is worth noting that at $r = g \in [0 \ \ R_L]$, both goods cannot be economic goods; one of them will *necessarily* be a free good. Here, the structure of demand intervenes only in determining which of them will be a free good while at $r = g \in [R_L \ \ R_0[$, it helps to find out whether there are free goods. Beyond RL we (may) find interval $[R_0 \ \ R]$ introduced earlier.

This case is particularly interesting since it shows that *labour values* may be negative (the labour-value ratio corresponds to the price ratio at $r = 0$), while production prices may be positive for values of r greater than R_L (we

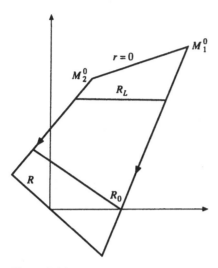

Figure 1.24

will return to this in chapter 6). Indeed, in I. Steedman's arithmetical example (1975), we have

$$A = \begin{bmatrix} 5 & 0 \\ 0 & 10 \end{bmatrix} \qquad L = \begin{bmatrix} 1 \\ 1 \end{bmatrix} \qquad B = \begin{bmatrix} 6 & 1 \\ 3 & 12 \end{bmatrix}$$

When $r \in [0 \ 10\%[$ the slope of the efficiency frontier is positive; we have $R_L = 10\%$, $R_0 = 20\%$ and $G = R = 44.4949\ldots\%$ (figure 1.25).

The difficulties underlined in the previous example also appear in the following example (see Schefold, 1978), where strong joint production prevails only in the first activity. Let

$$A = \begin{bmatrix} \frac{1}{2} & 1 \\ \frac{3}{10} & \frac{1}{5} \end{bmatrix} \qquad B = \begin{bmatrix} \frac{9}{2} & 2 \\ \frac{3}{10} & \frac{4}{5} \end{bmatrix} \qquad L = \begin{bmatrix} 1 \\ 1 \end{bmatrix} \qquad d = (79 \ 4)$$

and, with $r = g$:

$$[B - (1+r)A] = \begin{bmatrix} \dfrac{9}{2} - \dfrac{(1+r)}{2} & 2 - (1+r) \\[2mm] \dfrac{3}{10} - \dfrac{3(1+r)}{10} & \dfrac{4 - (1+r)}{5} \end{bmatrix} = \begin{bmatrix} 4 - \dfrac{r}{2} & 1 - r \\[2mm] -\dfrac{3r}{10} & \dfrac{3-r}{5} \end{bmatrix}$$

Several cases can be contemplated

$$r = 0 \qquad [B - (1+r)A] = [B - A] = \begin{bmatrix} 4 & 1 \\ 0 & \frac{3}{5} \end{bmatrix}$$

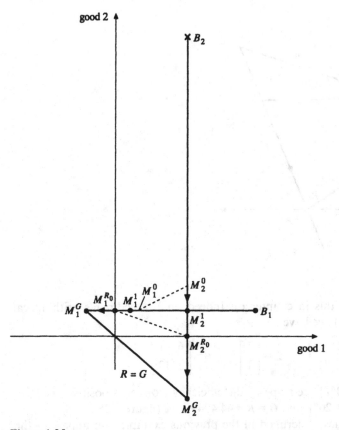

Figure 1.25

The slope of the efficiency frontier $M_1^0 M_2^0$ is then positive (see figure 1.26); owing to the free disposal[2] assumption only method 1 can be used. Moreover, since the structure of demand is $d=(79 \quad 4)$, method 1 produces an excess supply of good 2, and only good 1 is an economic good.

The slope of the efficiency frontier remains positive as long as the net surplus of good 2, produced by method 2, is less than method 1's; when it cancels out, the price of good 2 stops being negative at a particular value of the rate of profit $r_1 = R_L$ such that

$$1-r = \frac{3-r}{5} \Rightarrow r_1 = \frac{1}{2}$$

Hence, the second particular case

$$\text{at } r = \tfrac{1}{2} \qquad [B-(1+r)A] = \begin{bmatrix} \frac{15}{4} & \frac{1}{2} \\ \frac{-3}{20} & \frac{1}{2} \end{bmatrix}$$

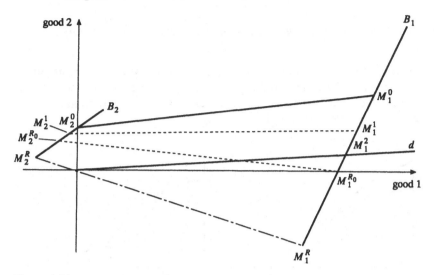

Figure 1.26

The efficiency frontier is parallel to the horizontal axis (see line $M_1^1 M_2^1$). *Owing to the structure of demand, only the first method is used, and the second good remains a free good.*

When the rate of profit (equal to the rate of growth) increases sufficiently, the second good becomes an economic good when the slope of method 1 net g production vector equals the final structure of demand, i.e., when $r = r_2$ such that $\dfrac{4 - r/2}{1-r} = \dfrac{79}{4}$, i.e., $r = 9/11$.

At $r = 9/11$, we have $M_1^2 = (79/22 \ 2/11)$. Then demand can be perfectly satisfied by using method 1 exclusively: one of either good will be arbitrarily considered as an economic good, while the other is a free good.

At $r = g > 9/11$, demand can be satisfied by using a combination of methods (1) and (2). When the rate of profit keeps on increasing, the excess supply of good 2 produced by method 1 decreases, it cancels out when $r = 1$.

At $r = 1$, we have a situation similar to weak joint production (see position $M_1^{R_0} M_0^{R_0}$), where using a combination of both methods allows to satisfy demand whatever its structure. Indeed, we have

$$[B - (1+r)A] = \begin{bmatrix} \frac{7}{2} & 0 \\ \frac{-3}{10} & \frac{2}{5} \end{bmatrix} \quad \text{and thus } R_0 = 1.$$

Finally, at $r = 2$, no surplus may emerge any more and we have $R = G = 2$ (see position $M_1^R M_2^R$). We note that: $[R_0 \ R] = [1 \ 2]$.

1.5.3 The choice of production method may depend on the structure of demand

We know that two techniques, two systems of activities, are compatible when they have the same consumption level at a given g: see point (c^*, g^*) on figure 1.27a. It is worth noting that there may be several compatibility points between techniques (figure 1.27b).

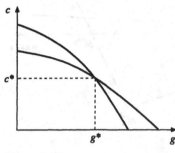

Figure 1.27a   Figure 1.27b

In a context of simple production (and weak joint production), the growth rates pertaining to points of compatibility between techniques are independent of the final structure of demand.

On the other hand, the situation may differ in a context of strong joint production: two techniques may be compatible at different growth rates if the structure of demand varies. In other words, *the choice of techniques does not necessarilly depend on the structure of demand*. This means that here the non-substitution theorem does not hold.

Let us revert to the previous example, we have

$$A = \begin{bmatrix} \frac{1}{2} & 1 \\ \frac{3}{10} & \frac{1}{5} \end{bmatrix} \quad B = \begin{bmatrix} \frac{9}{2} & 2 \\ \frac{3}{10} & \frac{4}{5} \end{bmatrix} \quad L = \begin{bmatrix} 1 \\ 1 \end{bmatrix}$$

(a) If $d = (79\ 4)$, we have seen earlier that with $r = g = 9/11$ two systems are compatible:

at $r \in [0\ 9/11]$ only method 1 is used, and only good 1 is an economic good,

at $r \in [9/11\ 2]$ both methods are used and both goods are economic goods with positive production prices.

(b) If $d = (0\ 1)$, the point of compatibility between techniques appears at $r = g = 1/2$ (see figure 1.26),

at $r \in [0\ 1/2]$ only method 1, which dominates method 2, is used and only good 2 is an economic good,

at $r \in [1/2\ 2]$ both methods are used simultaneously; both goods are economic goods with positive production prices (note that good 1 has a positive price, but its final demand is not positive).

(c) If $d = (1 \ 0)$ techniques are compatible with $r = g = 1$,

at $r \in [0 \ 1]$ method 1 dominates method 2 in the production of good 1 which is the sole economic good,

at $r \in [1 \ 2]$ both methods are used and both goods are economic goods.

This illustration demonstrates that the point of compatibility between two techniques depends on the rate of growth (which, remember, equals the rate of profit). However, this is true only in some intervals:

Indeed, when $r = g \in [1 \ 2]$, weak joint production prevails; in interval $[R_0 \ R[$ (when it is available), compatibility points between techniques are independent of the structure of demand. And beyond the maximum rate of profit $R = 2$, there are no systems allowing production of a positive surplus.

When $r = g \in [0 \ 1/2]$ we can see that activity 1 always dominates activity 2 (the slope of the efficiency frontier would be positive if both activities were simultaneously used). Thus, on this interval, the choice of techniques is independent of demand: the structure of demand matters only in determining which of either good is an economic good, the other being a free good.

Finally, we can check that both techniques are compatible at $r = 4/5$ if $d = (18 \ 1)$ and at $r = 2/3$ if $d = (11 \ 1)$. More generally, both techniques are compatible when the value of the rate of profit is such that the structure of the first activity perfectly satisfies demand d (while the second activity is specialized in the production of good 2). Figure 1.26 also shows that two systems are always compatible when $r = g = 1/2$ if $d_2/d_1 > 2/15$; indeed at $r = 1/2$ the slope of the efficiency frontier is zero and the production structure of the first activity is $(15/4 \ 1/2)$ or $(15/2 \ 1)$.

In any case, curve (c, g) is decreasing; it consists in the (outside) envelopes of curves (c, g) pertaining to each system of production allowing to satisfy demand with positive production prices.

It is worth noting that the problems of compatibility between the two techniques outlined above do not threaten the continuity of the curve; at g_1^* as at g_2^* (see figure 1.27), curve $c(g)$ cannot be derived. It remains continuous. However, the continuity of frontier $c(g)$ may be altered; let us now contemplate such a problem.

1.5.4 The discontinuity of the consumption–accumulation envelope curve (c, g)

This phenomenon was first illustrated by T. Bromek (1974). Let us use his example

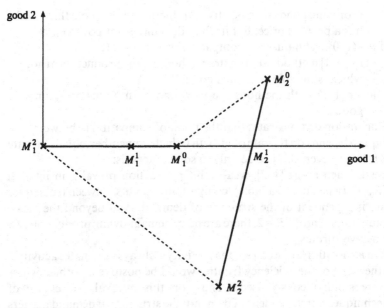

Figure 1.28

$$A = \begin{bmatrix} 1 & 0 \\ \frac{1}{3} & \frac{3}{2} \end{bmatrix} \qquad L = \begin{bmatrix} 1 \\ 1 \end{bmatrix} \qquad B = \begin{bmatrix} 2 & 0 \\ 2 & 2 \end{bmatrix} \qquad d = [1 \ 0]$$

As a result, for

$$r_0 = 0 \quad \text{we have} \quad B - A = M(0) = \begin{bmatrix} 1 & 0 \\ \frac{5}{3} & \frac{1}{2} \end{bmatrix}$$

$$r_1 = \tfrac{1}{3} \quad \text{we have} \quad B - (1 + r_1)A = M = \tfrac{1}{3} = \begin{bmatrix} \frac{2}{3} & 0 \\ \frac{14}{9} & 0 \end{bmatrix}$$

$$r_2 = 1 \quad \text{we have} \quad B - (1 + r_2)A = M(1) = \begin{bmatrix} 0 & 0 \\ \frac{4}{3} & -1 \end{bmatrix}$$

Figure 1.28 shows the different values of the net g-products of these three values of $g = r$.

Owing to the structure of demand $d = (1 \ 0)$, which merges with the horizontal axis, it appears clearly that as long as the second activity is productive, i.e., when $r \in [0 \ 1/3]$, it dominates the first and is the only one to be used, with the second good being a free good.

At $r \in [1/3 \ 1]$ the first activity is the only one that can be used; then, owing to the structure of demand, good 1 is the only good produced. This activity

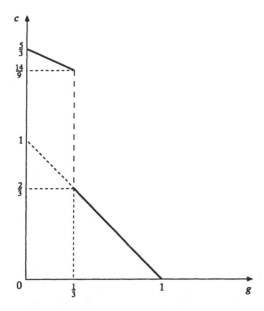

Figure 1.29

stops being productive at $r = 1$, which appears to be the maximum rate of profit of the system.

At $r = g = 1/3$, a discontinuity appears; since, when the rhythm of accumulation g has a greater value, the second activity stops being productive and is replaced by activity 1 which is much less productive at values of $r = g$ less than the critical value; hence, curve $c(g)$ on figure 1.29. Let us emphasise that both segments forming the curve represent curves (c, g) pertaining to two techniques (though reduced to one activity, which have nothing in common but to produce the same goods).

As emphasised by S. Takeda (1983), such a discontinuity is due, not to the fact that one technique stops being optimal (as in a case of switch in techniques), but to the fact that it stops being productive beyond that rate of profit. Such a phenomenon cannot happen when system (A, B) is indecomposable.

It may happen, however, in a simpler case where only one method of production is available to produce both goods.

Let

$$a_i = (1/3 \ 3/2) \quad 1_i = 1 \quad b_i = (2 \ 2) \text{ with } d = (1 \ 0)$$

These data are the same as those characterising the second method in the previous example. We can see that the level of consumption, the structure

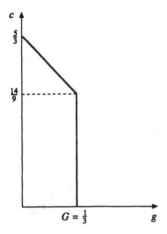

Figure 1.30

for which is $d=(1 \quad 0)$,[3] is positive at the maximum growth rate $G=1/3$. It may be amazing to find out that at the maximum growth rate G as defined by von Neumann in a model which ignores consumption, the consumption level is however positive. The fact is that in the present case consumption applies exclusively to the first good which appears as over-abundant in von Neumann's model (see figure 1.30).

1.5.5 Is the existence of a maximum rate of profit ensured?

If under simple production (and weak joint production) the mere productivity of the system suffices to ensure the existence of a positive maximum rate of growth, the issue is worth examining again under strong joint production. The counter example due to Manara (1968) does show well that there are joint production systems in which there is no maximum rate of profit. Indeed, let

$$A = \begin{bmatrix} 1 & 1.1 \\ 1.1 & 1 \end{bmatrix} \qquad B = \begin{bmatrix} 1.09 & 1.144 \\ 1.144 & 0.99 \end{bmatrix}$$

The determinant of matrix $B-(1+r)A$ equals

$$-0.002836 + 0.0168r - 0.21r^2 < 0 \qquad \forall r$$

Thus the determinant never cancels out and system (A, B) has no maximum rate of profit.

Let us consider this problem again. Since it is assumed that a situation of golden rule prevails $r=g$, and our purpose is to find the maximum rate of growth, we have a von Neumann model.

But we know that as long as system (A, B) is technologically and economically indecomposable, there is a maximum rate of growth G equal to a rate of profit R such that at this rate no activity makes any surplus profits.

This existence theorem, leads to a reconsideration of the model due to Manara. We can demonstrate that there is a maximum rate of profit that is equal to the rate of growth and find its value provided (1) we distinguish between economic and free goods and (2) we assume that labour is necessary to make the system work.

Let us first assume that the second hypothesis is satisfied and let $L = \begin{bmatrix} l_1 \\ l_2 \end{bmatrix} > 0$: at $r = g = 0$, we can determine the net product vectors of both activities M_1^0 and M_2^0. We write:

(a) At $r = g = 0$, the first activity yields a positive net surplus of both goods, that is per unit of labour: $(0.09/l_1 \quad 0.044/l_1)$. When $r = g$ becomes positive the coordinates of the net product vector become

$$\begin{bmatrix} \dfrac{(1.09 - (1+g).1}{l_1} & \dfrac{1.144 - (1+g).1.1}{l_1} \end{bmatrix} = \begin{bmatrix} \dfrac{0.09 - g}{l_1} & \dfrac{0.044 - 1.1g}{l_1} \end{bmatrix}$$

Note that:
  at $g_{12} = 4\%$ the activity's net surplus of good 2 equals zero and becomes negative at $g > 4\%$
  at $g_{11} = 9\%$ the activity's net surplus of good 1 equals zero and becomes negative at $g > 9\%$

(b) At $r = g = 0$, the second activity shows a net product vector that is non-positive $(0.044/l_2 \quad -0.01/l_2)$. When g becomes positive the coordinates of the net g-product vector become

$$\begin{bmatrix} \dfrac{1.144 - (1+g)1.1}{l_2} & \dfrac{0.99 - (1+g).1}{l_2} \end{bmatrix} = \begin{bmatrix} \dfrac{0.044 - 1.1g}{l_2} & \dfrac{-0.01 - g}{l_2} \end{bmatrix}$$

Thus at $g = 0$, this activity only produces a positive net surplus of good 1 while at $g_{22} = 4\%$ the net surplus of good 1 of the same activity is zero and becomes negative at $g > 4\%$.

Figure 1.31 shows the case when $l_1 = 1$ and $l_2 = 1/3$. Indeed, we can show that the efficiency frontier has a negative slope, ensuring positive prices, only when $l_2/l_1 \in [0 \quad 44/90]$. This is demonstrated in the following example (though it is not really significant compared to the topic of our analysis, as we shall see later on).

When g increases, the efficiency frontier $M_1^g M_2^g$ shifts 'south-west'; note that there is no surplus any more when $g = 4\%$. For such a value of g

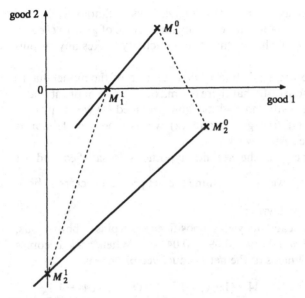

Figure 1.31

(independent of the structure l_1/l_2 considered) the first activity is the only one that can be used.

Thus, the maximum rate of growth (and profit) is 4%. At this rate, only the first activity is used and supplies a net surplus of components (0.05   0). Then good 1 is a free good, and good 2 is the only economic good (here, the structure of demand does not have to be taken into account since, when we seek for the maximum rate of growth, we assume a zero consumption).

Thus, distinguishing free goods from economic goods and the golden rule hypothesis allow us to wave the paradox underlined by Manara and agree with von Neumann's rule. When the system is indecomposable (or for the indecomposable part of a decomposable system), there is always a maximum rate of growth G equal to the rate of profit (and growth) in the sense of Sraffa; to emphasise this, it may happen that some activities (as in Manara's model) are not used because they do not produce any net surplus.

It is worth noting that two activities can be simultaneously used provided (a) demand is satisfied and (b) production prices are positive; in other words, when the efficiency frontier has a negative slope.

But, in the example above (figure 1.32),[4] this requirement is satisfied only if $g \in [0 \ 1.82608\%]$. Beyond that value, the first activity dominates the second and is the only one to be used.

Thus Manara's paradox can be relaxed. It is due to the fact that his model is the opposite extreme of the simple production system in which each

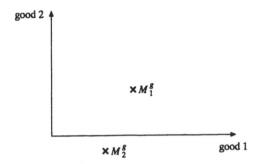

Figure 1.32

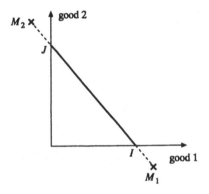

Figure 1.33

activity is specialised in the production of one good. In the case contemplated by Manara both activities produce both goods but they are virtually specialised in the production of the same good: when g increases, both points representing the net g-products move in the same direction in a particular way: they leave the positive quadrant crossing the same axis, that of good 1; this illustrates the fact that both activities first produce good 1 and incidentally good 2. This explains why when $g = G$ the good that is supplied in excess becomes a free good.

1.6 Separately reproducible goods and strong joint production

The simple model with two goods allows to underline the notion of separately reproducible goods. At a given g, let M_1 and M_2 be the net g-products of both activities. If, as shown on figure 1.33, each of the activities is specialised in the production of a specific good, simple production or weak joint production prevails. We know that the intersec-

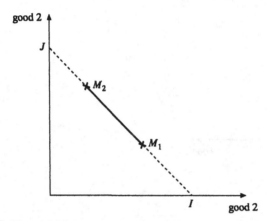

Figure 1.34

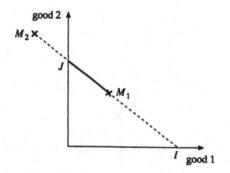

Figure 1.35

tion between M_1M_2 and the positive quadrant represent the line of consumption possibilities: as I and J are the intersection points between M_1M_2 and the axes, we can see that at I and J, good 1 and good 2 respectively, are separately reproducible.

On the other hand, if strong joint production prevails in both activities, none of the goods is separately reproducible (see figure 1.34): points I and J representing the separate production of either good, are not located on line M_1M_2. This situation is economically impossible since it implies a negative use of labour. Therefore, under strong joint production, none of the goods is seperately reproducible. Note also that none of the methods is necessary because a strictly positive net surplus can be obtained through the use of only one of them, which is out of question under simple production or weak joint production.

Of course, we could also analyse the case shown on figure 1.35, with only one of the methods of production being specialised. Then, only one of the goods is separately reproducible.

We can restate this analysis in general terms by introducing the notion of sub-systems definied by Sraffa (1960, appendix A) in *Production of Commodities by Means of Commodities*. Remember that Sraffa calls sub-system i the whole set of activities to which there are coefficients such that the net product of sub-system i consists in one unit of good i.

Let $e_i = (0, \ldots, 0, 1, \ldots, 0)$ be the net product of the system at a given g. Thus we have: $e_i = y[B - (1 + g)A]$

$$y(e_i) = e_i[B - (1 + g)A]^{-1}$$

If the ith line of matrix $[B - (1 + g)A]^{-1}$ obtained from $e_i[B - (1 + g)A]^{-1}$ is positive, good i is *g-separately reproducible*. If $y(e_i)$ has a negative component, good i is said to *be residual*.[5]

It appears clearly that if $[B - (1 + g)A]^{-1} > 0$ all the commodities are g-separately reproducible. Otherwise, some goods would be residual: an increase in good i of the original surplus can be obtained through a decrease in the level of some activities.

We have to underline that if we consider systems with more than two goods, all of the goods can be separately reproducible even though one activity produces a net surplus of more than one good. Thus, in the following example due to Schneider (1985), we can see that at $g = 0$ we have $[B - (1 + g)A]^{-1} = (B - A)^{-1} > 0$, activity 1 produces a net surplus of goods 1 and 3.

$$\text{For } (B - A) = \begin{bmatrix} 3 & -1 & \frac{1}{10} \\ -1 & 3 & -1 \\ -1 & -1 & 3 \end{bmatrix} \text{ we have } (B - A)^{-1} = \begin{bmatrix} 0.329 & 0.142 & 0.034 \\ 0.196 & 0.446 & 0.142 \\ 0.196 & 0.196 & 0.392 \end{bmatrix}$$

In the following case, two activities produce a net surplus of two goods. However, we can see that $(B - A)^{-1} > 0$

$$\text{For } (B - A) = \begin{bmatrix} 3 & -1 & \frac{1}{10} \\ -1 & 3 & -1 \\ \frac{1}{10} & -1 & 3 \end{bmatrix} \Rightarrow (B - A)^{-1} = \begin{bmatrix} 0.378 & 0.137 & 0.033 \\ 0.137 & 0.424 & 0.137 \\ 0.033 & 0.137 & 0.378 \end{bmatrix}$$

As underlined by Schefold (1978b), at $g = 0$, all the goods are separately reproducible in systems where $(B - A)^{-1} > 0$ (and more particularly in systems of simple production or weak joint production). Such a system is said to be 'all-engaging' because a net product can be obtained only if all the activities are actually used. If this requirement is not satisfied, the joint production systems include activities that are not necessary; which was emphasised in a simple example with two goods and two activities.[6]

Thus, the important opposition of production systems cannot be based, at a given g, on the simple production–joint production criterion. Indeed, we have seen that weak joint production does not pose any more problems than simple production. However, we cannot limit ourselves to comparing weak joint production to strong joint production, making of simple production a peculiar case of weak joint production.

Indeed, we have seen that, beyond the simple case of an economy with two goods and two activities, all the properties of simple production appear while some activities, at a given g, produce a net surplus of several goods. To obtain this suffices, but the condition is important, that all goods are separately reproducible, or, which is equivalent, that all the methods of production are necessary. Mathematically, this comes down to knowing whether matrix $[B - (1 + g)A]^{-1}$ has non-positive elements.

We have to underline that we have been reasoning with a given g. But as we have seen, and we will revert to this in chapter 3, with a value of g close to the maximum rate of growth, we can obtain in a golden rule situation, the usual and safe framework of simple production systems. Paradoxically, when the rhythm of accumulation becomes sufficient, all the goods become g-separately reproducible.

2 Systems of production prices

In this chapter we shall examine the problem of the determination of prices following Sraffa's (1960) approach in *Production of Commodities by Means of Commodities*.[1] We will first contemplate the problem of the determination of prices in a case of production for subsistence, a world of robots where there is no final consumption. There is no surplus, and prices which make it possible for the production process to be repeated spring directly from the methods of production. In a sense, we have here pure production prices. As soon as the economic system produces more than the minimum that is necessary to replace what was used up for production, the exchange values cannot be determined as in the previous case: there is a fundamental interaction between prices and distributive variables. The notion of 'wage-prices' will allow us to specify the relationship between wage and profit, the form of which depends on the numeraire chosen to evaluate prices and wages. After we will show that production prices may be considered as dated quantities of labour (this is the problem of 'reduction') and that we can easily shift from the hypothesis of wages as a share of surplus to the hypothesis of 'advanced' wages.

Our framework of analysis here is simple production with specialised activities, while industry systems under joint production are developed in chapter 4. Finally, since irregular decomposable systems are addressed in detail in chapter 3, we shall limit the analysis of the present chapter to regular indecomposable systems.

2.1 A world of robots: production for subsistence

Consider a society which produces just enough to maintain itself, that is to say, every commodity produced is entirely consumed either as a means of production or for subsistence. The system is said to be in a self-replacing state.

More generally, we consider k commodities, each of which is produced by a separate industry. Let a_{ij} be the quantity of good j necessary to produce one unit of good i; the vector of inputs needed to produce one unit of good i is $(a_{i1}, a_{i2}, \ldots, a_{ij}, \ldots, a_{ik})$, and we need not assume that every good enters into the production of every other. Consequently, some a_{ij} may be zeros.

Note that for every commodity, we have $\sum\limits_{i=1}^{k} a_{ij} = 1$ since, by assumption, in a self-replacing system, the quantity of goods consumed $\sum\limits_{i=1}^{k} a_{ij}$ and the quantity of goods j produced (equal to unity, as seen earlier) is equal.

We assume that every quantity produced and consumed is known; the unknowns to be determined are $p_1, p_2, \ldots, p_k$, representing the values of units of k commodities which, if adopted, restore 'the original distribution of the products and makes it possible for the process to be repeated; such values spring directly from the methods of production' (P.S. 1).

Indeed k prices are the solution to the following system

$$\begin{cases} a_{11}p_1 + \ldots + a_{1j}p_j + \ldots + a_{1k}p_k = p_1 \\ \ \cdots\cdots\cdots\cdots\cdots\cdots\cdots\cdots\cdots\cdots \\ a_{i1}p_1 + \ldots + a_{ij}p_j + \ldots + a_{ik}p_k = p_i \\ \ \cdots\cdots\cdots\cdots\cdots\cdots\cdots\cdots\cdots\cdots \\ a_{k1}p_1 + \ldots + a_{kj}p_j + \ldots + a_{kk}p_k = p_k \end{cases}$$

Let $Ap = p$ where $A = [a_{ij}]$ and $p = [p_j]$.
$\qquad\qquad\qquad\quad (k,k)\qquad\qquad (k,1)$

The price vector p appears as the eigenvector of matrix A corresponding to the dominant eigenvalue 1 of A. Vector p is defined up to the multiplication by scalars, since we can choose any value of any good (or any combination of goods), as the standard of value: this leaves only $k-1$ unknowns.[2]

Further there are k equations, but only $(k-1)$ of them are independent; indeed, since we assume that the system is in a self-replacing state, the sum of each column is equal to 1. By adding up all the equations, the same quantities occur on both sides: then, any one of the equations can be inferred from the sum of the other $(k-1)$. This leaves only '$k-1$ independent linear equations which uniquely determine the $k-1$ prices'.[3]

Having equal numbers of equations and unknowns is not sufficient to ensure the positivity of prices. However, we have implicitly assumed that matrix A is indecomposable. In such conditions, we know that the eigenvector corresponding to the dominant eigenvalue of an indecomposable matrix is strictly positive. Thus all the prices are strictly positive and uniquely defined (up to the multiplication by scalars).

As an illustration, matrix

$$A = \begin{bmatrix} 8/15 & 4/7 & 3/10 \\ 1/5 & 2/7 & 1/5 \\ 4/15 & 1/7 & 1/2 \end{bmatrix}$$

has 1 as its dominant eigenvalue because the sum of every column is equal to 1; the corresponding eigenvector is $p = \begin{bmatrix} 1.5 \\ 0.7 \\ 1 \end{bmatrix}$ (or any homothetic vector),

which satisfies $Ap = p$.

Note related to the change of units

The example above is one of those given by Sraffa when he analyses production for subsistence; but our presentation is a little different and lets us address the problem of switch in (and choice of) units of different commodities. The economic system presented by Sraffa is:

240 quarters wheat + 12 tons iron + 18 pigs → 450 quarters wheat

90 quarters wheat + 6 tons iron + 12 pigs → 21 tons iron

120 quarters wheat + 3 tons iron + 30 pigs → 60 pigs

Besides, the author adds that the exchange values which ensure replacement all round are

10 quarters wheat = 1 ton iron = 2 pigs.

Using one formulation or the other and obtaining matrix A is rather easy if the unit used is the produced quantity of each commodity, that is to say, 450 quarters of wheat, 21 tons of iron, and 60 pigs respectively. Technically this means that matrix A is obtained by dividing every figure of every column of Sraffa's system by the quantity of output used as unit (returns to scale are not considered here; if we assumed constant returns to scale, this would come down to multiplying or dividing every *line* of the previous system by the same number). Such a treatment is interesting for it allows us to apply linear algebra theorems which assume that the production matrix is the unit matrix I.

It is worth noting that the price vector obtained as the solution to $Ap = p$, concerns the relative prices of the quantities chosen as units. In the example above this would mean that if 1 is the 'cost' of 60 pigs, then 0.7 is the 'cost' of 21 tons of iron and 1.5 is the 'cost' of 450 quarters of wheat. If we want to obtain prices p_1, p_2, p_3 of 1 quarter of wheat, 1 ton of iron and 1 pig, suffice to divide every element of the price vector previously obtained by the corresponding quantity; hence

$$p_1 = \frac{1.5}{450} \qquad p_2 = \frac{0.7}{21} \qquad p_3 = \frac{1}{60}$$

or also, since this vector is defined up to the multiplication by scalars,

$$p_1 = 0.2 \qquad p_2 = 2 \qquad p_3 = 1$$

As the ratio of exchange values x_1, x_2, x_3 is the opposite of the price ratio, as indicated by Sraffa, the exchange value required is 10 quarters of wheat for 1 ton of iron and/or 2 pigs. Indeed, by definition we have $p_1 x_1 = p_2 x_2 = p_3 x_3$, hence the figures above.

Thus, the solution is unique and always positive. The exchange values are determined by the production (and reproduction) conditions of the system, each industry exactly covering its production costs without surplus or deficit. The problem is different when there is a surplus.

2.2 Sharing out the surplus

If the economic system produces more than the minimum necessary for replacement of what was used up in production and there is a surplus to be distributed,[4] the exchange values cannot be determined as in a context of production for subsistence.

2.2.1 Assuming a uniform rate of profit

The relationship between prices and distributive variables appears here with the problem of distributing any surplus. Sraffa assumes that 'the surplus (or profit) must be determined through the same mechanism and at the same time as are the prices of commodities' (P.S. 4–5).

Indeed, if we add the rate of profit r (which must be uniform for all industries) as an unknown, the system becomes

$$\begin{cases} a_{11}p_1 + \ldots + a_{1j}p_j + \ldots + a_{1k}p_k(1+r) = p_1 \\ \ldots\ldots\ldots\ldots\ldots\ldots\ldots\ldots\ldots\ldots\ldots \\ a_{i1}p_1 + \ldots + a_{ij}p_j + \ldots + a_{ik}p_k(1+r) = p_i \\ \ldots\ldots\ldots\ldots\ldots\ldots\ldots\ldots\ldots\ldots\ldots \\ a_{k1}p_1 + \ldots + a_{kj}p_j + \ldots + a_{kk}p_k(1+r) = p_k \end{cases}$$

or in matrix notation

$$Ap(1+r) = p \Rightarrow Ap = \frac{1}{1+r}p$$

which means that p is the eigenvector corresponding to the dominant eigenvalue $1/(1+r)$.[5] Accordingly, we simultaneously determine the dominant eigenvalue $1/(1+r)$ of A, i.e., the rate of profit r and the corresponding eigenvector p, and $(k-1)$ relative prices.

As an example, let us use Sraffa's two-commodity system, wheat and iron, where there is a surplus of 175 quarters of wheat and no surplus of iron. By assumption the resulting production equations are the following

$$\begin{cases} 280 \text{ quarters wheat} + 12 \text{ tons iron} \rightarrow 575 \text{ quarters wheat} \\ 120 \text{ quarters wheat} + 8 \text{ tons iron} \rightarrow 20 \text{ tons iron} \end{cases}$$

Prices and the rate of profit can be easily determined simultaneously by writing the system under the following form

$$Ap = \frac{1}{1+r} p$$

or also[6]

$$\begin{bmatrix} \frac{56}{115} & 0.6 \\ \frac{24}{115} & 0.4 \end{bmatrix} \begin{bmatrix} p_1 \\ p_2 \end{bmatrix} = \frac{1}{1+r} \begin{bmatrix} p_1 \\ p_2 \end{bmatrix}$$

By calling $\alpha = 1/(1+r)$ the dominant eigenvalue of matrix A, the characteristic equation $\det(A - \alpha I) = 0$ allows us to determine $\alpha = 92/115$ and thus $r = 25\%$.[7]

The eigenvector $\begin{bmatrix} p_1 \\ p_2 \end{bmatrix}$ corresponding to $\frac{1}{1+r} = \frac{92}{115}$ is such that $\frac{56}{115} p_1 + 0.6 p_2 = \frac{92}{115} p_1$ or also $0.6 p_2 = \frac{36}{115} p_1$. Then, $p_2 = \frac{60}{115} p_1 = \frac{12}{23} p_1$ that is to say $\begin{bmatrix} p_1 \\ p_2 \end{bmatrix} = \begin{bmatrix} 23 \\ 12 \end{bmatrix}$. Which means that we will need 575 quarters of wheat to get 20 tons of iron, the relative price ratio of both quantities is given in the previous relation. As a result, prices p_1 and p_2 of 1 quarter of wheat and 1 ton of iron are respectively $p_1 = 23/575 = 1/25$ and $p_2 = 12/20 = 0.6$, or by multiplying both elements of the price vector by 25, we obtain: $p_1 = 1$, $p_2 = 15$. Accordingly, the exchange value of 15 quarters of wheat (good 1) is 1 ton of iron (good 2).

2.2.2 Workers' wages

How can worker's wages be taken into account?

As Sraffa puts it 'we have up to this point regarded wages as consisting of the necessary subsistence of the workers and thus entering the system on the same footing as the fuel for the engines or the feed for the cattle' (P.S. 8). We may also consider that they include a share of the surplus. In view of this, he continues, it would be appropriate to separate the two component parts of the wage and regard only the 'surplus' part as variable. However, Sraffa immediately abandons this assumption and then treats the whole of the wage as variable, that is to say, paid post-factum as a part of the annual product while the classics considered that the wage was advanced from capital.

The subsistence quantities do not appear in the technology matrix any more. The quantity of labour employed in each industry has now to be represented explicitly by assuming, for the moment, a uniform quality of labour.

We call $l_1, l_2, \ldots, l_k$, the quantities of labour necessary to produce one unit of each good.

We call 'w' the wage per unit of labour, which, as prices, will be expressed in terms of the chosen numeraire.

On this basis, the equations take the form

$$\begin{cases} a_{11}p_1 + \ldots + a_{1j}p_j + \ldots + a_{1k}p_k(1+r) + wl_1 = p_1 \\ a_{i1}p_1 + \ldots + a_{ij}p_j + \ldots + a_{ik}p_k(1+r) + wl_i = p_i \\ a_{k1}p_1 + \ldots + a_{kj}p_j + \ldots + a_{kk}p_k(1+r) + wl_k = p_k \end{cases}$$

which can be reformulated as follows

$$(1+r)Ap + wl = p$$

$$\text{with } p = \begin{bmatrix} p_1 \\ \vdots \\ p_i \\ \vdots \\ p_k \end{bmatrix} \quad L = \begin{bmatrix} l_1 \\ \vdots \\ l_i \\ \vdots \\ l_k \end{bmatrix}$$

2.2.3 *The numeraire: arbitrary and necessary*

We have here a system of k equations (i.e., k production equations since we assume that only one method of production[8] is available to produce each good), with $k+2$ unknowns: k prices and both distributive variables (w and r). Since we are interested in the exchange ratio, i.e., the structure of relative prices, it is always possible to express all the prices in terms of the price of a particular commodity by making $p_i = 1$, or more exactly by making the value of a quantity of the ith commodity u_i equal to unity, that is to say, $u_i p_i = 1$ (of course, suffice to choose a quantity equal to unity, $u_i = 1$, to obtain the traditional formulation); more generally the normalisation condition can be written as follows

$$up = 1 \quad \text{with} \quad u = (u_1, u_2, \ldots, u_i, \ldots, u_k) \geq 0$$

Then, it is the value of the composite commodity u which is set equal to unity. Note that in chapter 2 of *Production of Commodities by Means of Commodities*, Sraffa chooses to normalise the system of prices by making the value of 'the set of commodities' which form 'the national income' equal to unity. If we let y be the row vector of activity levels in the economy in question, namely $y = (y_1, y_2, \ldots, y_i, \ldots, y_k)$, then the normalisation condition proposed by Sraffa leads to choosing $u = y(I - A)$ where $y(I - A)p = 1$.

Thus, owing to the normalisation condition, the system of equations writes

$$p = (1 + r)Ap + wL \quad \text{with} \quad up = 1$$

This gives $k + 1$ equations (k production equations and the normalisation equation) with $k + 2$ unknowns (k prices and two distributive variables).

The result of this is that *the equation system is not sufficient to determine the unknowns*; one of the unknowns is taken to be fixed, the other is exogenously fixed and the system presents a degree of freedom.

It is generally convenient to consider that one of the distributive variables is exogenous; as the need arises, Sraffa alternatively considers the rate of profit and the wage as being exogenous. At such a level of abstraction, what is important is to emphasise that once the value of one of the two distributive variables is set, the value of the other is fixed *at the same time* as the set of production prices (here, matrix A is taken to be indecomposable and thus all goods are 'basic' goods; the decomposability of the technology matrix is addressed in chapter 3). Further, it is frequently more convenient to consider r, which is a percentage, as exogenous; while the level of wages, as prices, is determined as a function of the chosen numeraire: assuming that w is exogenous implies that the numeraire has already been determined.

A different way of addressing the problem consists in taking the wage level as the numeraire of the whole set of prices; prices are then determined in terms of wages; this is what we can call for short 'wage-prices'; then the system of equations writes

$$p = (1 + r)Ap + wL \quad \text{with} \quad w = 1$$

or

$$\frac{p}{w} = (1 + r)A \frac{p}{w} + L$$

Under either of these forms, it appears clearly that the system presents a degree of freedom and we can directly consider the distortion in the price system as a function of the rate of profit taken to be exogenous.[9]

2.2.4 *Prices of production: existence, uniqueness and positivity*

In what follows, we shall limit our analysis to cases of economic interest, namely the incomes distributed between different social groups (capitalists and workers) cannot be negative.

If wages equal zero, the whole surplus goes to capitalists; profit is then at a maximum rate and is written R, the system of production prices then becomes

$$p=(1+R)Ap \qquad \text{or also} \quad \frac{1}{1+R}p=Ap$$

The vector of production prices p is the eigenvector corresponding to the dominant eigenvalue $\alpha = 1/(1+R)$ of the indecomposable matrix A; according to the Perron-Frobenius theorem, this vector is unique (up to the multiplication by scalars) and strictly positive. We can see that in the case of production for subsistence contemplated earlier, we had $R=0 \Leftrightarrow \alpha = 1$: we note that

$$\alpha = \frac{1}{1+R} < 1 \Rightarrow R > 0$$

When profit equals zero, the whole surplus goes to workers; the wage is at a maximum rate $w(0)=W$, with $r=0$, the system of production prices then becomes

$$p=Ap+wL$$

We then revert to Leontief prices and since matrix $(I-A)$ has an inverse, we have

$$p=w(I-A)^{-1}L$$

and $\frac{p}{w}(I-A)^{-1}L=(I+A+A^2+...+A^n+...)L$.

When $r=0$, wage prices appear as the quantities of indirect and direct labour entering the production of the different commodities, that is to say, the labour values in the sense of Marx.

Let

$$\frac{p(0)}{w}=L=(I-A)^{-1}L$$

For all r included between 0 and the maximum value R, the system of production prices becomes

$$p=(1+r)Ap+wL \quad \text{with } up=1$$

from which we obtain $[I-(1+r)A]p=wL$ with $up=1$.

Matrix $[I-(1+r)A]$ has an inverse when $r\in[0 \ R[$ and its inverse is positive; Thus the production prices of the commodities are defined uniquely up to the multiplication by scalars and are strictly positive

$$\begin{cases} p = w[I - (1+r)A]^{-1} L \text{ for all } r \in [0 \quad R[\\ up = 1 \end{cases}$$

Remember that at $r = R$, matrix $[I - (1+r)A]$ has no inverse; the existence, uniqueness and positivity of every price is ensured by the Perron-Frobenius theorem since then $p = (1+R)Ap$.

2.3 Wage prices and wage–profit relations

2.3.1 Characteristics of wage prices

Wage prices are all *positive* and *decreasing functions of the rate of profit* at $r \in [0 \quad R[$. Indeed, from the definition of the system of wage prices

$$\frac{p}{w} = (1+r)A \frac{p}{w} + L$$

we obtain $[I - (1+r)A] \dfrac{p}{w} = L$, and matrix $[I - (1+r)A]$ having an inverse in

the interval where r is analysed, we have

$$\frac{p}{w} = [I - (1+r)A^{-1}]L$$

$$= [I + (1+r)A + (1+r)^2 A^2 + \ldots + (1+r)^n A^n + \ldots]L$$

We know that when $r = 0$, wage prices are equal to labour values in the sense of Marx. When $r \to R$ wage prices are increasing towards infinity; their increase does not obey any law, which means that the structure of relative prices is altered when r increases; figure 2.1 shows a possible evolution of some wage prices. Remember that at $r = R$, wage prices are not defined but the structure of relative prices can be determined by the Perron-Frobenius theorem.

2.3.2 The wage–profit relation

We can enhance an implicit relation, or rather a series of implicit relations between the wage (w) and the profit (r). Indeed, for a given set of methods of production represented by matrix A and vector L, there are as many wage–profit relations as there are numeraires of prices; all these curves are decreasing and intersect point ($r = R, w = 0$). Indeed, from the k equations of prices, we obtain

$$[I - (1+r)A]p = wL \text{ that is, } p(r) = w(r)[I - (1+r)A]^{-1}L$$

where for $r \in [0, R[, [I - (1+r)A]^{-1} > 0$.

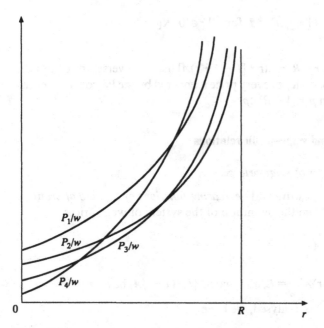

Figure 2.1

From the normalisation condition $up = 1$, we obtain

$$1 = up = wu[I - (1 + r)A]^{-1}L$$

hence

$$w_u = \frac{1}{u[I - (1 + r)A]^{-1}L}$$

which is a decreasing function of r in interval $[0, R[$ since $[I - (1 + r)A]^{-1}$ is an increasing function of r in this interval.

It appears clearly that the wage is a decreasing function of the rate of profit in the considered interval, whatever the commodity u chosen as a standard. The curve (figure 2.2) intersects the axis for $r = R$ which is independent of the numeraire and for the maximum wage $w_u(0)$ written $W_u = 1/u\Lambda$ since at $r = 0$ $[I - (1 + r)A]^{-1}$, $L = [I - A]^{-1}L = \Lambda$, the vector of labour values. The exact form of the wage–profit relation also depends on the chosen standard u; this is the reason why we have chosen to write it $w_u(r)$.

In this connection, let us revert to the normalisation condition of the system of prices initially imposed by Sraffa. We have already seen (see 2.2.3.) that this condition consisted in setting the value of the whole set of

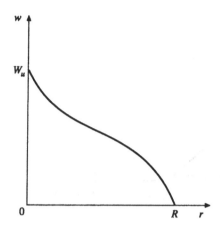

Figure 2.2

commodities forming the national income equal to 1, i.e., with the previous notations

$$y(I - A)p = 1$$

From the definition equation of the system of prices, we have $yp = (1 + r)yAp + wyL$ and $ryAp + wyL = yp - yAp = y(I - A)p$ and thus $ryAp + wyL = 1$.

The total value of the national income, the sum of wages and profits, is set equal to unity, whatever the wage or the rate of profit. In the peculiar case when the rate of profit is zero ($r = 0$) the wage is then at a maximum level W such that $W = 1/yL$. Further, it may be convenient to assume that the total labour is equal to 1, which comes down to taking the total annual labour of society as unit (see P.S. 10). In such conditions, the wage–profit curve intersects point ($r = 0$, $W = 1$) and the wage (at $r > 0$) represents fractions of the national income (P.S. 13).

Such a process can be generalised; whatever the commodity chosen as a standard, we can make sure that curve $w_u(r)$ crosses point ($r = 0$, $W_u = 1$). Such a condition comes down to writing $up(0) = 1$.

Since $p(0) = W(I - A)^{-1}L = (I - A)^{-1}L$ with $W = 1$ and $\Lambda = (I - A)^{-1}L$

$$up(0) = uL = 1 \Leftrightarrow W = 1$$

Then, all the curves $w_u(r)$ cross point ($r = 0$, $W = 1$). It is worth noting that we could have chosen to make the wage–profit curve (and thus all the curves $w(r)$) cross another point. Indeed, for any given structure of u, we can always choose the level of u by writing: $u[I - (1 + r_0)A]^{-1}L = C$ (C being any

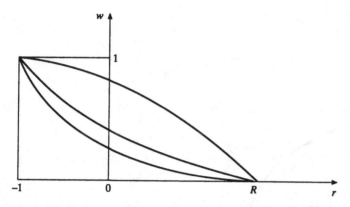

Figure 2.3

positive scalar) for $r_0 \in [-1, R[$, an interval in which matrix $[I - (1 + r_0)A]^{-1}$ is positive.

Thus, the choice of numeraire poses both a problem of structure and a problem of level that it would be convenient (but not necessary) to separate. We can note that choosing the standard comes down to making all the curves $w_u(r)$ cross a common intersection point different from R (which is already common to all the wage–profit curves).

Example

If we choose $r_0 = -1$ and $C = 1$, the normalisation condition of prices writes

$$u[I - (1-1)A]^{-1}L = uL = 1$$

That is $W_u = 1$ for $r_0 = -1$ whatever the value of u.

This gives the following wage–profit curves (see figure 2.3) characterising the considered technique at different numeraires.

The exact form of the curve depends both on the structure of production (of matrix A and vector L) and on the numeraire. We have shown (Abraham-Frois and Berrebi, 1980, pp. 12 and 13) that, in the specific model with two goods and two activities, the wage–profit curve was convex, linear or concave depending on whether the ratio uAL/uL was greater than, equal to or less than the dominant eigenvalue a of matrix A. Decreasing wage–profit relations, whatever the numeraire, express an increase in every wage price in the interval $[0, R[$. Indeed, from the normalisation condition of production prices $up = 1$, we can also obtain $up/w = 1/w$, hence

$$w = \cfrac{1}{u\dfrac{p}{w}} = \cfrac{1}{u_1\dfrac{p_1}{w} + u_2\dfrac{p_2}{w} + \ldots + u_i\dfrac{p_i}{w} + \ldots + u_k\dfrac{p_k}{w}}$$

The wage–profit relation can thus be defined as the inverse of a linear combination of wage prices, the weighting of which depends on the numeraire chosen for prices $u = (u_1, u_2, \ldots, u_i, \ldots, u_k)$.

2.3.3 Linearisation of the wage–profit relation

If curve (w, r) is always decreasing, its exact form depends on the chosen numeraire. However, as previously mentioned, the latter is arbitrary and may be represented by a semi-positive row-vector with k components.

We can show that in a system with single-product industries and circulating capital, the wage–profit relation can always be made linear provided we choose as a standard of prices (and of course, of wages) a particular composite commodity, a homothetic commodity, which is also Sraffa's balanced commodity.

Let us revert to the definition and the properties of the eigenvector corresponding to the dominant eigenvalue of an indecomposable and semi-positive matrix. Let q be the eigenvector on the left, corresponding to the dominant eigenvalue α of matrix A taken to be indecomposable. By definition, we have $qA = \alpha q$ or, with $\alpha = \dfrac{1}{1 + R}$

$$q = (1 + R)qA$$

By the Perron-Frobenius theorem, this vector is unique, strictly positive and defined up to the multiplication by scalars; which means that the previous system allows us to determine the structure of the basket of goods q, but not its level; the latter is determined by the additional condition $qL = 1$.

From now on, the system of production prices will be normalised by using as a standard of prices (and wages) not any commodity, but the net surplus which would emerge if the considered economy provided a gross production vector q (thus requiring an intermediate consumption qA). The value of such a net surplus $q(I - A)p$ is taken to be equal to unity; hence the normalisation condition $q(I - A)p = 1$; then, the system writes

$$\begin{cases} p = (1 + r)Ap + wL \\ i = q(I - A)p \end{cases}$$

Now, we have a system of $k + 1$ equations with $k + 2$ unknowns, from which we can quite easily obtain a linear relation between wage and profit. Indeed, by multiplying (on the left) the first system of equations by q and by rearranging the terms, we obtain

$$qp - qAp = rqAp + wqL$$

This expression can be considerably simplified; indeed:
(a) $qp - qAp = q(I - A)p = 1$
(b) $qL = 1$ as indicated previously
(c) finally, $qAp = 1/R$, since from $q = (1 + R)qA$ we obtain

$$qp = (1 + R)qAp \text{ and } RqAp = q(I - A)p = 1$$

hence by replacing

$$1 = \frac{r}{R} + w \quad \text{or also} \quad w = 1 - \frac{r}{R}$$

Thus, relation (w, r) can always be made linear provided we choose Sraffa's balanced commodity as a numeraire of prices, that is to say, $q(I - A)$, with the basket of goods having the same structure as the eigenvector on the left corresponding to the dominant eigenvalue of the indecomposable matrix A. It is the value of such a commodity $q(I - A)$ which we set equal to unity to normalise prices.

Remark
We can write: $qL = 1 \Leftrightarrow W = 1$ when $u = q(I - A)$.
Indeed, since, as indicated earlier, we have in the general case

$$u\Lambda = 1 \Leftrightarrow W = 1$$

owing to the definition of $\Lambda = (I - A)^{-1}L$, we obtain

$$1 = u\Lambda = q(I - A)(I - A)^{-1}L = qL$$

2.4 Reduction to dated quantities of labour

'We shall call "Reduction to dated quantities of labour" [or "Reduction" for short] an operation by which in the equation of a commodity the different means of production used are replaced with a series of quantities of labour, each with its appropriate "date"' (P.S. 46).
The equation of prices: $p = (1 + r)Ap + wL$ also writes

$$p - (1 + r)Ap = wL$$

or

$$[I - (1 + r)A]p = wL$$

that is, when $r \in [0 \ R[$

$$p = w[I - (1 + r)A]^{-1}L$$

since then $[I - (1 + r)A]^{-1} > 0$.

We can then develop $[I-(1+r)A]^{-1}$ for $r\in[0\ R[$, and we obtain

$$p(r)=w[I-(1+r)A]^{-1}L$$
$$=w[I+(1+r)A+(1+r)^2A^2+\ldots+(1+r)^nA^n+\ldots]L$$

that is

$$p(r)=w[L+(1+r)AL+(1+r)^2A^2L+\ldots+(1+r)^nA^nL+\ldots]$$

We shall study the evolution of the value of each term composing price $p_i(r)$ of good i as a function of r and show that in fact the price of $p(r)$ only depends on the first k layers of labour, $L, AL, A^2L,\ldots,A^{k-1}L$.

2.4.1 Evolution of the value of each term with a change in the rate of profit

The price of good i is $p_i(r)$, and

$$p_i(r)=e_ip(r)$$
$$=we_i[L+(1+r)AL+(1+r)^2A^2L+\ldots+(1+r)^nA^nL+\ldots]$$

where vector e_i is equal to $(0,0,\ldots,0,1,0,\ldots,0)$. Thus we have

$$p_i(r)=w[1_i+(1+r)e_iAL+(1+r)^2e_iA^2L+\ldots+(1+r)^ne_iA^nL+\ldots]$$

or $\hspace{10cm}$ (1)

$$p_i(r)=w[1_i^{(0)}+(1+r)l_i^{(1)}+(1+r)^2l_i^{(2)}+\ldots+(1+r)^nl_i^{(n)}+\ldots]$$

where $l_i^{(j)}$ represents each 'layer' of labour

$$l_i^{(j)}=e_iA^jL \quad \text{with } j\in N$$

If we choose commodity $q(I-A)$ as a standard of prices with $q(I-A)p=1$,

we have $w=1-\dfrac{r}{R}$ and

$$p_i(r)=\left(1-\frac{r}{R}\right)\sum_{n=0}^{\infty}(1+r)^nl_i^{(n)}=\sum_{n=0}^{\infty}L_i^{(n)}(r)$$

where $L_i^{(n)}(r)=\left(1-\dfrac{r}{R}\right)(1+r)^nl_i^{(n)}$.

By deriving $L_i^{(n)}(r)$ in relation to r we obtain

$$\frac{\partial L_i^{(n)}(r)}{\partial r}=-\frac{1}{R}(1+r)^nl_i^{(n)}+n\left(1-\frac{r}{R}\right)(1+r)^{n-1}l_i^{(n)}$$

$$=(1+r)^{n-1}1_i^{(n)}\frac{[n(R-r)-(1+r)]}{R}$$

Thus if $n < (1+r)/(R-r)$ we have $\partial L_i^{(n)}(r)/\delta r < 0$; more particularly if $n < 1/R$, we have $\partial L_i^{(n)}(0)/\delta r < 0$ and since $n < 1/R < (1+r)/(R-r) \forall r \in [0 \ R[$ we have $\partial L_i^{(n)}(r)/\partial r < 0 \forall r \in [0 \ R[$, i.e., if $L_i^{(n)}(r)$ decreases at the beginning (at $r = 0$) it constantly decreases for $r \in [0 \ R[$.

However, if $r = 0$ and $n > 1/R$, $\partial L_i^{(n)}(0)/\delta r > 0$ and $L_i^{(n)}(r)$ is increasing in the neighbourhood of $r = 0$. Since $(1+r)/(R-r)$ increases with r and tends towards infinity when $r \to R$, there exists a rate of profit r_0 such that $n = (1+r_0)/(R-r_0)$.

This means that for a *given* n greater than $1/R$, $L_i^{(n)}(r)$ increases when r varies from 0 to r_0 and decreases when r varies from r_0 to R. The term $L_i^{(n)}(r)$ reaches its *maximum value* at a rate of profit r_0 defined by $1 + r_0 = (R - r_0)n$ or

$$r_0 = \frac{nR-1}{1+n} = \frac{(1+n)R-(1+R)}{1+n} = R - \frac{1+r}{1+n}$$

Thus we can see that 'with the rise of the rate of profits, terms devide into two groups: those that correspond to a labour done in a more recent past' $(n < 1/R)$, 'which begin at once to fall in value and fall steadily throughout; and those representing labour more remote in time' $(n > 1/R)$, 'which at first rise and then, as each of them reaches its maximum value, turn and begin the downward movement' (P.S. 47).

This is best shown in figure 2.4 given by Sraffa with curves representing terms of widely different periods (n) and different quantities of labour. In this example Sraffa assumed that R was equal to 25%.

2.4.2 Expression of $p(r)$ as a function of the first k layers of labour

By the Cayley–Hamilton theorem every square matrix A of order k satisfies its characteristic equation

$$\phi(\lambda) = |A - \lambda I| = \lambda^k + c_1\lambda^{k-1} + c_2\lambda^{k-2} + \ldots + c_{k-1}\lambda + c_k = 0$$

Thus we have $\phi(A) = A^k + c_1A^{k-1} + c_2A^{k-2} + \ldots + c_{k-1}A + c_kI = 0$. That is $A^k = -[c_1A^{k-1} + c_2A^{k-2} + \ldots + c_{k-1}A + c_kI]$, where the c_i(s) are constants which only depend on matrix A. Accordingly, vector A^kL is a linear combination of vectors $L, AL, \ldots, A^{k-1}L$ since $A^kL = -[c_1A^{k-1}L + c_2A^{k-2}L + \ldots + c_{k-1}AL + c_kL]$ and we can show that, by iteration, vectors $A^{k+1}L, A^{k+2}L \ldots, A^nL, \ldots$ are also linear combinations of $L, AL, A^2L, \ldots, A^{k-1}L$. Thus equation (1) representing $p(r)$ as a function of successive layers of labour can always be expressed as

$$p(r) = w [\beta_0 L + b_1 AL + \ldots + \beta_j A^j L + \ldots + b_{k-1} A^{k-1} L] \qquad (2)$$

While according to (1), $p(r)$ seems to depend on an infinity of layers of

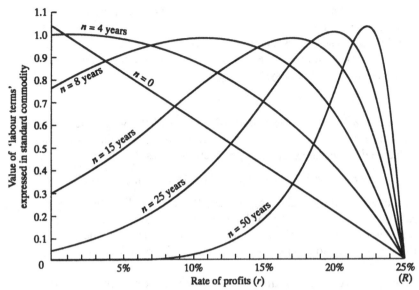

Figure 2.4

Note: Variation in the value of 'reduction terms' of different periods $[L_n w(1+r)^n]$ relative to the standard commodity as the rate of profits varies between zero and R (assumed to be 25%). The quantities of labour (L_n) in the various 'terms', which have been chosen so as to keep the curves within the page, are as follows: $L_0 = 1.04$; $L_4 = 1$; $L_8 = 0.76$; $L_{15} = 0.29$; $L_{25} = 0.0525$; $L_{50} = 0.0004$.

Source: Reproduction of figure 2 from Sraffa, *Production of Commodities by Means of Commodities*

labour (as indicated by Sraffa), (2) shows that $p(r)$ depends at most on the first k layers of labour L, $AL, \ldots, A^{k-1}L$. The coefficients β_0, $\beta_1, \ldots, \beta_j, \ldots, \beta_{k-1}$ are functions of $(1+r)$ and we have[10]

$$\beta_j = \frac{(1+r)^j + c_1(1+r)^{j+1} + \ldots + c_{k-1-j}(1+r)^{k-1}}{|I-(1+r)A|}$$

Where $|I-(1+r)A| = 1 + c_1(1+r) + c_2(1+r)^2 + \ldots + c_k(1+r)^k$ is the determinant of the square matrix $|I-(1+r)A|$.

2.5 'Advanced' wages and wages paid 'post factum'

We have already noted that, from the very beginning of *Production of Commodities by Means of Commodities*, Sraffa abandons the classical economists' idea of a wage *'advanced* from the capital' and retains the assumption that the 'wage is paid *post factum* as a share of the annual product' (section 9).

What differences does a change of hypothesis entail?

By writing p^S and w^S the system of prices and the wage retained in Sraffa's assumption, the system of production prices (S) writes

$$(S) \qquad p^S = (1+r)Ap^S + Lw^S$$

If we call p^M and w^M the system of prices and the wage retained in the assumptions of the classical school, and more particularly of Marx, of 'advanced wage', the system of production prices then becomes

$$(M) \qquad p^M = (1+r)(Ap^M + Lw^M) = (1+r)Ap^M + Lw^M(1+r)$$

In the latter notation, the wage is actually 'advanced' in the sense that the rate of profit applies both to the amount of wages paid and to the set of other 'advances'; then, this assumption does vary from the one expressed by the former notation (S) where the wage is paid 'post factum' as a share of the surplus.

In order to compare both systems of prices more precisely, prices have to be expressed in terms of the same standard, in short we need

$$up^M = 1 = up^S$$

At a given rate of profit, the comparison of both systems (M) and (S) shows that *the relative prices of the goods are identical in both systems M and S and only vary in the proportion* $(1+r)$; that is to say

$$w^S = (1+r)w^M \Leftrightarrow w^M = \frac{w^S}{1+r}$$

This first result allows easy derivation of an advanced-wage/profit relation, i.e., (w^M, r). We have already seen that if we retain Sraffa's assumption of a wage paid as a share of the surplus, the wage–profit relation (w^S, r) writes

$$w^S = \frac{1}{u[I - (1+r)A]^{-1}L}$$

From which we obtain

$$w^M = \frac{w^S}{1+r} = \frac{1}{(1+r)u[I - (1+r)A]^{-1}L}$$

As a matter of fact, these two curves have two intersection points; indeed at $r = 0$ we have $w^S = w^M$. Further, for $w^S = w^M = 0$ we have $r = R = (1-\alpha)/\alpha$. Thus we can see that, on the basis of that formulation, *the maximum rate of*

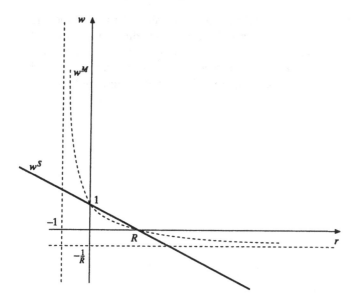

Figure 2.5

profit is identical whatever the assumption retained (advanced wage or wage paid on surplus).

If we choose to express prices by $u = q(I-A)$, we obtain $q(I-A)p^S = 1$; owing to system (S) and the definition of q we then obtain the well-known relation

$$w^S = 1 - \frac{r}{R}$$

And, as $w^M = w^S/(1+r)$, if we express system (M) in terms of the same commodity, $q(I-A)p^M = 1$, we obtain

$$w^M = \left(1 - \frac{r}{R}\right)/(1+r) = \frac{R-r}{R+rR}$$

In these conditions, the $w-r$ relation stops being linear and is now of homographic type. Thus the curve $w-r$ is an equilateral hyperbola. We write

$w^M = w^S = 0 \Rightarrow r = R$

$r = R \Rightarrow w^M = w^S = 0$

if $r \to -1 \Rightarrow w^M \to +\infty$

if $r \to +\infty \Rightarrow w^M = \dfrac{R/r - 1}{R/r + R} \to -1/R$ since $R/r \to 0$

Linear relation in one case and equilateral hyperbola in the other, the representation of the wage–profit relation is thus very different according to the assumption retained. *But in neither case does the form of the wage profit relation depend on the technology*, the characteristics of system (A, I, L); in one case it is a line, in the other case it is a branch of equilateral hyperbola (figure 2.5).

3   Irregular and decomposable systems

The purpose of the present chapter is to analyse peculiar technology configurations and their effects on systems of production prices and systems of activity levels. Some of them only concern the technology matrices, or more precisely, system $[A, I]$. This is a problem of decomposability and indecomposability. Some other peculiarities can be underlined if we integrate into the analysis the structure of the needs of labour for the various activities or the structure of the final consumption; hence the distinction between regular and irregular systems which brings to light two types of irregularities.

3.1 Decomposable systems

In order to distinguish between two types of goods, basics and non-basics, it is desirable to specify the properties of decomposable and indecomposable matrices. Indeed, under the assumption of decomposability, the production prices of all goods are not determined simultaneously. However, since the basic sector plays a dominant role that we shall specify, the maximum rate of profit is not necessarily determined by the production conditions of basic commodities; a detailed analysis of Sraffa's famous 'beans' example will help us emphasise this. More generally, we will show the importance of a classification of basic goods of different degrees in a k-sector model; the maximum rate of profit R is determined by a set of goods, basics or not, that we shall call 'blocking goods'.

The decomposability of the technology matrix does not only affect the determination of prices and the distinction between basic and non-basic commodities, it also affects the determination of activity levels; we will then be led to underline two types of activities, or processes: the 'antibasic' process on the one hand, and the 'non-antibasic' process, on the other hand (this terminology obviously refers to Sraffa's distinction of commodities), but the distinction is not necessarily symmetric. We will also show that there may be several (independent) numeraires of prices and activity levels making the $w-r$ and $c-g$ relations linear.

3.1.1 Determination of prices

Basics and non-basics

'Luxury' goods are not used, whether as means of production or as articles of subsistence, in the production of other commodities. Such a category of goods could not exist in a context of production for subsistence, where, the surplus being by assumption zero, all commodities were 'bound' to be found among both the products and the means of production.

When a surplus emerges, all commodities do not necessarily rank equally. Luxury goods have a purely passive role: they have no part in the determination of the system of prices. If an invention were to decrease the quantity of means of production required to produce one unit of a luxury commodity, the price of that commodity will also decrease, but there would be no further consequences. The price relations of the other products and the distributive variables would remain unaffected while they would be altered if such a change occurred in the means of production of the other products.

Therefore, we understand the importance of distinguishing between basics and non-basics, this term being more appropriate than that of 'luxury' goods for their passive role can readily be extended to such 'luxuries' as are merely used in their own reproduction or merely for the production of other luxuries. 'The criterion is whether a commodity enters (no matter whether directly or indirectly) into the production of *all* commodities. Those that do we shall call *basic*, and those that do not, *non-basic* products' (P.S. 6).

This criterion, as we shall see, refers to the concept of a decomposable matrix. The objective is to identify and gather within two seperate sectors, basic and non-basic products. To separate the basic sector from the non-basic sector we only need to rearrange the technology matrix by a simultaneous permutation of the rows and columns.

Decomposable matrices

Definition

A square matrix is said to be *decomposable* or that it can be reduced if there exists a permutation[1] $\bar{A}$ of matrix A with the form

$$\bar{A} = \begin{bmatrix} A_1^1 & 0 \\ A_2^1 & A_2^2 \end{bmatrix}$$

where A_1^1 and A_2^2 are square matrices of dimension $k - m$ and m respectively.

$\bar{A}$ is said to be a *quasi-triangular* matrix which means that it includes zeros only at the intersection of its first rows and last columns.

If $\bar{A}$ is a $k \times k$ matrix and A_2^2 an $m \times m$ matrix, the fact that $\bar{A}$ is quasi-triangular means that indexes $\{1, 2, \ldots, k\}$ are divided into two non-empty classes $\{i_1, i_2, \ldots, i_{k-m}\}$ and $\{j_1, j_2, \ldots, j_m\}$ such that

$$a_{ij} = 0 \, \forall i \in \{i_1, i_2, \ldots, i_{k-m}\} \text{ and } \forall j \in \{j_1, j_2, \ldots, j_m\}$$

More particularly, if at the same time we have

$$a_{ij} = 0 \text{ and } a_{ji} = 0 \, \forall i \in \{i_1, i_2, \ldots, i_{k-m}\} \text{ and } \forall j \in \{j_1, j_2, \ldots, j_m\}$$

matrix A is said to be *totally decomposable*. In that case there is a permutation $\bar{A}$ of matrix A which can write as

$$\bar{A} = \begin{bmatrix} A_1^1 & 0 \\ 0 & A_2^2 \end{bmatrix} \text{ where } A_1^1 \text{ and } A_2^2 \text{ are square matrices.}$$

When a square matrix is not decomposable it is said to be *indecomposable or irreducible*.

Now, for the semi-positive square matrices, let us recall some properties of the indecomposable and decomposable matrices.

Properties of indecomposable matrices

Property 1

If the square matrix A is indecomposable, there are two possibilities whatever the index pair (i, j):

either $a_{ij} > 0$

or there exists a series of subscripts $j_1, j_2, \ldots, j_n$ such that $a_{ij_1} a_{j_1 j_2}, \ldots, a_{j_n j} > 0$. In that case every commodity of model $[A, I, L]$ enters directly (if $a_{ij} > 0$) or indirectly (if $a_{ij_1} a_{j_1 j_2}, \ldots, a_{j_n j} > 0$) in the production of every commodity j and every commodity of the system is a basic commodity.

Note that if matrix A is (strictly) positive $(A > 0)$ it is of course indecomposable and every commodity enters directly or indirectly the production of every other.

Property 2 (Frobenius theorem)

Any *indecomposable* semi-positive square matrix A possesses a positive eigenvalue $\alpha(A)$ and positive eigenvectors q on the left and $\bar{p}$ on the right corresponding to $\alpha(A)$. The positive number $\alpha(A)$, the only eigenvalue of matrix A with an associated positive eigenvector, is a simple root of the characteristic equation $|A - \alpha I| = 0$.[2] The absolute values of the other $k - 1$

eigenvalues of matrix A are not greater than $\alpha(A)$. $k-1$ is said to be the dominant eigenvalue of matrix A.

Properties of decomposable matrices

When the semi-positive square matrix A of order k is decomposable,[3] there exists a permutation $\bar{A}$ of matrix A with the form

$$\bar{A} = \begin{bmatrix} A_1^1 & 0 \\ A_2^1 & A_2^2 \end{bmatrix}$$

where A_1^1 is a square *indecomposable* matrix of order $k-m$ and A_2^2 is a square matrix of order m. If we write matrices $\bar{A}$ and I as follows

$$\bar{A} = \begin{bmatrix} A_1^1 & 0 \\ A_2^1 & A_2^2 \end{bmatrix} \quad \text{and} \quad I = \begin{bmatrix} I_{k-m} & 0 \\ 0 & I_m \end{bmatrix}$$

the following properties appear.

Property 1

$$\text{Matrix } [A^2, I^2] = \begin{bmatrix} 0 & 0 \\ A_2^2 & I_m \end{bmatrix}$$

composed of the last m columns of $\bar{A}$ and I is of rank m, that is to say, when matrix A is decomposable there exists a number m and a permutation of the columns of A such that matrix $[A^2, I^2]$ of the form $(k, 2m)$ composed of the last m columns of A (after permutation) and of I is of rank m.

Property 2

When $A_2^1 \geq 0$ and A_2^2 is *indecomposable* the $k-m$ commodities produced by the system (A_1^1, I_{k-m}) enter the production of the other m commodities and are basic commodities since A_1^1 is indecomposable.

Production prices

The system of price equations of model $[A, I, L]$ can be decomposed as follows

$$(1+r)Ap + wL = p$$

from the new configuration of the technology matrix

$$A = \begin{bmatrix} A_1^1 & 0 \\ A_2^1 & A_2^2 \end{bmatrix}$$

By distinguishing L_1 and L_2, the quantity vectors of direct labour used in the basic sector and non-basic sector respectively, namely $L = \begin{bmatrix} L_1 \\ L_2 \end{bmatrix}$, and by

considering p_1 and p_2, the price vectors in the basic sector and non-basic

sector respectively, namely $p = \begin{bmatrix} p_1 \\ p_2 \end{bmatrix}$ we deduce

$$(1+r)\begin{bmatrix} A_1^1 & 0 \\ A_2^1 & A_2^2 \end{bmatrix} \begin{bmatrix} p_1 \\ p_2 \end{bmatrix} + w\begin{bmatrix} L_1 \\ L_2 \end{bmatrix} = \begin{bmatrix} p_1 \\ p_2 \end{bmatrix}$$

Hence the following vector systems

$$\begin{cases} (1+r)A_1^1 p_1 + wL_1 & = p_1 \\ (1+r)(A_2^1 p_1 + A_2^2 p_2) + wL_2 = p_2 \end{cases}$$

The first system of $(k-m)$ equations simultaneously determines the $(k-m-1)$ relative prices of the basic goods and both distributive variables. Provided we chose an appropriate numeraire, there are $(k-m)$ equations for $(k-m-1+2) = (k-m+1)$ unknowns; thus the system has one degree of freedom and suffice to set one of the $(k-m+1)$ unknowns to determine the $(k-m)$ others.

The second system of m equations allows us to obtain the m prices of the non-basic goods as a function of the prices of the basic products and of the distributive variables which have all been determined in the first system.[4]

In that case matrix $[A^1, I^1] = \begin{bmatrix} A_1^1 & I_{k-m} \\ A_2^1 & 0 \end{bmatrix}$ is of a rank strictly greater than $k-m$.

As a result, a *necessary* condition for at least one basic good to exist in the system is that rank $[A^1, I^1] > k-m$. Note that this condition is not sufficient, for if the square matrix A can be decomposed as follows

$$A = \begin{bmatrix} A_1^1 & 0 & 0 \\ 0 & A_2^2 & 0 \\ A_3^1 & A_3^2 & A_3^3 \end{bmatrix} \begin{matrix} k-m \\ \\ m \end{matrix}$$

none of the goods is basic even though rank $[A^1, I^1] > k-m$. This is due to

the fact that matrix $\begin{bmatrix} A_2^2 & 0 \\ A_3^2 & A_3^3 \end{bmatrix}$ is not indecomposable.

Property 3

Any decomposable semi-positive square matrix A possesses a non-negative eigenvalue $\alpha(A)$ and semi-positive eigenvectors q on the left and $\bar{p}$ on the right corresponding to $\alpha(A)$. The absolute values of the other $k-1$ eigenvalues of matrix A are not greater than $\alpha(A)$.

Owing to properties 1 and 2, if matrices A_1^1 and A_2^1 are indecomposable and if matrix $A_2^1 \geq 0$, system $[A, I, L]$ where A may, after permutation, write:

$$A = \begin{bmatrix} A_1^1 & 0 \\ A_2^1 & A_2^2 \end{bmatrix} \begin{matrix} {}^{k-m} \\ {}_m \end{matrix}$$

possesses m non-basic products and $(k - m)$ basic products since the first $(k - m)$ commodities, and only they, directly or indirectly enter the production of all the goods.

If $m = k - 1$, there exists $(k - 1)$ non-basic commodities and one basic commodity: A_1^2 which generally has $(k - m)$ rows and m columns becomes a row-vector with $m = k - 1$ components, all zeros of course, since $k - m = k - (k - 1) = 1$.

If $m = 0$ it is not possible to obtain a configuration that is a quasi-triangular matrix through simultaneous permutation of the rows and columns of A, and the system is indecomposable. Then, the economy only includes basic commodities.

Finally, if matrix A is totally decomposable, there are only non-basic commodities; no product is basic. In that case the production system could be divided into several sub-sets having no technical relations and thus constituting as many independent 'sub-economies' as there would be sub-sets having at least one specific basic product. The configuration of the technology matrix would then be

$$\begin{bmatrix} A_1^1 & 0 & 0 & 0 \\ 0 & A_2^2 & 0 & 0 \\ 0 & 0 & A_3^3 & 0 \\ 0 & 0 & 0 & A_4^4 \end{bmatrix}$$

which means that we would have to analyse several elementary sub-economies represented above by sub-matrices of type A_1^1, A_2^2, A_3^3, A_4^4. We shall see later on that there is a maximum rate of profit R for the whole model, which is determined by the blocking sector.

The following table shows the conditions of decomposability of a matrix A and the conditions of existence of basic commodities in the model of simple production $[A, I, L]$.

Decomposability of matrix A and existence of basic commodities

Is there an $m < k$ and a permutation of A such that matrix $[A^2, I^2]$ of dimension $k \times 2m$ is such that rank $[A^2, I^2] = m < k$?	$\rightarrow$ no: A is *indecomposable* and all the goods are basic. $\rightarrow$ yes: A is *decomposable*.

m being the greatest number such that $[A^2, I^2] = m < k$, is rank $[A^1, I^1] > k - m$?	→ no: A is totally decomposable and there are no basic goods. → yes: there is at least one basic good if A_2^2 is indecomposable.[5]

This presentation allows us to understand as Sraffa states it (P.S. 7):

why the ratios which satisfy the conditions of production have been called values or prices rather than, as might be thought more appropriate, costs of production.

The latter description would be adequate so far as *non*-basic products were concerned, since ... their exchange ratio is merely a reflection of what must be paid for means of production, labour and profits in order to produce them – there is no mutual dependence ...

In other words, the price of a non-basic product depends on the prices of its means of production, but these do not depend on it. Whereas in the case of a basic product the prices of its means of production depend on its own price no less than the latter depends on them.

The prices of the non-basic products are then determined by the conditions in which they are produced; on the other hand, the technology matrix being taken to be known and unchanged, the prices of basic goods determine as much the endogenous distributive variable as the latter determines them.

Classification of goods in a decomposable system

In model $[A, I, L]$ where matrix A is decomposable, Sraffa distinguishes basic goods which directly or indirectly enter into the production of all goods, and non-basic goods which do not enter into the production of basic goods but may enter into the production of non-basic goods.

In a decomposable model, a refined classification of non-basic goods is needed. For simplicity's sake, we shall analyse a simple decomposable production model with four sectors $[A, I, L]$.

In order to avoid complex notations, we shall first comment upon the simple table representing inter-industrial relationships, where (C) stands for the production of coal, (P) phosphate, (F) fertiliser and (W) wheat. The needs in labour are not represented here, we shall simply assume that each production requires a certain quantity of labour.

Inputs	Outputs
C	C
CP	P
CPF	F
CPFW	W

Coal is produced with coal and labour; Phosphate is produced with coal, phosphate and labour; fertiliser with the same inputs and fertiliser; wheat with coal, phosphate, fertiliser, wheat and labour. Coal is the only basic good, while the others are non-basic.

However, the traditional distinction between basic and non-basic goods is far from being satisfactory. First, because it does not determine clearly the hierarchy of the determination of prices; second, there is no reason why the maximum rate of profit should be determined by the basic sector only.

The example above shows clearly that the hierarchy of the determination of prices is to be further specified. Indeed, if we write the price equations, it appears that for a given r, the wage and the price of coal are determined simultaneously. Then the price of phosphate is determined, then the price of fertiliser and finally the price of wheat. Phosphate is then considered as a non-basic good of degree 1, fertiliser is a non-basic of degree 2, and so on. Note that we can compare basic goods and non-basic goods of degree 0 and we obtain the following rule: The prices of non-basic goods of degree d are independent of the prices of non-basic goods of a degree greater than d and only depend on the prices of non-basic goods of a degree less than or equal to d. We can then classify the goods of this decomposable model into two categories: basic goods (or non-basic goods of degree 0) and non-basic goods of increasing degree 1, 2 and 3 (possibly 0, 1, 2 and 3). Thus, the role of basic goods appears less basic. Their role is further weakened, if we take a closer look at the conditions in which prices are determined.

Blocking goods and the maximum rate of profit

Unforeseen difficulties can, however, appear concerning 'self-reproducing non-basics'. This is Sraffa's famous 'beans' example which, as we shall see, merits some attention. In Sraffa's terms:

Consider a commodity which enters to an unusually large extent into the production of itself. It may be imagined to be some crop such as a species of beans or of corn the wastage on which is so great that for every 100 units sown no more than 110 are repeated. It is clear that this would not admit of a rate of profits higher than, or indeed, since other means of production must be used as well, as high as 10%.

If, the product in question is a basic one there is no problem; it simply means that the maximum rate of profits of the system will have to be less than 10%.

If, however, it is a non-basic product, complications arise. The way in which a non-basic is produced has, as we have seen, no influence on the general rate of profits, so that there would be nothing to prevent the Maximum rate of the system being higher than 10%: and yet the product in question is incompatible with a rate as high as 10% (P.S. Appendix B).

If the input matrix of model $[A, I, L]$ is

$$A = \begin{bmatrix} \frac{20}{23} & 0 \\ a_{21} & \frac{10}{11} \end{bmatrix}$$

with $a_{21} > 0$, the dominant eigenvalue of matrix A is $\alpha(A) = 10/11$ and the maximum rate of profit is $R = (1 - \alpha)/\alpha = 0.10$. But the basic sector has $\alpha(A_1^1) = 20/23$ as its dominant eigenvalue and the rate of profit corresponding to the basic good is $R^1 = \dfrac{1 - 20/23}{20/23} = 0.15$. If $L = \begin{bmatrix} L_1 \\ L_2 \end{bmatrix}$, at a rate of profit r, the system that gives the production prices p_1 and p_2 of the basic product and of the beans as a function of r is $(1 + r)Ap + wL = p$, that is to say

$$(1 + r) \begin{bmatrix} \frac{20}{23} & 0 \\ a_{21} & \frac{10}{11} \end{bmatrix} \begin{bmatrix} p_1 \\ p_2 \end{bmatrix} + w \begin{bmatrix} L_1 \\ L_2 \end{bmatrix} = \begin{bmatrix} p_1 \\ p_2 \end{bmatrix}$$

or

$$\begin{cases} (1 + r) \frac{20}{23} p_1 + wL_1 = p_1 \Leftrightarrow p_1[1 - (1 + r)\frac{20}{23}] = wL_1 \\ (1 + r)(a_{21}p_1 + \frac{10}{11} p_2) + wL_2 = p_2 \Leftrightarrow p_2[1 - (1 + r)\frac{10}{11}] = wL_2 + (1 + r)a_{21}p_1 \end{cases}$$

Thus we have $p_1 = \dfrac{23}{3 - 20r} wL_1 = \dfrac{23}{20[0.15 - r]} wL_1$ and

$$p_2 = \dfrac{11}{1 - 10r} [wL_2 + (1 + r)a_{21}p_1]$$

If we normalise prices and wages by $w = 1$, which comes down to taking into account wage prices, we have

$$\hat{p}_1(r) = \frac{p_1}{w} = \frac{23}{20(0.15 - r)} L_1$$

and

$$\hat{p}_2(r) = \frac{p_2}{w} = \frac{11}{1 - 10r} [L_2 + (1 + r)a_{21}\hat{p}_1(r)]$$

Price $\hat{p}_1(r)$ is positive and an increasing function of r in the interval $[0 \ \ 0.15]$; and if we only take into account the first good which is the only basic good, the rate of profit would be 15%, as shown by Sraffa. But by observing the

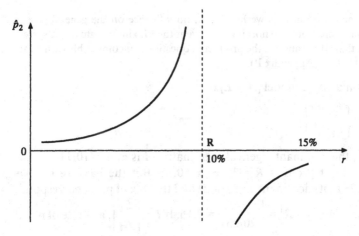

Figure 3.1

expression of $\hat{p}_2(r)$ we notice that if $\hat{p}_2(r)$ is positive and an increasing function of the rate of profit when r varies from 0 to 10%, it becomes negative when r is included between 10% and 15%. More precisely (figure 3.1) the curve representing $\hat{p}_2$ as a function of r has the following shape and has line $r = 10\%$ as its asymptote.

It appears clearly that the maximum rate of profit of the system must be equal to $R = 0.10 = (1 - \alpha)/\alpha$ where α is the dominant eigenvalue of matrix A and not only the basic sector's.

Suffice to reason within a golden rule context that beyond $r = g = 10\%$ the net surplus of beans is necessarily negative; the negative wage price of beans shows the economic impossibility of obtaining a higher rate of profit than the average 10%, except of course in the case when no 'bean' is consumed. Then why bother producing non-basic goods? The problem disappears on its own.

The 'beans' example is a peculiar case of a decomposable model where blocking goods are not basic goods. Indeed, let A be a decomposable square matrix of order seven (actually including four sectors) with non-negative terms which, after a simultaneous permutation of rows and columns, writes

$$A = 0.1 \begin{bmatrix} 5 & 1 & 0 & 0 & 0 & 0 & 0 \\ 2 & 6 & 0 & 0 & 0 & 0 & 0 \\ 1 & 1 & 6 & 0 & 0 & 0 & 0 \\ 0 & 1 & 2 & 5 & 2 & 0 & 0 \\ 1 & 0 & 2 & 4 & 7 & 0 & 0 \\ 1 & 1 & 0 & 0 & 1 & 4 & 2 \\ 0 & 1 & 1 & 0 & 1 & 1 & 3 \end{bmatrix}$$

We can see that matrix A can be broken down into blocks

$$A = 0.1 \begin{bmatrix} 5 & 1 & 0 & 0 & 0 & 0 & 0 \\ 2 & 6 & 0 & 0 & 0 & 0 & 0 \\ 1 & 1 & 6 & 0 & 0 & 0 & 0 \\ 0 & 1 & 2 & 5 & 2 & 0 & 0 \\ 1 & 0 & 2 & 4 & 7 & 0 & 0 \\ 1 & 1 & 0 & 0 & 1 & 4 & 2 \\ 0 & 1 & 1 & 0 & 1 & 1 & 3 \end{bmatrix}$$

so that the four square matrices

$$A(1\ 1) = \begin{bmatrix} 0.5 & 0.1 \\ 0.2 & 0.6 \end{bmatrix}, \quad A(2\ 2) = [0.6]$$

$$A(3\ 3) = \begin{bmatrix} 0.5 & 0.2 \\ 0.4 & 0.7 \end{bmatrix}, \quad A(4\ 4) = \begin{bmatrix} 0.4 & 0.2 \\ 0.1 & 0.3 \end{bmatrix}$$

which are on the 'main diagonal', are indecomposable.

The system of prices (1) can then be broken down into four matrix equations

(1.1) $p(1) = (1+r)\, A(1\ 1)p(1) + wL_1$

(1.2) $p(2) = (1+r)[A(2\ 1)p(1) + A(2\ 2)p(2)] + wL_2$

(1.3) $p(3) = (1+r)[A(3\ 1)p(1) + A(3\ 2)p(2) + A(3\ 3)p(3)] + wL_3$

(1.4) $p(4) = (1+r)[A(4\ 1)p(1) + A(4\ 2)p(2) + A(4\ 3)p(3)$
$\qquad\qquad\qquad\qquad\qquad + A(4\ 4)p(4)] + wL_4$

where L_1, L_2, L_3 and L_4 represent the four sectors's needs for direct labour.

We can thus divide the goods of this decomposable model into two categories: basic goods (or non-basics of degree 0) and non-basic goods of increasing degrees 1, 2 and 3.

Now we need to find out under what conditions the prices of the seven goods are positive. Let us first start with $p(1)$. According to equation (1.1), we have

$$[I - (1+r)A(1\ 1)]p(1) = wL_1 > 0$$

and since matrix $A(1\ 1) = \begin{bmatrix} 0.5 & 0.1 \\ 0.2 & 0.6 \end{bmatrix}$ has $\alpha[A(1\ 1)] = 0.7$ as an eigenvalue, the prices $p(1)$ of the first two goods are positive if

$$r \le R(1) = (1 - 0.7)/0.7 = 3/7 = 0.42857\ldots$$

Note that $0.42857\ldots$ is the maximum rate of profit of matrix $A(1\ 1)$ which represents the quantities of both basic goods entering into their own production. Let us now take a look at the conditions for $p(2)$, the price of the third good which is a non-basic good of degree 1, to be positive. According to equation (1.2), we have

$$[1-(1+r)A(2\ 2)]p(2)=(1+r)A(2\ 1)p(1)+wL_2$$

or

$$[1-(1+r)0.6]p(2)=(1+r)A(2\ 1)p(1)+wL_2$$

that is to say

$$[0.4-0.6r]p(2)=(1+r)A(2\ 1)p(1)+wL_2$$

since $p(1)>0$ when $r\leq R(1)=0.42857...$ and $A(2\ 1)=[1\ 1]>0$, we have $(1+r)A(2\ 1)p(1)+wL_2>0$ when $r\leq R(1)$. As a result, $p(2)>0$ when $0.4-0.6>0$ or $r<2/3=0.66666....$

Note that $R(2)=0.66666...=(1-0.6)/0.6$ where 0.6 is the eigenvalue of the square matrix of order 1, $A(2\ 2)=[0.6]$ which represents the quantity of the third good entering into its own production. Since price $p(1)$ is positive only if $r\leq R(1)=0.42857...$ and price $p(2)$ is positive when $r<R(2)=0.66666...$ prices $p(1)$ and $p(2)$ are positive when $r\leq R(1)=0.42857...$ since $r\leq R(1)$ and $r<R(2)$.

In order to determine the conditions of positivity of prices $p(3)$ of the non-basic goods of degree 2, we use equation (1.3) and we obtain

$$[I-(1+r)A(3\ 3)]p(3)=(1+r)[A(3\ 1)p(1)+A(3\ 2)p(2)]+wL_3$$

Since the dominant eigenvalue of matrix $A(3\ 3)=\begin{bmatrix}0.5 & 0.2\\0.4 & 0.7\end{bmatrix}$ is $\alpha(A(3\ 3))$

$=0.9$, prices $p(3)$ of both non-basic goods of degree 2 are positive if and only if $r<(1-0.9)/0.9=0.11111...$ Note that $0.11111...$ is the maximum rate of profit of matrix $A(3\ 3)$ which represents the quantity of both non-basic goods of degree 2 entering into their own production.

As a result, prices $p(1)$, $p(2)$ and $p(3)$ are all positive provided $r<0.11111...$

Finally, in order to determine the conditions of positivity of prices $p(4)$ of the non-basic goods of degree 3, we use equation (1.4) and we obtain

$$[I-(1+r)A(4\ 4)]p(4)=(1+r)[A(4\ 1)p(1)+A(4\ 2)p(2)$$
$$+A(4\ 3)p(3)]+wL_4$$

Since the dominant eigenvalue of matrix $A(4\ 4)=\begin{bmatrix}0.4 & 0.2\\0.1 & 0.3\end{bmatrix}$ is $\alpha(A(4\ 4))$

$=0.5$, *prices $p(4)$ of both non-basic goods of degree 3 are positive if and only if $r<(1-0.5)/0.5=1$. Note that 1 is the maximum rate of profit of matrix $A(4\ 4)$ which represents the quantity of both non-basic goods of degree 3 entering into their own production. Since $1 > 0.11111\ldots$, the prices of the seven goods are all positive if and only if the rate of profit of economy r is less than $0.11111\ldots$ i.e., the maximum rate of profit of the model is $R = 0.11111\ldots$

As we can see, non-basic goods of degree 2 have the lowest maximum rate of profit. We call them blocking goods because the rate of profit of economy r must be less than the maximum rate of profit $R(2) = 0.11111\ldots$, otherwise the prices of those goods would be negative. Thus, the maximum rate of profit R of model $[A, I, L]$ must be equal to the maximum rate of profit $R(2) = 0.11111\ldots$ of the blocking goods, and this enhances the vital role they play.

Further, note that the dominant eigenvalue of matrix A, which equals the greatest of the four dominant eigenvalues of matrices $A(i\ i)$, is 0.9, which is the dominant eigenvalue of matrix $A(3\ 3)$. The latter characterises non-basic goods of degree 2. Thus the maximum rate of profit R of model $[A, I, L]$ equals the maximum rate of profit $R(2) = 0.11111\ldots$ of blocking goods, or, non-basic goods of degree 2.

Linearisation of the wage–profit relation

When a matrix A is indecomposable, to its dominant eigenvalue $\alpha(A)$ correspond the positive eigenvectors q on the left and $\bar{p}$ on the right. As a result, every eigenvector q_i on the left corresponding to an eigenvalue $\alpha_i \neq \alpha$ has necessarily components with opposite signs otherwise the scalar product $q_i\bar{p}$ would always be zero.[6] On the other hand, if matrix A is decomposable, to its dominant eigenvalue $\alpha(A)$ correspond semi-positive eigenvectors on the left and on the right; one of these vectors at the most being positive. As a result, a decomposable matrix can have several semi-positive eigenvectors on the left that are not homothetic. More particularly, if the dominant eigenvalue of matrix A_2^2 corresponding to the non-basic sector is greater than the dominant eigenvalue of matrix A_1^1 corresponding to the basic sector, this would ensure at least two independent numeraires allowing the linearisation of relation (w, r).

Let us revert to the 'beans' example, that is to model $[A, I, L]$, where

$$A = \begin{bmatrix} \frac{20}{23} & 0 \\ a_{21} & \frac{10}{11} \end{bmatrix}$$

A has two eigenvalues $\alpha = \dfrac{10}{11}$ and $\alpha_2 = \dfrac{20}{23}$.

To the dominant eigenvalue $\alpha = 10/11$ corresponds the eigenvector on the left $q = (q_1, q_2)$ satisfying $qA = 10/11q$

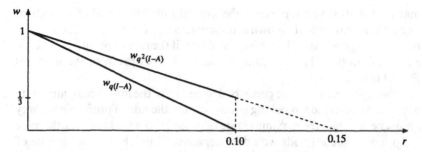

Figure 3.2 The wage–profit curve of model $[A, I, L]$ corresponding to numeraires $q(I-A)$ and $q(I-A)$

$$\frac{20}{23} q_1 + a_{21}q_2 = \frac{10}{11} q_1 \Leftrightarrow a_{21}q_2 = \frac{230-220}{253} q_1 = \frac{10}{253} q_1$$

or

$$\frac{10}{11} q_2 = \frac{10}{11} q_2 \Leftrightarrow q_2 \text{ arbitrary}$$

thus we have $q = \lambda(25, 3a_{21}, 1) > 0$ if $\lambda > 0$ since $a_{21} > 0$. If we choose as a numeraire of prices, vector $q(I-A)$ such that $qL = \lambda(25, 3a_{21}, 1)L = 1$, then the wage–profit curve $w_{q(I-A)}$ is the segment connecting points $(r=0, w=1)$ and $(r=0, 1\ w=0)$.

To eigenvalue $\alpha_2 = 20/23$ corresponds the eigenvector on the left $q^2 = (q^2_1, q^2_2)$ satisfying $q^2 A = (20/23)q^2$ or

$$\frac{20}{23} q^2_1 + a_{21}q^2_2 = \frac{20}{23} q^2_1 \Leftrightarrow \text{any } q^2_1$$

$$\frac{10}{11} q^2_2 = \frac{20}{23} q^2_2 \Leftrightarrow q^2_2 = 0$$

thus $q^2 = \lambda(1, 0) \geq 0$ when $\lambda > 0$.

Let us now choose vector $q^2(I-A)$ as a numeraire, such that $q^2 L = \lambda(1.0)L = 1$; the wage–profit curve $w^2_q(I-A)$ is the segment of line connecting points $(r=0, w=1)$ and $(r=0.10, w=1/3)$ which extends to point $(r=0.15, w=0)$. Recall that for $r > 0.10$, $p_2(r) < 0$ (figure 3.2).

Now let us consider the three sector model $[A, I, L]$, where

$$A = \begin{bmatrix} 0.4 & 0 & 0 \\ 0.1 & 0.5 & 0 \\ 0.1 & 0.1 & 0.6 \end{bmatrix} \quad \text{and} \quad L = \begin{bmatrix} 3 \\ 2 \\ 1 \end{bmatrix}$$

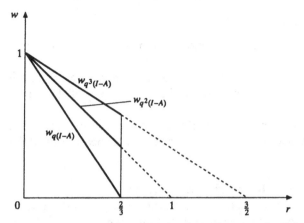

Figure 3.3 Wage–Profit curves corresponding to each of the three numeraires

Matrix A has three eigenvalues: $\alpha = 0.6$, which is the dominant eigenvalue, $\alpha_2 = 0.5$ and $\alpha_3 = 0.4$, which is the eigenvalue of the basic sector matrix.

To each of these values correspond the respective positive eigenvectors on the left $q = (\frac{1}{6} \; \frac{1}{6} \; \frac{1}{6})$, $q^2 = (\frac{1}{5} \; \frac{1}{5} \; 0)$ and $q^3 = (\frac{1}{3} \; 0 \; 0)$. In interval $[0 \; R]$ where $R = (1-\alpha)/\alpha = 2/3$, there are three numeraires $q(I-A)$, $q^2(I-A)$ and $q^3(I-A)$ which will make the wage–profit curve linear, as shown on figure 3.3.

We can see that the wage corresponding to the maximum rate of profits is not necessarily zero when prices are normalised with one of the eigenvectors corresponding to one of the non-dominant eigenvalues. Thus, at $r = R = 2/3$, the price equation $p = (1+r)Ap + wL$ to which is associated the normalisation condition $1 = q^2(I-A)p$ (where q^2 is the eigenvector on the left of A corresponding to the dominant eigenvalue $\alpha_2 = 0.5$ satisfying $q^2L = 1$) leads to

$$1 = q^2(I-A)p = rq^2Ap + wq^2L = \frac{r}{R^2} + w$$

for $q^2Ap = \alpha_2 q^2 p = \alpha_2 \frac{q^2p}{1} = \frac{\alpha_2 q^2 p}{(1-\alpha_2)q^2p} = \frac{\alpha_2}{1-\alpha_2} = \frac{1}{R^2}$. Thus at $r = R$, we have

$$w_q^2(I-A) = 1 - \frac{R}{R^2} = 1 - \frac{2}{3} = \frac{1}{3} \neq 0$$

Similarly

$$wq^3(I-A) = 1 - \frac{R}{R^3} = 1 - \frac{2}{3} \cdot \frac{2}{3} = \frac{5}{9} \neq 0$$

Thus the wage corresponding to the system's maximum rate of profit $R = 2/3$ is not necessarily zero when prices are expressed in terms of

$$q^2(I-A)p=1 \text{ or } q^3(I-A)p=1$$

As a conclusion, in a decomposable model it is proper to distinguish two cases:

(a) The model's maximum rate of profit is also the basic sector's. Then there is only one numeraire ensuring the linearisation of the wage–profit relation.

(b) The model's maximum rate of profit is also the non-basic sector's. Then, there are at least two numeraires ensuring the linearisation of the wage–profit relation.

Coincidence of the basic and blocking sectors

Up to now we have assumed that the rate of profit r is identical in all the sectors of the economy. If we relax this assumption, we will be able to find conditions in which the basic sector is the blocking sector.

Let us revert to the beans example where the input matrix is

$$A = \begin{bmatrix} \frac{20}{23} & 0 \\ a_{21} & \frac{10}{11} \end{bmatrix} \qquad L = \begin{bmatrix} l_1 \\ l_2 \end{bmatrix}$$

Assume that the rates of profit of both activities are different and respectively equal to r and μr where $r \in [0 \ 0.15]$ and μ is a constant to be determined. $p = \begin{bmatrix} p_1 \\ p_2 \end{bmatrix}$ is the price vector and the price equations are

$$p_1 = (1+r)\frac{20}{23}p_1 + wl_1 \tag{1}$$

$$p_2 = (1+\mu r)\left(a_{21}p_1 + \frac{10}{11}p_2\right) + wl_2 \tag{2}$$

From equation (1) we deduce $p_1 = \dfrac{wl_1}{1-(1+r)\dfrac{20}{23}}$ which is positive for all

$r \in [0 \ 0.15[$ and equation (2) gives $\left[1-(1+\mu r)\dfrac{10}{11}\right]p_2 = wl_2 + (1+\mu r)a_{21}p_1$,

that is

$$p_2 = \frac{wl_2 + (1+\mu r)a_{21}p_1}{1-(1+\mu r)\dfrac{10}{11}} \tag{3}$$

At $r \in [0 \ 0.15[$ the numerator of (3) is positive while its denominator $1-(1+\mu r)\dfrac{10}{11}$ is positive provided

$$1 + \mu r < \frac{11}{10} \quad \text{or} \quad \mu r < \frac{11}{10} - 1 = \frac{1}{10} \text{ or } r < \frac{1}{10.\mu}.$$

If we choose μ such that $\frac{1}{10.\mu} > 0.15$ or $10\mu \leq \frac{1}{0.15} = \frac{100}{15} = \frac{20}{3}$ that is $\mu \leq \frac{2}{3}$, both prices and the wage are positive.

Thus, if we choose μr as the rate of profit of the activity producing beans, where $\mu \leq \frac{2}{3}$, when the rate of profit of the activity producing basic goods is r, then at $r \in [0 \ 0.15[$ the prices of both goods and the wage will all be positive.

In such conditions, the basic sector determines the model's maximum rate of profit $R = 15\%$ and with an exogenous rate of profit $r \in [0 \ R[$, price p_1 of the basic good, as well as the wage w.

Equation (2) will then allow us to calculate p_2 which is necessarily positive.

Suffice it to assume that the capitalists producing beans accept a lower rate of profit than the rest of the economy, to allow the basic sector to determine the maximum rate of profit.

Consider the general case of a decomposable model with k goods where the blocking sector has a maximum rate of profit R that is less than R_f, the rate of profit of the basic sector. At any rate of profit r of the basic sector, included between 0 and R_f, we obtain positive prices and wages for all the goods, provided we choose a rate of profit $\rho = \mu r$, where $\mu \leq \frac{R}{R_f}$, in all the non-basic sectors.

Anyway, the role of blocking goods is essential. It is explicit if we assume that the rate of profit is uniform in all the industries of the model. It is implicit if we relax that assumption since in that condition the rate of profit in the non-basic sector must be less than μr where $\mu = \frac{R}{R_f}$ depends on the internal return of blocking goods.

3.1.2 Determination of activity levels

Antibasic and non-antibasic processes

Let us contemplate the case when matrix A is decomposable, and after permutation of its rows and columns, it writes as

$$A = \begin{bmatrix} A_1^1 & 0 \\ A_2^1 & A_2^2 \end{bmatrix} \begin{matrix} n \\ k-n \end{matrix}$$
$$\begin{matrix} n & k-n \end{matrix}$$

where A_2^2 is an *indecomposable*[7] square matrix of order $k-n$ and A_1^1 is a square matrix of order n; all the activites are not on the same footing. We then have to distinguish between antibasic processes and non-antibasic processes as we have distinguished between basic goods and non-basic goods. Indeed, the equation systems of activity levels can now be written by distinguishing between y_1 and y_2, the vectors of activity levels respectively producing the first n and the last $(k-n)$ commodities with $y=(y_1,y_2)$.

Similarly, d_1 and d_2 are respectively the consumption structures of the first n and the last $(k-n)$ commodities with $d=(d_1,d_2)$

$$(1+g)(y_1,y_2) \qquad A=\begin{bmatrix} A_1^1 & 0 \\ A_2^1 & A_2^2 \end{bmatrix}+c(d_1,d_2)=(y_1,y_2)$$

Hence the two equation systems

$$\begin{cases} (1+g)(y_1A_1^1+y_2A_2^1)cd_1=y_1 \\ (1+g)y_2A_2^2+cd_2=y_2 \end{cases}$$

The *second* system of $(k-n)$ equations simultaneously determines the $(k-n)$ activity levels, the rate of growth g and the consumption level c.

Provided we choose a proper numeraire, there is one degree of freedom and we only have to determine one of the unknowns to obtain the others. In this case, therefore, the rate of growth is determined by the system of $(k-n)$ equations whatever the level of consumption c (if the exogeneous variable is the level of consumption). The processes forming the last $(k-n)$ rows after permutation (i.e., A_2) are thus 'basic' processes, as far as the determination of the rate of growth of the activity and consumption levels is concerned; while the commodities forming the first n columns (i.e., A^1) were 'basic' for the determination of the rate of profit, prices and wages. To avoid any ambiguity, we call the processes forming A_2 'antibasic'. We shall see later that they do not necessarily correspond to the processes producing luxury goods, or non-basic goods.

If we revert to the two equation system that we have just emphasised, the *first* (with n equations) allows to obtain the activity levels of what we shall call non-antibasic processes as a function of the activity levels of the antibasic processes and of the rate of growth determined within the antibasic system only.

Let us look more closely at the distinction between antibasic and non-antibasic processes to clarify the characteristics of an antibasic process. Sraffa defines a *basic good as a good entering, directly or indirectly, the production of all goods. Similarly, a process will be called antibasic if it uses all goods directly or indirectly.*[8] If this condition is not fulfilled, the process is said to be *non-antibasic*.

Existence and characteristics of non-antibasic processes

Let us revert to the decomposable matrix A. By writing matrices A and I as follows

$$A = \begin{bmatrix} A_1^1 & 0 \\ A_2^1 & A_2^2 \end{bmatrix} \text{ and } I = \begin{bmatrix} I_n & 0 \\ 0 & I_{k-n} \end{bmatrix}$$

The following properties appear:

Property 1

Matrix $\begin{bmatrix} A_1 \\ I_1 \end{bmatrix} = \begin{bmatrix} A_1^1 & 0 \\ I_n & 0 \end{bmatrix}$ composed of the first n rows of A and I, is

of rank n, which means that, when a matrix A is decomposable, there exists a number n and a permutation of the rows of A such that matrix $\begin{bmatrix} A_1 \\ I_1 \end{bmatrix}$ of dimension $(2n \times k)$ composed of the first n rows of A and I is of rank n.

Property 2

When $A_2^1 \geq 0$ and A_1^1 is *indecomposable* each of the last $(k-n)$ activities uses, directly or indirectly, *all* the goods since A_2^2 is indecomposable. These $(k-n)$ activities are antibasic and in this case $\begin{bmatrix} A_2 \\ I_2 \end{bmatrix} = \begin{bmatrix} A_2^1 & A_2^2 \\ 0 & I_{k-n} \end{bmatrix}$

is of rank strictly greater than $(k-n)$.

Thus, the condition for at least one antibasic process to exist in the system is that the rank of matrix $\begin{bmatrix} A_2 \\ I_2 \end{bmatrix}$, composed of the last $k-n$ rows of matrices A and I, is strictly greater than $k-n$. Of course this condition is not sufficient, as shown in the third configuration of case $\beta.2$ below. However, this condition is sufficient if the square matrix A_1^1 is indecomposable.

The determination of an antibasic process needs to be specified, all the more because antibasic processes do not necessarily coincide with those producing non-basic goods and, symmetrically, non-antibasic processes do not always correspond to those producing basic goods.

Several cases may be distinguished:

α. *matrix A is indecomposable: all processes are antibasic and all goods are basic.*

β. *matrix A is decomposable.*

$\beta.1$. *A is totally decomposable*: the economy can be considered as a juxtaposition of independent 'sub-economies' without any link between them. Then *there is no antibasic process and no basic good.*

$\beta.2$. *A is not totally decomposable.*

$\beta.2$. 1st configuration contemplated: A_1^1 and A_2^2 are indecomposable and $A_2^1 \geq 0$. Then, there are m antibasic processes and $(k-m)$ non-basic processes. In this case all non-basic goods are produced by antibasic processes and all basic goods are produced by non-basic processes.

$(k-m)$	A_1^1	0
(m)	A_2^1	A_2^2

$\beta.2$.2nd possible configuration[9]

$k-(m_1+m_2)$	A_1^1	0	0
m_2	A_2^1	A_2^2	0
m_1	A_3^1	A_3^2	A_3^3
	$k-(m_1+m_2)$	m_2	m_1

with A_1^1 and A_3^3 not entirely composed of zeros.
    In this case there are:

$k-(m_1+m_2)$	basic goods
m_1	antibasic processes
m_1+m_2	non-basic goods
$k-m_1$	non-antibasic processes

$\beta.2$.3rd configuration

$k-(m_1+m_2)$	A_1^1	0	0
m_2	A_2^1	A_2^2	0
m_1	A_3^1	0	A_3^3
	$k-(m_1+m_2)$	m_2	m_1

with A_2^1 and A_3^1 not entirely composed of zeros.
    In this case there are:

$k-(m_1+m_2)$	basic goods
m_1+m_2	non-basic goods

Note that in this configuration there are no antibasic processes.

β.2–4th configuration

$k-(m_1+m_2)$	A_1^1	0	0
m_2	0	A_2^2	0
m_1	A_3^1	A_3^2	A_3^3
	$k-(m_1+m_2)$	m_2	m_1

with A_3^1 and A_3^2 not entirely composed of zeros.

In this case there are m_1 antibasic processes, $k-m_1$ non-antibasic processes, and no basic good.

β.2–5th configuration

$k-(m_1+m_2)$	A_1^1	0	0
m_2	0	A_2^2	0
m_1	A_3^1	0	A_3^3
	$k-(m_1+m_2)$	m_2	m_1

Then, there are no basic goods and no antibasic processes. In fact we revert to the case of a totally decomposable matrix A. Suffice simultaneously to permute the first $k-(m_1+m_2)$ rows with the following m_2 rows and the first $k-(m_1+m_2)$ columns with the following m_2 ones to notice that after permutation A becomes

$$A = \begin{bmatrix} A_2^2 & 0 & 0 \\ 0 & A_1^1 & 0 \\ 0 & 0 & A_3^3 \end{bmatrix}$$

The table below reveals the conditions of decomposability of matrix A and the conditions of existence of antibasic processes in the simple production model $[A, I, L]$.

Decomposability of matrix A and existence of antibasic processes

Is there $m<k$ and a permutation of A such that matrix $[A^2, I^2]$ of dimension $k \times 2m$ is such that rank $[A^2, I^2] = m < k$?	no $\rightarrow$ A is *indecomposable* and all the goods are basic yes $\rightarrow$ A is *decomposable*.

As m is the greatest number such that rank $[A^2, I^2] = m < k$, is rank $[A^1, I^1] > k - m$?	no $\rightarrow$ A is *totally decomposable* and there is no basic good. yes $\rightarrow$ there is at least one basic good if A_2^2 is indecomposable.[10]

We can add that there are non-antibasic processes of different degrees. In the example developed on pages 68–71 we emphasised the existence of non-basic goods of degrees 1, 2 and 3. Similarly, we note that the last two activities are antibasic while the five others are non-antibasic of degrees 1, 2 and 3. We can see that both non-basic goods are produced by non-basic activities of the highest degree (3), the non-basic good of degree 1 is produced by the non-antibasic activity of degree 2, etc.

The activity levels are all positive only with a growth rate g that is less than the maximum growth rate $G = R = 0.111\ldots$ of the model defined by the blocking sector.

Note   We may always revert to the case when the antibasic sector is also the blocking sector. An analysis similar to that of section 1.1.7 leads to relaxing the assumption of a uniform growth rate in the model. In such conditions, if g is the growth rate of the antibasic sector, which means that it is included between 0 and G_a (the maximum growth rate of the sector), suffice to choose mg as the growth rate of the non-basic sector, where

$$m \leq \frac{G}{G_a},$$

G being the maximum growth rate of the blocking goods.

Choice of numeraire and the $c-g$ relation
In a k-sector model $[A, I, L, d]$ the system of activity levels writes

$$y = (1+g)yA + cd \tag{S}$$

where y is a row vector with k components which represents the vector of activity levels; d is a row vector with k components which represents consumption when $g = 0$; c is the level of consumption; g is the uniform rate of growth of the means of production.

System (S) with k equations, includes $k + 2$ unknowns: the k components of y, g and c. Thus we have two degrees of freedom.

As we have defined a standard $u \geq 0$ of prices p by writing $up = 1$, we shall define a numeraire of activity levels $v \geq 0$ which is a row vector of dimension k, by writing

$$yv = 1 \tag{1}$$

Note that in chapter 1 we wrote $yL = 1$ to show that the quantity of labour used by the system was equal to 1. In fact, this comes down to normalising the activity levels with the labour vector L.

From system (S) we obtain

$$y[I - (1 + g)A] = cd$$

or

$$y = cd[I - (1 + g)A]^{-1} \text{ if } g \in [0 \ \ G[\text{ where } G = R = \frac{1 - \alpha}{\alpha}$$

this results in

$$1 = yv = cd[I - (1 + g)A]^{-1}v$$

or

$$c = \frac{1}{d[I - (1 + g)A]^{-1}v}$$

It appears that c depends on g and since $[I - (1 + g)A]^{-1}$ is positive and an increasing function of g for $g \in [0 \ \ G[$, the relation $c - g$ is decreasing.

Of course, the exact shape of curve $c - g$ depends on the numeraire v. We may contemplate the case where the relation $c - g$ is linear. By analogy with relation $w - r$, it seems quite normal to choose $(I - A)\bar{p}$ as the numeraire of activity levels, where $\bar{p}$ is the eigenvector on the right of matrix A corresponding to its dominant eigenvalue $\alpha(A)$.

On this basis we add to the system

$$y = (1 + g)yA + cd \tag{S}$$

the normalisation equation

$$y(I - A)\bar{p} = 1 \tag{1'}$$

where $\bar{p}$ satisfies the relations

$$A\bar{p} = \alpha p = \frac{1}{1 + G}\bar{p} \text{ and } d\bar{p} = 1$$

From equation (S) we deduce

$$y\bar{p} = (1 + g)yA\bar{p} + cd\bar{p}$$

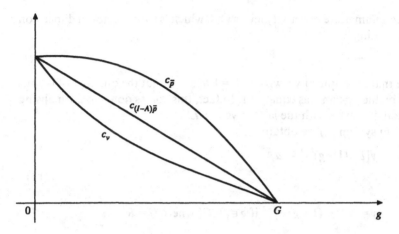

Figure 3.4

or

$$y(I-A)\bar{p}=gyA\bar{p}+c$$

that is

$$1=\frac{g}{G}+c$$

for $(1+G)A\bar{p}=\bar{p}$ implies $(1+G)yA\bar{p}=y\bar{p}$ or $GyA\bar{p}=y(I-A)\bar{p}=1$.

The shape of curve $c-g$ changes with the numeraire chosen, as shown on figure 3.4.

If matrix A is indecomposable, the eigenvector $\bar{p}$ is positive and only the numeraire $(I-A)\bar{p}$ makes the relation $c-g$ linear.[11]

If matrix A is decomposable there may be several numeraires making relation $c-g$ linear, as shown in the example below.

> *Example*
> Consider model $[A, I, L, d]$ where
>
> $$A=\begin{bmatrix} 0.6 & 0 \\ 0.2 & 0.4 \end{bmatrix} \qquad L=\begin{bmatrix} 1 \\ 1 \end{bmatrix}$$

and $d=[1,1]$.

There is a correspondence between the eigenvalues 0.6 and 0.4 respectively and the eigenvectors on the right $\bar{p}=\begin{pmatrix} 1 \\ 1 \end{pmatrix}>0$ and $\bar{p}_2=\begin{pmatrix} 0 \\ 1 \end{pmatrix}\geq 0$ satisfying $d\bar{p}=1$ and $d\bar{p}_2=1$. We show that the curve $c-g$ is also linear if we

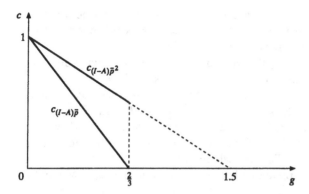

Figure 3.5

choose $(I-A)\bar{p}_2$ as a numeraire.[12] The maximum growth rate of the first good is $G = \dfrac{1-0.6}{0.6} = \dfrac{3}{2}$ while that of the second good is $\dfrac{1-0.4}{0.4} = \dfrac{3}{2}$.

We have here the same problem for determining the activity levels as for calculating production prices in the beans example; the exogenous variable g must be less than $G = \dfrac{3}{2}$ (and not only less than $G_2 = 1.5$) so that the activity level y_1 of the non-antibasic process is positive as c and y_2.

Thus, we have two numeraires of activity levels $(I-A)\bar{p}$ and $(I-A)\bar{p}_2$ allowing us to represent the relation $c-g$ by a segment of the line on the interval $[0\ \ G] = [0\ \ \frac{2}{3}]$ (see figure 3.5).

3.1.3 The role of blocking goods in the system

In the model that we have just developed, there were two numeraires of activity levels making the relation $c-g$ linear. We notice that in this model there is only one numeraire of prices, $(I-A)q$, where $q = (1\ \ 0)$ is defined by $qA = aq$ and $qL = 1$. Indeed, both components of q_2, the second eigenvector on the left of A, have opposite signs.

However, note that the maximum rate of profit R and the maximum growth rate G are equal and defined on the basis of the blocking sector which is composed of the sub-model $[0.6\ \ 1]$ describing the production of the first good in the first activity.

In the beans example where the input matrix is

$$A = \begin{bmatrix} \frac{20}{23} & 0 \\ a_{21} & \frac{10}{11} \end{bmatrix}$$

we have established the existence of two numeraires of prices making relation $w - r$ linear and we can easily show that there is only one numeraire of activity levels which makes relation $c - g$ linear.

The maximum rate of profits R and the maximum growth rate G are equal and defined by the blocking sector consisting here in model $[\begin{smallmatrix} 10 \\ 11 \end{smallmatrix} \ 1]$ which describes the production of the second good in the second activity.

In both cases the blocking sector determines R and G which are necessarily equal. Further, we can see that the beans example does make some sense for if it is not true for production prices it is true for activity levels (except for the peculiar case where $\alpha_2 = \alpha$).

We may now contemplate the three-sector model $[A, I, L, d]$ where

$$A = \begin{bmatrix} 0.4 & 0 & 0 \\ 0.1 & 0.6 & 0 \\ 0.1 & 0.6 & 0.5 \end{bmatrix} \qquad L = \begin{bmatrix} 2 \\ 1 \\ 1 \end{bmatrix} \qquad \text{and } d = [1 \ 1 \ 1]$$

The blocking sector is different from both the basic and the non-basic sectors.

Matrix A has three eigenvalues: $\alpha = 0.6$ which is the dominant eigenvalue of A, $\alpha^2 = 0.5$ which is the dominant eigenvalue of the antibasic sector $\alpha(A_3^3)$ and $\alpha^3 = 0.4$ which is the basic sector's, $\alpha(A_1^1)$. Thus, in this model we have both the problem that is dual to the 'beans' problem for the production prices since $\alpha(A_1^1) < \alpha$ and the problem that is dual to the 'beans' problem for the activity levels since $\alpha(A_3^3) < \alpha$. We need to choose $r < R = (1 - 0.6)/0.6 = 2/3$ so that the prices of non-basic goods are positive (while for $r < (1 - 0.4)/0.4 = 1.5$ the prices of basic goods and the wage are positive) and $g < G = (1 - 0.6)/0.6 = 2/3$ so that the activity levels of the non-antibasic processes are positive (while for $r < (1 - 0.5)/0.5 = 1$ the activity levels of anti-basic processes and the consumption level are positive).

In this model we have two numeraires $q = (I - A)$ and $q^3 = (I - A)$ making the wage–profit relation linear; we have $q = \left(\dfrac{1}{4}, \dfrac{1}{2}, 0 \right)$ defined by $qA = 0.6q$ and $qL = 1$ which corresponds to $R = \dfrac{1 - 0.6}{0.6} = \dfrac{2}{3}$ and $q^3 = (1/2, 0, 0)$ defined by $q^3 A = 0,4q^3$ and $q^3 L = 1$ which corresponds to $R^3 = (1 - 0.4)/0.4 = 1.5$.

Similarly, there are two numeraires $(I - A)\bar{p}$ and $(I - A)\bar{p}^2$ making relation $c - g$ linear; we have $\bar{p} = \begin{bmatrix} 0 \\ 1/2 \\ 1/2 \end{bmatrix}$ defined by $A\bar{p} = 0.6\bar{p}$ and $d\bar{p} = 1$ which corresponds to $G = (1 - 0.6)/0.6 = 2/3$ and $\bar{p}^2 = \begin{bmatrix} 0 \\ 0 \\ 1 \end{bmatrix}$ defined by

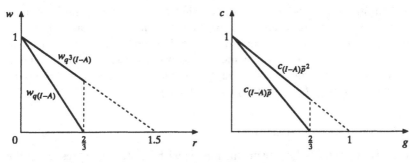

Figure 3.6a   Figure 3.6b

$A\bar{p}^2 = 0.5\bar{p}^2$ and $d\bar{p}^2 = 1$ which corresponds to $G^2 = (1 - 0.5)/0.5 = 1$.

Thus we have two $(w-r)$ relations and two $(c-g)$ relations which are represented by straight lines in the interval $[0\ R[= [0\ G[= [0\ 2/3[$ (see figure 3.6).

To sum up, in a decomposable model (A, I, L, d) containing at least one basic good and an antibasic process,[13] there is always a dominant eigenvalue α to which corresponds an eigenvector on the left $q \geq 0$ and an eigenvector on the right $\bar{p} \geq 0$, which means that the model has a numeraire of prices and a numeraire of activity levels associated with $R = G = (1 - \alpha)/\alpha$, which respectively make relations $w - r$ and $c - g$ linear.

This is at variance with the case when matrix A is indecomposable where there may exist other numeraires making relations $w - r$ and/or $c - g$ linear.

More precisely, when matrix A has the following configuration

$$A = \begin{bmatrix} A_1^1 & 0 & 0 \\ A_2^1 & A_2^2 & 0 \\ A_3^1 & A_3^2 & A_3^3 \end{bmatrix}$$

where A_1^1, A_2^2 and A_3^3 are indecomposable matrices, we know that:

if the dominant eigenvalue $\alpha(A_1^1)$ of the basic sector is inferior to the dominant eigenvalue α of matrix A, there always are other numeraires making relation $w - r$ linear;

if the dominant eigenvalue $\alpha(A_3^3)$ of the antibasic sector is inferior to the dominant eigenvalue α of matrix A, there always are other numeraires ensuring the linearisation of relation $c - g$;

if $\alpha(A_1^1)$ and $\alpha(A_3^3)$ are both less than the dominant eigenvalue $\alpha = \alpha(A_2^2)$ of matrix A, we always have both properties.

3.2 Irregular systems

If we integrate the structure of the needs in labour of the various activitites into the analysis, thus contemplating system (A, I, L), new peculiarities may appear; the systems where they appear are called 'irregular'. Similarly, taking into account the structure of the final consumption will lead to studying systems (A, I, d) in which these peculiarities may also appear. Thus, we shall distinguish two types of irregularities, *irregular price systems* (A, I, L) and *irregular activity systems* (A, I, d).

3.2.1 Irregular price systems

We have to define a labour profile matrix with k columns representing the first k successive layers of labour. If there are only m independent layers of labour (with $m < k$), the system is said to be irregular and two specific features may be emphasised.

On the one hand, *when r varies*, only price vectors $p(r_1), p(r_2), \ldots, p(r_m)$ corresponding to m rates of profit $r_1, r_2, \ldots, r_m$, all different, vary independently from one another. On the other hand, the price vector $p(r_{m+1})$ corresponding to any $(m+1)^{th}$ rate of profits r will be a linear combination of $p(r_1), p(r_2), \ldots, p(r_m)$. Further, for a given r, only m equations of prices can be considered as independent: the determination of the prices of m of the k goods entails, when the system is irregular, the determination of the prices of the $(k-m)$ other goods. It is only when the system is regular that no additional constraints are imposed on the determination of prices and that the k prices are determined by linearly independent k equations.

Matrix K of labour profile

The price vector $p(r)$ of a k-sector model $[A, I, L]$ can write as follows (see proposition 1, mathematical appendix)

$$p(r) = w[\beta_0 L + \beta_1 AL + \ldots + \beta_j A^j L + \ldots + \beta_{k-1} A^{k-1} L] \qquad (1)$$

or

$$bj = \frac{(1+r)^j + c_1(1+r)^{j+1} + \ldots + c_{k-1+j}(1+r)^{k-1}}{1 + c_1(1+r) + \ldots + c_k(1+r)^k}$$

$$= \frac{(1+r)^j [1 + \sum_{i=1}^{k-1-j} c_i(1+r)^i]}{1 + \sum_{i=1}^{k} c_i(1+r)^i}$$

Then, the price wage writes

$$\hat{p}(r) = \frac{p(r)}{w} = \sum_{j=0}^{k-1} = \beta_j A^j L$$

Thus, whatever the distribution, price $p(r)$ only depends on the first k layers of labour $L, AL, A^2L, ..., A^{k-1}L$.

Definition
We call labour profile matrix the square matrix

$$K = [L, AL, A^2L, ..., A^{k-1}L]$$

the k columns of which represent the first k layers of labour of model $[A, I, L]$.

Expression of $\hat{p}(r)$ as a function of K   By calling $\beta(r)$ the column vector $(\beta_0, \beta_1, \beta_2, ..., \beta_{k-1})'$, where M' stands for the transpose of M, the vector $\hat{p}(r)$ then writes

$$\hat{p}(r) = K\beta(r)$$

Rank of matrix K   We call *rank m* of matrix K the number of column vectors *independent* of matrix K.

Note that from relation (1) we deduce that price $p(r)$ only depends on the first m layers of labour – where $1 \leq m \leq k$ – when matrix K is of rank m.

Rank m of matrix K is going to play an important role in the behaviour and the evolution of prices $p(r)$ as a function of the rate of profit r.

Regular system
System $[A, I, L]$ is said to be regular when the labour profile matrix K is of full rank, that is rank k.

Note that if an eigenvector q_i on the left of matrix A corresponding to an eigenvalue α_i, is orthogonal to L, we have $q_i A^j L = \alpha_i^j q_i L = 0$ for all $j = 0, 1, 2, ...$ The k vectors $L, AL, A^2L, ..., A^{k-1}L$ which are orthogonal to q_i, belong to a vector sub-space of R^k of dimension $k - 1$ othogonal to q_i.

Then, matrix K, the rank of which is at most equal to $k - 1$, is not of full rank and system $[A, I, L]$ is not regular if L is orthogonal to an eigenvector on the left q_i of A.[14]

In fact matrix K is of full rank if and only if all the eigenvalues of matrix A are semi-simple and none of the eigenvectors q_i on the left of A is orthogonal to L.

Irregular system
System $[A, I, L]$ is said to be irregular when K is of rank $m < k$.

Before addressing the evolution of $p(r)$, we will first recall the definition and the properties of a kernel of linear application associated with a matrix.

Kernel of linear applications associated with K and $\hat{p}(r)$ The *application* which associates vector $xK = (xL, xAL, ..., xA^{k-1}L)$ representing the first k layers of labour used to produce x to any activity level vector (or gross production) $x = (x_1, x_2, \ldots, x_k)$, is *linear*.

Kernel of the linear application associated with K We call kernel of the linear application defined by matrix K, the vector sub-space of R^k

$$N(K) = \{z \in R^k | zK = 0\} \qquad (2)$$

Since $zK = [zL, zAL, \ldots, zA^{k-1}L]$ if $z \in N[K]$ we have $zK = 0$ which is equivalent to

$$zA^nL = 0 \qquad \forall n = 0, 1, 2, \ldots, k-1 \qquad (3)$$

Further (see chapter 2, section 5)

$$A^k = [c_1 A^{k-1} + c_2 A^{k-2} + \ldots + c_{k-1} A + c_k I]$$

As a result

$$zA^kL = [c_1 z A^{k-1}L + c_2 z A^{k-2}L + \ldots + c_{k-1} AL + c_k zL] = 0$$

when we have inequalities (3).

We can see that these inequalities imply

$$zA^nL = 0 \qquad \forall n = 0, 1, 2, \ldots \qquad (4)$$

and relations (2), (3) and (4) are equivalent.

Kernel of the linear application associated with $\hat{p}(r)$ The application which associates its wage price $x\hat{p}(r)$ with every gross production vector $x = (x_1, \ldots, x_k)$ is linear.[15] The kernel of this linear application

$$N(\hat{p}(r)) = \{z \in R^k | zk = 0\} \qquad (5)$$

is a vector sub-space of R^k

We have

$$N[K] = N[\hat{p}(r)] = N[p(r)] \qquad (6)$$

Number of independent prices for a given rate of profit

For every $r \in [-1 \ R[$ we have $N[p(r)] = N[K]$ and if matrix K is of rank m the kernel $N[p(r)] = N[K]$ is a vector sub-space of R^k of dimension $k - m$. Thus, to any base $z_1, \ldots, z_h, \ldots, z_{k-m}$ of $N[p(r)]$ we can make the $(k - m)$ *independent equations* correspond

$$\begin{cases} z_1 p(r) = 0 & z_{11} p_1(r) + \ldots + z_{1i} p_i(r) + \ldots + z_{1k} p_k(r) = 0 \\ \ldots \\ z_h p(r) = 0 & \Leftrightarrow z_{h1} p_1(r) + \ldots + z_{hi} p_i(r) + \ldots + z_{hk} p_k(r) = 0 \\ \ldots \\ z_{k-m} p(r) = 0 & z_{k-m,1} p_1(r) + \ldots + z_{k-m,i} p_i(r) + \ldots + z_{k-m,k} p_k(r) = 0 \end{cases} \qquad (7)$$

which link the prices of the k goods.

As a result, with the aid of relation (7), we can deduce the price of the $k-m$ other goods when the prices of m of the k goods are known, i.e., there exists a decomposable model with m basic goods which has the same price system as the indecomposable irregular model $[A, I, L]$.

Indeed, if k is of rank m any square matrix Z of order k such that $ZK=0$, has its k rows orthogonal to m linearly independent row vectors of K. Thus, matrix K is totally determined as soon as k of its columns are determined arbitrarily. If we choose $k-m$ columns of Z equal to the $k-m$ corresponding columns of matrix A, the matrix $A-Z$ will have $k-m$ zero columns and will be decomposable. Further, since $ZK=0$ we have $Zp(r)=0$ for every $r \in [-1 \ R[$ and the price system of model $[A, I, L]$

$$p(r) = (1+r)Ap(r) + wL$$

also writes

$$p(r) = (1+r)[Ap(r) - Zp(r)] + wL = (1+r)(A-Z)p(r) + wL$$

This means that $p(r)$ is also a price system of the decomposable model $[A-Z, I, L]$ which has m basic goods and $k-m$ non-basic goods since $A-Z$ has $k-m$ zero columns. Of course there are $k!/m!(k-m)!$ decomposable systems $[A-Z, I, L]$ equivalent to the irregular indecomposable system $[A, I, L]$, where the rank of K is equal to m since there are $k!/m!(k-m)!$ ways of choosing $k-m$ columns among the k columns of matrix A.

Example of irregular indecomposable model $[A, I, L]$ Consider the model $[A, I, L]$ where

$$A = \begin{bmatrix} \frac{1}{2} & \frac{4}{15} & \frac{1}{8} \\ \frac{5}{18} & \frac{5}{18} & \frac{5}{16} \\ \frac{2}{9} & \frac{4}{45} & \frac{5}{12} \end{bmatrix} \quad \text{and} \quad L = \begin{bmatrix} 0.74 \\ 0.10 \\ 0.16 \end{bmatrix}$$

We have $AL = \frac{1}{3} \begin{bmatrix} 1.25 \\ 0.85 \\ 0.72 \end{bmatrix}$ and $A^2 L = \frac{1}{9} \begin{bmatrix} 2.825 \\ 2.425 \\ 1.96 \end{bmatrix}$; we notice $A^2 L = AL - (5/36)L$ meaning that matrix $K = [L, AL, A^2 L]$ is of rank 2. The indecomposable system $[A, I, L]$ is thus irregular. Since the rank of the labour profile matrix K is equal to 2, there exists a non-zero square matrix Z such that $ZK=0$ and which shares any $(=3-2)$ column with A.

If Z and A share the last column, it has the following form

$$Z = \begin{bmatrix} z_{11} & z_{12} & \frac{1}{8} \\ z_{21} & z_{22} & \frac{5}{16} \\ z_{31} & z_{32} & \frac{5}{12} \end{bmatrix} \quad \text{where}$$

z_{11} and z_{12} are solutions to $z_1 K = 0$ or $z_1 L = 0$ and $z_1 AL = 0$, that is

$$\begin{cases} 0.74z_{11} + 0.10z_{12} + \frac{1}{8}.0.16 = 0 \\ \\ 1.25z_{11} + 0.85z_{12} + \frac{1}{8}.0.72 = 0 \end{cases}$$ hence $z_{11} = \frac{-1}{63}$ and $z_{12} = \frac{-5.2}{63}$

z_{21} and z_{22} are solutions to $z_2 K = 0$ or $z_2 L = 0$ and $z_2 AL = 0$, that is

$$\begin{cases} 0.74z_{21} + 0.10z_{22} + \frac{5}{16}.0.16 = 0 \\ \\ 1.25z_{21} + 0.85z_{22} + \frac{5}{16}.0.72 = 0 \end{cases}$$ hence $z_{21} = \frac{-2.5}{63}$ and $z_{22} = \frac{-13}{63}$

z_{31} and z_{32} are solutions to $z_3 K = 0$ or $z_3 L$ and $z_3 AL = 0$, that is

$$\begin{cases} 0.74z_{31} + 0.10z_{32} + \frac{5}{12}.0.16 = 0 \\ \\ 1.25z_{31} + 0.85z_{32} + \frac{5}{12}.0.72 = 0 \end{cases}$$ hence $z_{31} = \frac{-10}{3.63}$ and $z_{32} = \frac{-52}{3.63}$

thus we have $Z = \frac{1}{63} \begin{bmatrix} -1 & -5.2 & 63\frac{1}{8} \\ -2.5 & -13 & 63\frac{5}{16} \\ \frac{-10}{3} & \frac{-52}{3} & 63\frac{5}{12} \end{bmatrix}$ and $A.Z = \frac{1}{63} \begin{bmatrix} 32.5 & 22 & 0 \\ 20 & 35.5 & 0 \\ \frac{52}{3} & \frac{68.8}{3} & 0 \end{bmatrix}$, and

the decomposable system $[A - Z, I, L]$ has the same price system as $[A, I, L]$ which is indecomposable and irregular.

If we choose a matrix $\bar{Z}$ sharing its second column with A, we have

$$\bar{Z} = \begin{bmatrix} z_{11} & \frac{4}{15} & z_{13} \\ z_{21} & \frac{5}{18} & z_{23} \\ z_{31} & \frac{4}{45} & z_{32} \end{bmatrix} \text{ where}$$

z_{i1} and z_{i3} are solutions to $z_i K = 0$, i.e., $z_i L = 0$ and $z_i AL = 0$, with $i = 1, 2, 3$. We obtain

$z_{11} = \frac{4.8}{93.6}$ $z_{13} = \frac{-37.8}{93.6}$

$z_{21} = \frac{5}{93.6}$ $z_{23} = \frac{-39.375}{93.6}$ and $\bar{Z} = \frac{1}{93.6} \begin{bmatrix} 4.8 & 93.6.\frac{4}{15} & -37.8 \\ 5 & 93.6.\frac{5}{18} & -39.375 \\ 1.6 & 93.6.\frac{4}{45} & -12.6 \end{bmatrix}$

$z_{31} = \frac{1.6}{93.6}$ $z_{33} = \frac{-12.6}{93.6}$

thus, we have $A - \bar{Z} = \frac{1}{93.6} \begin{bmatrix} 42 & 0 & 49.5 \\ 21 & 0 & 68.625 \\ 19.2 & 0 & 51.6 \end{bmatrix}$.

And the decomposable system $[A - \bar{Z}, I, L]$ has the same price system as the indecomposable and irregular system $[A, I, L]$.

While in model $[A-Z,I,L]$ the first two goods are basic goods and the third is non-basic, in model $[A-\bar{Z},I,L]$ the first and the third goods are basic goods and the second is non-basic.

Similarly, we can determine matrix

$$\bar{\bar{Z}}=\begin{bmatrix} \frac{1}{2} & 2.6 & -3.9375 \\ \frac{5}{18} & \frac{13}{9} & -2.1875 \\ \frac{2}{9} & \frac{10.4}{9} & -1.75 \end{bmatrix}$$

which shares the first column with A, and such that $\bar{\bar{Z}}K=0$.

Thus we have $A-\bar{\bar{Z}}=\begin{bmatrix} 0 & \frac{-7}{3} & 4.0625 \\ 0 & \frac{-7}{6} & 2.5 \\ 0 & \frac{-16}{15} & \frac{13}{6} \end{bmatrix}$ and in the decomposable system

$[A-\bar{\bar{Z}},I,L]$ which is equivalent to the indecomposable and irregular system $[A,I,L]$, the last two goods are basic goods while the first good is not.

Now, let us consider a model $[A,I,L]$ where we still have

$$A=\begin{bmatrix} \frac{1}{2} & \frac{4}{15} & \frac{1}{8} \\ \frac{5}{18} & \frac{5}{18} & \frac{5}{16} \\ \frac{2}{9} & \frac{4}{45} & \frac{5}{12} \end{bmatrix}$$

but $L=\begin{bmatrix} 1.1 \\ 1 \\ 0.8 \end{bmatrix}$

We have $AL=(5/6)L$ and $A^2L=(5/6)AL=(25/36)L$, which means that matrix $K=[L,AL,A^2L]$ is of rank 1. The indecomposable system $[A,I,L]$ is thus irregular. Since K, the labour profile matrix, is of rank 1, there exists a non-zero square matrix Z such that $ZK=0$ which shares two $(=3-1)$ columns with A.

If Z shares its last two columns with A it has the form

$$Z=\begin{bmatrix} z_{11} & \frac{4}{15} & \frac{1}{18} \\ z_{21} & \frac{5}{18} & \frac{5}{16} \\ z_{31} & \frac{4}{45} & \frac{5}{12} \end{bmatrix}$$

z_{11} is the solution to $z_1K=0$ or $z_1L=0$, that is

$$1.1z_{11}+\tfrac{4}{15}+\tfrac{1}{8}.0.8=0$$

hence $z_{11}=\frac{-5}{15}=\frac{-1}{3}$.

z_{21} is the solution to $z_2K=0$ or $z_2L=0$, that is

$$1.1z_{21}+\tfrac{5}{18}+\tfrac{5}{16}.0.8=0$$

hence $z_{21} = \frac{-95}{198}$.

z_{31} is the solution to $z_3 K = 0$ or $z_3 L = 0$, that is

$$1.1 z_{31} + \frac{4}{45} + \frac{5}{12}.0.8 = 0$$

hence $z_{31} = \frac{-38}{99}$.

Thus we have

$$Z = \begin{bmatrix} \frac{-1}{3} & \frac{4}{15} & \frac{1}{8} \\ \frac{-95}{198} & \frac{5}{18} & \frac{5}{16} \\ \frac{-38}{99} & \frac{4}{45} & \frac{5}{12} \end{bmatrix}$$

and

$$A - Z = \begin{bmatrix} \frac{5}{6} & 0 & 0 \\ \frac{25}{33} & 0 & 0 \\ \frac{20}{33} & 0 & 0 \end{bmatrix}$$

and the decomposable model $[A - Z, I, L]$ has the same price system as the indecomposable and irregular system $[A, I, L]$.

If we choose a matrix $\bar{Z}$ sharing its first two columns with A, it has the following form

$$\bar{Z} = \begin{bmatrix} \frac{1}{2} & \frac{4}{15} & z_{13} \\ \frac{5}{18} & \frac{5}{18} & z_{23} \\ \frac{2}{9} & \frac{2}{45} & z_{33} \end{bmatrix}$$

z_{i3} is the solution to $z_i K = 0$, that is, $z_i L = 0$, with $i = 1,2,3$. We obtain $z_{13} = -49/48$, $z_{23} = -35/48$ and $z_{33} = -20/48$, and

$$\bar{Z} = \begin{bmatrix} \frac{1}{2} & \frac{4}{15} & \frac{-49}{48} \\ \frac{5}{18} & \frac{5}{18} & \frac{-35}{48} \\ \frac{2}{9} & \frac{2}{45} & \frac{-20}{48} \end{bmatrix}$$

$$\text{matrix } A - \bar{Z} = \begin{bmatrix} 0 & 0 & \frac{55}{44} \\ 0 & 0 & \frac{50}{48} \\ 0 & 0 & \frac{40}{48} \end{bmatrix}$$

and the decomposable model $[A - \bar{Z}, I, L]$ has the same price system as $[A, I, L]$.

While in model $[A - Z, I, L]$ only the first good is basic, in model $[A - \bar{Z}, I, L]$ only the third good is basic. These two examples show quite well that an indecomposable and irregular model $[A, I, L]$ has the same price system as several decomposable systems $[A - Z, I, L]$ where $ZK = 0$. If the rank of matrix $K = [L, AL, A^2 L, \ldots, A^{k-1} L]$ is equal to m, we can always find a decomposable system $[A-Z,I,L]$ equivalent to $[A,I,L]$, with m basic goods (which can be chosen arbitrarily) and $k-m$ non-basic goods. In this case any numeraire is a price standard since L is the eigenvector on the right of A.

As far as the determination of prices is concerned, we can see that at a given rate of profit, in irregular or decomposable systems, only some of the goods have their prices vary independently from one another. There is a difference between decomposable models and irregular systems though. In any decomposable model, there are non-basic goods, the prices of which are deduced from that of basic goods. While in an irregular system, whose matrix K is of rank m, the m goods, the price of which vary independently, can be chosen arbitrarily among the k goods produced by the system.

Variations of $p(r)$ as a function of r

We have established that $zp(r)=0$ is equivalent to $zK=0$. Let us consider k rates of profit $r_1,r_2,\ldots,r_k$, all different, and the square matrix: $P(r_1,\ldots,r_h,\ldots,r_k)=[p(r_1),\ldots,p(r_h),\ldots,p(r_k)]$. Since $zP=0 \Leftrightarrow zp(r_h)=0$ $\forall h=1,2,\ldots,k \Leftrightarrow zK=0$, we have $N[P]=N[K]$ and matrices P and K have the same rank. Consequently, if K is of rank m, the price vectors $p(r_1),p(r_2),\ldots,p(r_m)$ corresponding to m rates of profit $r_1,r_2,\ldots,r_m$, all different, move *independently* of one another. On the other hand, the price vector $p(r)$ corresponding to any $(m+1)^{\text{th}}$ rate of profit r, will be a linear combination of $p(r_1),p(r_2),\ldots,p(r_m)$. Since the rank of matrix K represents the number of independent layers of labour, when distribution varies, the price vector $p(r)$ takes as many independent values as there are independent layers of labour.

More particularly, if the rank of matrix K is equal to 1, that is to say, $AL=\alpha L$. The price vector $p(r)$ is homothetic to L whatever the value of r. In that case the price system does not change. However, if the rank of matrix K is equal to k, the rank of matrix $P[r_1,\ldots,r_2,\ldots,r_k]$ is also equal to k and we obtain the maximum number k of linearly independent price vectors $p(r_1),p(r_2),\ldots,p(r_k)$.

3.2.2 Irregular systems of activity levels

As we have distinguished irregular and regular price systems when the input matrix A of model $[A,I,L]$ was indecomposable, we shall now distinguish regular and irregular systems of activity levels. We have to define the square matrix $C=[d,dA,dA^2,\ldots,dA^{k-1}]$, that we call the matrix of consumption profile.

In this case, where d is the eigenvector on the left of the indecomposable square matrix A of order k, matrix $C = [d, dA, dA^2, \ldots, dA^{k-1}]$, which we call the consumption profile matrix, is of rank 1.

If the k columns $d, dA, dA^2, \ldots, dA^{k-1}$ representing the first k successive layers of consumption associated to gross production y are independent, the system of activity levels of model $[A, I, d]$ is said to be regular.

Otherwise matrix C is of rank n where $1 \le n < k$ and the system is said to be irregular for the activity levels. If we consider k rates of growth $g_1, g_2, \ldots, g_k$ all different, the activity level vectors $y(g_1), y(g_2), \ldots, y(g_n)$ corresponding to the n rates of growth $g_1, g_2, \ldots, g_n$ vary *independently* of one another. On the other hand, the activity level $y(g)$ corresponding to any $(n+1)^{\text{th}}$ rate of growth g is a linear combination of $y(g_1), y(g_2), \ldots, y(g_n)$.

Similarly, for any $g \in [-1 \ \ G[$ the k activity levels $y_1(g), y_2(g), \ldots, y_k(g)$ are linked by $k - n$ *independent equations* if matrix C is of rank n. As soon as we know the activity levels of n of the k processes we can deduce those of the $k - n$ other processes.

In other words, there exists a *decomposable* model with n antibasic processes having the same system of activity levels $y(g)$ as the irregular indecomposable model $[A, I, d]$.

Example of irregular indecomposable model $[A, I, d]$

Let us consider the model $[A, I, d]$ where

$$A = \begin{bmatrix} \frac{1}{2} & \frac{4}{15} & \frac{1}{8} \\ \frac{5}{18} & \frac{5}{18} & \frac{5}{16} \\ \frac{2}{9} & \frac{4}{45} & \frac{5}{12} \end{bmatrix} \text{ and } d = [1 \ \ 0.8 \ \ 0.5]$$

We have $dA = 1/3[2.5 \ \ 1.6 \ \ 1.75]$ and $dA^2 = 1/9[6.25 \ \ 3.8 \ \ 4.625]$. We can see that $dA^2 = dA - \frac{1.25}{9} d$ which means that matrix $C = [d \ \ dA \ \ dA^2]$ is of rank 2. The indecomposable system $[A, I, d]$ is thus irregular. Since C, the rank of the consumption profile matrix, is equal to 2, there exists a non-zero square matrix Z sharing with A any $(= 3 - 2)$ row such that $CZ = 0$.

$$\bar{Z} = \begin{bmatrix} \frac{-1}{3} & \frac{-2}{15} & \frac{-5}{8} \\ \frac{5}{18} & \frac{1}{9} & \frac{25}{48} \\ \frac{2}{9} & \frac{4}{45} & \frac{5}{12} \end{bmatrix} \text{ satisfies } CZ = 0 \text{ and shares its third row with } A.$$

$$\text{Matrix } A - Z = \frac{1}{120} \begin{bmatrix} 100 & 48 & 90 \\ 0 & 20 & -25 \\ 0 & 0 & 0 \end{bmatrix}$$

has its third row composed of zeros, and the decomposable model $[A - Z, I, d]$ has the same system of activity levels y as the irregular and indecomposable model $[A, I, d]$ since $y = (1+g)yA + cd = (1+g)y(A-Z)$ $+ cd$, owing to the fact that $CZ = 0$ implies $yZ = 0$.[16]

$$\bar{Z} = \begin{bmatrix} \frac{-1}{3} & \frac{-1}{3} & \frac{-3}{8} \\ \frac{5}{18} & \frac{5}{18} & \frac{5}{16} \\ \frac{2}{9} & \frac{2}{9} & \frac{1}{4} \end{bmatrix}$$ satisfies $C\bar{Z} = 0$ and shares its second row with A.

$$\text{Matrix } A - \bar{Z} = \tfrac{1}{30} \begin{bmatrix} 25 & 18 & 15 \\ 0 & 0 & 0 \\ 0 & -4 & 5 \end{bmatrix}$$

has its second row composed of zeros and the decomposable model $[A - \bar{Z}, I, d]$ has the same activity level system as the irregular and indecomposable model $[A, I, d]$. We can see that in model $[A - \bar{Z}, I, d]$ the first and the third processes are antibasic and the second process is non-antibasic while in model $[A - Z, I, d]$ the first two processes are antibasic and the third is non-antibasic.

$$\bar{\bar{Z}} = \begin{bmatrix} \frac{1}{2} & \frac{4}{45} & \frac{1}{8} \\ \frac{-5}{12} & \frac{-2}{27} & \frac{-5}{48} \\ \frac{-1}{3} & \frac{-8}{135} & \frac{-1}{12} \end{bmatrix}$$ satisfies $C\bar{\bar{Z}} = 0$ and shares its first row with A.

$$\text{Matrix } A - \bar{\bar{Z}} = \tfrac{1}{108} \begin{bmatrix} 0 & 0 & 0 \\ 75 & 38 & 45 \\ 60 & 16 & 54 \end{bmatrix}$$

has its first row composed of zeros and in the decomposable model $[A - \bar{\bar{Z}}, I, d]$, which is equivalent to the irregular indecomposable model $[A, I, d]$, the last two processes are antibasic while the first process is non-antibasic.

Now let us consider model $[A, I, d]$ where we always have

$$A = \begin{bmatrix} \frac{1}{2} & \frac{4}{15} & \frac{1}{8} \\ \frac{5}{18} & \frac{5}{18} & \frac{5}{16} \\ \frac{2}{9} & \frac{4}{45} & \frac{5}{12} \end{bmatrix} \text{ but } d = [1 \ \ 0.6 \ \ 0.75]$$

We have $dA = [5/6 \ \ 1/2 \ \ 5/8] = 5/6[1 \ \ 0.6 \ \ 0.75]$ and $dA^2 = dA.A = 5/6dA$ $= 25/36d$, which means that matrix $C = [d \ dA \ dA^2]$ is of rank 1. The indecomposable system $[A, I, d]$ is thus irregular. Since C, the rank of the consumption profile matrix, is equal to 1, there exists a non-zero square matrix Z sharing with A any two $(=3-1)$ rows, such that $CZ = 0$.

$$\text{matrix } Z = \begin{bmatrix} \frac{1}{2} & \frac{4}{15} & \frac{1}{8} \\ \frac{5}{18} & \frac{5}{18} & \frac{5}{16} \\ \frac{-8}{29} & \frac{-26}{45} & \frac{-5}{12} \end{bmatrix}$$ satisfies $CZ = 0$ and shares its first two rows

with A.

$$\text{Matrix } A - Z = \tfrac{1}{18} \begin{bmatrix} 0 & 0 & 0 \\ 0 & 0 & 0 \\ 20 & 12 & 15 \end{bmatrix}$$

has its first two rows composed of zeros and the decomposable model $[A - Z, I, d]$ has the same system of activity levels y as the irregular indecomposable model $[A, I, d]$.

$$\bar{Z} = \begin{bmatrix} \tfrac{-1}{2} & \tfrac{4}{15} & \tfrac{1}{8} \\ \tfrac{-10}{9} & \tfrac{-5}{9} & \tfrac{-35}{48} \\ \tfrac{2}{9} & \tfrac{4}{45} & \tfrac{5}{12} \end{bmatrix} \text{ satisfies } C\bar{Z} = 0 \text{ and shares its first and third rows}$$

with A.

$$A - \bar{Z} = \tfrac{5}{72} \begin{bmatrix} 0 & 0 & 0 \\ 20 & 12 & 15 \\ 0 & 0 & 0 \end{bmatrix}$$

has its first and last rows composed of zeros and the decomposable model $[A - \bar{Z}, I, d]$ is equivalent to model $[A, I, d]$ which is irregular and indecomposable.

While in model $[A - Z, I, d]$ only the last process is antibasic, in model $[A - \bar{Z}, I, d]$, only the second process is antibasic.

Similarly, the decomposable model $[A - \bar{\bar{Z}}, I, d]$, where

$$A - \bar{\bar{Z}} = \tfrac{1}{24} \begin{bmatrix} 20 & 12 & 15 \\ 0 & 0 & 0 \\ 0 & 0 & 0 \end{bmatrix}$$

is equivalent to system $[A, I, d]$ and its first process is antibasic and the last two processes are non-antibasic. These two examples show that an irregular indecomposable model $[A, I, d]$ has the same system of activity levels as several decomposable models $[A - Z, I, d]$ where $CZ = 0$. If the rank of matrix $C = [d \ dA \ dA^2 \ldots dA^{k-1}]$ is equal to n, we can always find a decomposable model $[A - Z, I, d]$, equivalent to $[A, I, d]$, which has n antibasic processes (that can be chosen arbitrarily) and $k - n$ non-antibasic processes.

Mathematical appendix

Proposition 1
If A is a square matrix of order k, we have

$$[I - (1 + r)A]^{-1}L = \sum_{j=0}^{k-1} \beta_j A^j L \qquad \forall r \in [-1 \ R]$$

where $bj = \dfrac{(1+r)^j + c_1(1+r)^{j+1} + \ldots + c_{k-1-j}(1+r)^{k-1}}{[I-(1+r)A]}$ (1)

By writing $\tilde{M}$ and $|M|$ the adjoint matrix and the determinant of a square matrix M, we have

$$[I-(1+r)A]^{-1} = \frac{[I-(1+r)A]}{|I-(1+r)A|} \qquad (2)$$

$$= \frac{M_0 + (1+r)M_1 + \ldots + (1+r)^i M_i + \ldots + (1+r)^{k-1}M_{k-1}}{1 + c_1(1+r) + c_2(1+r)^2 + \ldots + c_i(1+r)^i + \ldots + c_k(1+r)^k}$$

Since[17] the minors of matrix $I-(1+r)A$ are determinants of the square matrix of order $(k-1)$ the terms of which are functions of $(1+r)$. As we have the identity $[I-(1+r)A].[I-(1+r)A]^{-1} = I$, we deduce

$$[1 + c_1(1+r) + c_2(1+r)^2 + \ldots + c_i(1+r)^i + \ldots + c_k(1+r)^k]I$$
$$= [I-(1+r)A][M_0 + (1+r)M_1 + \ldots + (1+r)^i M_i + \ldots + (1+r)^{k-1}M_{k-1}]$$

By identifying the terms $(1+r)^0, (1+r), (1+r)^2, \ldots, (1+r)^k$ we obtain between matrices $M_0, M_1, \ldots, M_j, M_{k-1}$, the following $(k-1)$ relations between matrices $M_0, M_1, \ldots, M_j, M_{k-1}$

$$\begin{aligned}
I &= M_0 &&\Rightarrow\quad M_0 = I \\
c_1 I &= M_1 - AM_0 &&\Rightarrow\quad M_1 = AM_0 + c_1 I = A + c_1 I \\
c_i I &= M_i - AM_{i-1} &&\Rightarrow\quad M_i = AM_{i-1} + c_i I \\
c_{k-1} I &= M_{k-1} - AM_{k-2} &&\Rightarrow\quad M_{k-1} = AM_{k-2} + c_{k-1}I \\
c_k I &= AM_{k-1}
\end{aligned}$$

Consequently, for any $i = 1, 2, \ldots, k-1$, we have

$$\begin{aligned}
M_i &= AM_{i-1} + c_i I = A[AM_{i-2} + c_{i-1}I] + c_i I \\
&= A^2[AM_{i-3} + c_{i-2}I] + c_{i-1}A + c_i I \\
&= A^3 M_{i-3} + c_{i-2}A^2 + c_{i-1}A + c_i I
\end{aligned}$$

that is $M_i = A^i + c_1 A^{i-1} + \ldots + c_{i-1}A + c_i I$

Thus we have

$$\begin{aligned}
I-(1+r)A &= M_0 + (1+r)M_1 + \ldots + (1+r)^{k-1}M_{k-1} \\
&= \sum_{i=0}^{k-1}(1+r)^i M_i = \sum_{i=0}^{k-1}(1+r)^i[A^i + c_1 A^{i-1} + \ldots + c_{i-1}A + c_i I] \\
&= I + (A + c_1 I)(1+r) + \ldots + (1+r)^i[A^i + c_1 A^{i-1} + \ldots \\
&\quad + c_{i-1}A + c_i I] + \ldots + (1+r)^{k-1}[A^{k-1} + c_1 A^{k-2} + \ldots + c_{k-1}I]
\end{aligned}$$

$$= [1 + c_1(1+r) + \dots + \varepsilon_i(1+r)^i + \dots + c_{k-1}(1+r)^{k-1}]I$$
$$+ [(1+r) + \dots + c_{i-1}(1+r)^i]A + \dots + (1+r)^{k-1}A^{k-1}$$

$$= \sum_{i=0}^{k-1} [(1+r)^j + c_1(1+r)^{j+1} + \dots + c_{k-1-j}(1+r)^{k-1}]A^j \quad \text{hence}$$

$$[I - (1+r)A]^{-1}L = \frac{[I - (1+r)A]L}{|I - (1+r)A|}$$

$$= \frac{[I(1+r)^j + c_1(1+r)^{j+1} + \dots + c_{k-1-j}(1+r)^{k-1}]}{|I - (1+r)A|}$$

$$= \sum_{i=0}^{k-1} \beta_j A^j L$$

$$\text{where } \beta_j = \frac{(1+r)^j + c_1(1+r)^{j+1} + \dots + c_{k-1-j}(1+r)^{k-1}}{[I - (1+r)A]}$$

$$= \frac{(1+r)^j + c_1(1+r)^{j+1} + \dots + c_{k-1-j}(1+r)^{k-1}}{1 + c_1(1+r) + c_2(1+r)^2 + \dots + c_k(1+r)^k}$$

Proposition 2

The kernels of the linear applications respectively corresponding to matrix K and vectors $p(r)$ and $\hat{p}(r)$ merge

$$N[K] = N[\hat{p}(r)] = N[p(r)] \tag{6}$$

Of course we have $N[p(r)] = N[\hat{p}(r)]$ since $\forall z \in N[p(r)]$ we have $zp(r) = 0 \Leftrightarrow$ $z\hat{p}(r) = z \dfrac{p(r)}{w} = 0 \; z \in N[\hat{p}(r)]$

Suffice to prove that $N[K] = N[\hat{p}(r)]$, namely, $N[K]$ is included in $N[\hat{p}(r)]$ and $N[\hat{p}(r)]$ is included in $N[K]$.

We do have $N[K]$ included in $N[\hat{p}(r)]$ since $\forall z \in N[K]$ we have $zK = 0$ and thus according to (1)

$$z\hat{p}(r) = z.K\beta(r) = zK.\beta(r) = 0 \text{ that is } z \in N[\hat{p}(r)]$$

Similarly if $z\hat{p}(r) = 0 \; \forall r \in [-1 \; R[$ we have $zK = 0$, i.e., $N[\hat{p}(r)]$ is included in $N[K]$.

Indeed if $z\hat{p}(r) = 0 \; \forall r \in [-1 \; R[$, we also have $\forall r \in [-1 \; R[$

$$\frac{d[z\hat{p}(r)]}{dr} = 0$$

and more generally

$$\frac{d^j[z\hat{p}(r)]}{dr^j} = 0 \qquad \forall j = 2,3,4,\dots,k-1$$

As a result, since $z\hat{p}(r) = z[I - (1+r)A]^{-1}L = zM^{-1}(r)$ where $M(r) = I - (1+r)A$

$$\frac{dM(r)}{dr} = -A$$

A and $M(r)$ are commutative

$$\frac{d[z\hat{p}(r)]}{dr} = zM^{-1}\frac{dM}{dr}M^{-1}L = zAM^{-2}(r)L$$

$$\frac{d^2[z\hat{p}(r)]}{dr^2} = 2zA^2M^{-3}(r)L$$

$$\frac{d^j[z\hat{p}(r)]}{dr^j} = j!zA^jM^{-(j+1)}(r)L$$

Since $M(-1) = I - (1-1)A = I$, we have $M^{-1}(-1) = I$ and $M^{-(j+1)}(-1) = I$.

Which implies

$$zL = zM^{-1}(-1)L = z\hat{p}(-1) = 0$$

$$zAL = zAM^{-2}(-1)L = \frac{[dz\hat{p}(r)]}{dr}(r = -1) = 0$$

$$zA^jL = zA^jM^{-(j+1)}(-1)L = \frac{1}{j!}\frac{d^j[z\hat{p}(r)]r = -1}{d^jr} = 0 \qquad \forall j = 2,3\ldots,$$

hence $zK = [zL, zAL, \ldots, zA^jL, \ldots, zA^{k-1}L] = 0$.

Thus $N[\hat{p}(r)] = N[K]$ \hfill (6)

4   The analysis of joint production

The analysis carried out in the previous chapter was restricted to single-product industries and circulating capital. It is not because we consider simple production as the rule and joint production as an exception that we have first comprehensively developed simple production models. It is rather for simplicity's sake, and this allowed us to obtain concise and elegant results from the assumption of system productivity alone.

In fact, the general rule is joint production and Steedman (1984) has listed the processes of joint production that can be encountered in various sectors of the economy, such as agriculture, fishing, chemistry, electricity, petrol, transportation, communications, etc. The emergence of fixed capital, of machines, in models of production also requires a joint production framework of analysis.

The analysis of joint production systems cannot be carried out without mentioning the phenomenon of truncation, or the suppression of methods of production. Analysing a specific system of joint production means assuming that supply is in conformity with demand and that there is no excess production; it also means that problems of efficiency, revealed by negative prices, have been solved.

Such issues have already been contemplated in the first chapter, and the issue of switch in methods of production will be dealt with in detail in chapter 7, so it is not taken into account in the present chapter: production systems are taken to be square, which means that unprofitable activities have been eliminated as well as the excess supply of goods. It is in this particular framework that we shall specify the determination of prices in joint production systems.

Then we shall analyse particular structures, up to now unknown in simple production where matrices A were either decomposable or indecomposable. However, in joint production, system (A, B) may be decomposable and at the same time broken down into basic and non-basic systems for the determination of prices and into antibasic and non-antibasic systems for the determination of activity levels. We shall then tackle the problem of the determination of the standard, or rather standards, in a joint production system.

More generally, we have to insist on the fact that simple production systems are exceptional and ... at the same time exceptionally simple. We shall see that for some structures of joint production (provided the system of production is both basic and non-basic) and for high enough rates of profit (or growth) we revert to the mere simplicity of simple production. This is a paradox that we have to emphasise for it is not in a stationary state that these properties are enhanced but with high enough rates of growth (or profit).

4.1 Prices in joint production

Sraffa[1] analysed circulating capital and joint production systems as a kind of preamble to the analysis of fixed capital and land. Thus, as in simple production we assume that the methods of production do not require either land or machines but only use circulating capital. However, since joint production prevails, we have to introduce an additional assumption so that the determination of prices is possible:

In Part 1 it has been assumed that each commodity was produced by a separate industry. We shall now suppose two of the commodities be jointly produced by a single industry (or rather a single process, as it will be more appropriate to call it in the present context). The conditions would no longer be sufficient to determine the prices. There would be more prices to be ascertained than there are processes, and therefore equations, to determine them.

In these circumstances there will be room for a second, parallel process which will produce the two commodities by a different method and, as we shall suppose at first, in different proportions. Such a parallel process will not only be possible, it will be necessary if the number of processes is to be brought to equality with the number of commodities so that the prices may be determined. We shall therefore go a step further and assume that in such cases a second process or industry does in fact exist. (P.S. 50)

More generally, if there are k commodities there must be k production equations so that the k prices can be determined: 'The assumption previously made of the existence of a "second process" can now be replaced by the more general assumption that the number of processes should be equal to the number of commodities' (*ibid.*).

This implies that the k activities allowing to produce the k commodities are known, that is, the choice of techniques has been made.

We are now in a stationary state economy and we want to determine prices and the scalar w for a given rate of profit r.

Such an economy is represented by $[A, B, L]$ where $A = [a_{ij}]$ and $B = [b_{ij}]$ respectively stand for the input and output matrices, both are square and of format $k \times k$.[2]

As in simple production, L represents the direct labour vector (taken to be homogeneous); w and r are respectively the wage and rate of profit.

Thus, the price equations write

$$\begin{cases} (a_{11}p_1 + a_{12}p_2 + \ldots + a_{1k}p_k)(1+r) + l_1 w = b_{11}p_1 + b_{12}p_2 + \ldots + b_{1k}p_k \\ (a_{21}p_1 + a_{22}p_2 + \ldots + a_{2k}p_k)(1+r) + l_2 w = b_{21}p_1 + b_{22}p_2 + \ldots + b_{2k}p_k \\ \ldots\ldots\ldots\ldots\ldots\ldots\ldots\ldots\ldots\ldots\ldots\ldots\ldots\ldots\ldots\ldots\ldots\ldots\ldots\ldots\ldots\ldots \\ (a_{k1}p_1 + a_{k2}p_2 + \ldots + a_{kk}p_k)(1+r) + l_k w = b_{k1}p_1 + b_{k2}p_2 + \ldots + b_{kk}p_k \end{cases}$$

or even

$$(1+r)Ap + wL = Bp$$
$$[B - (1+r)A]p = wL$$

At a given rate of profit r prices $p(r)$ are determined uniquely (up to the multiplication by scalars) if matrix $B - (1+r)A$ has an inverse. In addition to this condition, we have to make sure that the model is productive and that the supply of goods perfectly satisfies demand. Therefore, in order to allow the determination of prices, model $[A, B, L]$ must meet the following three conditions:

Productivity of the system

The productivity of model $[A, B, L]$ is guaranteed if there is at least one activity level $y \geq 0$ permitting a surplus $s > 0$ of all the goods, that is if

$$\exists y \geq 0 \,|\, y(B - A) \geq s > 0 \tag{N1}$$

Satisfaction of demand

Once the productivity requirement is satisfied (N1), and whatever demand $cd = c(d_1, d_2, \ldots, d_k) \geq 0$, we can find an activity vector $y = (y_1, y_2, \ldots, y_k) > 0$ satisfying

$$\begin{cases} y(B - A) \geq cd \\ y(B - A)^i = cd_i \quad \text{for at least one } i \in \{1, 2, \ldots, k\} \end{cases}$$

where $(B - A)^i$ represents the ith column of matrix $B - A$, that is to say the net surplus of good i in each activity. The relation $y(B - A)^i = cd_i$ means that the supply of good i is *perfectly equal* to its demand cd_i and this good is an *economic good*. On the other hand, a good j such that $y(B - A)^j > cd_j$ is a *free good* since it is overabundant owing to the fact that the supply $y(B - A)^j$ is greater than its demand cd_j. For prices to be positive there must be *no surplus* of any good.

Thus there is joint production in the economic sense of the word if demand is perfectly satisfied, i.e., in a stationary state, if

$$\exists y \geq 0 | y(B - A) = cd \tag{N2}$$

Note that in simple production $[A, I, L]$ the productivity requirement (N1) is ascertained if the dominant eigenvalue $\alpha(A)$ of matrix A is included between 0 and 1. Condition (N2) is then satisfied whatever the demand cd since matrix $I - A$ has an inverse and $(I - A)^{-1} > 0$ which implies that vector $y = (I - A)^{-1} cd > 0$ always satisfies $y(I - A) = cd$.

However, in joint production, before considering the positivity of prices we have to make sure that supply and demand are in conformity, in other words, that demand cd satisfies requirement (N2), or assuming growth at rate g, the condition (N'2)

$$\exists y \geq 0 | y[B - (1 + g)A] = cd \tag{N'2}$$

In this chapter, we assume that it is possible to satisfy demand perfectly; in chapter 8 we will show that if this assumption is not satisfied one method of production will have to be superseded, one of the goods becoming in some conditions a free good.

Regularity of matrix $M(r)$
Requirements (N1) and (N2) being satisfied, the price matrix equation

$$[B - (1 + r)A]p = wL$$

has at least one solution if there exists at least one rate of profit r such that matrix $M(r) = B - (1 + r)A$ has an inverse. Therefore, we asume that the following condition is always satisfied[3]

$$\exists r \geq 0 | M(r) = B - (1 + r)A \text{ has an inverse} \tag{N3}$$

Furthermore, vector L must be such that $M^{-1}(r)L > 0$ so that prices are positive. Otherwise, some prices may be negative which proves the lack of efficiency of the system, a bad selection of methods of production that has to be remedied (the analysis of switch in methods of production is developed in chapter 7). But if the previous assumption is satisfied, if the prices are positive (as assumed in the present chapter), we can no longer revert to the reassuring simplicity of simple production systems.

Indeed, we know that in that case $r \in [0 \ R[\ M^{-1}(r) > 0$, which is sufficient for $\hat{p}(r) = M - 1(r)L$ to be positive. Such a condition is also sufficient to ensure the growth of $\hat{p}(r)$. Indeed, since

$$\frac{dM^{-1}(r)}{dr} = M^{-1} \frac{dM(r)}{dr} . M^{-1}$$

where $\dfrac{dM(r)}{dr} = -A$, we have

$$\frac{d\hat{p}(r)}{dr} = \frac{dM^{-1}(r).L}{dr} = -M^{-1}(r).(-A).M^{-1}(r).L$$

$$= M^{-1}(r).A.M^{-1}(r)L > 0$$

And relation $w(r)$ is decreasing in interval $(0\ R)$, whatever the numeraire u retained for prices: indeed, we have

$$w_u = \frac{1}{u.M^{-1}(r).L}$$

But generally, in joint production, there is no interval $(0\ R)$ in which the system has these characteristics: usually $M^{-1}(0) = (B-A)^{-1}$ is not positive. Even if prices are positive, as assumed from the beginning, wage prices are not necessarily increasing functions of the rate of profit, the wage–profit relation can be increasing for one numeraire and decreasing for another.

However, for a great number of joint production systems, there exists an interval $(R_0\ R)$ (R_0 being positive) in which we can find the properties specific to the simple production systems. It is quite paradoxical to find out that in a golden rule situation, joint production systems that are not viable in a stationary state (for $r = g = 0$) become so at high enough rates of profit (and growth) – though they are less than the maximum rate.

Recall that we have already defined R_0 as the 'minimum' rate of profit in the sense that all the properties of simple production are ascertained on the interval $(R_0\ R)$ (see chapter 1, section 5.1).

If demand is not appropriate or the system is inefficient, the system under question will have to be truncated, which means that some inefficient activities will have to be superseded at a specific rate of profit.

When an activity is suppressed, the system changes dimensions from (k,k) to $(k-1,k)$. A surplus of one of the goods emerges and the latter is available at zero price. Therefore, we have a system with $k-1$ activities, producing $k-1$ goods and a free good.

If all the economic goods do not have positive prices or if demand cannot be perfectly satisfied, a second activity will have to be suppressed. Consequently, there will be $k-2$ activities producing $k-2$ economic goods and two free goods. We can go on that way until when at a given rate of profit r, there are as many activities as there are economic goods to produce at positive prices.

We may also be led to a situation where a unique activity produces k goods and among them $k-1$ are free and only one is an economic good. It goes without saying that the exegonous rate of profit r retained for the economy must not have a higher value than R as seen in section 1.5.5.

The issue of suppressing some methods will be dealt with in detail in chapter 7 and the determination of the maximum rate of profit R will be addressed in chapter 5.

Thus the link between prices and the rate of profit is more complex than in a simple production context; such complexity will also appear when analysing the basic or non-basic characteristics of the system.

4.2 Basic and non-basic systems

In a single product system with circulating capital each commodity was produced by a single method of production which defined the industry. Because there was a one to one correspondence between commodities and industries there was an identity between the sector of basic industries and the sector of basic commodities which was independent of the rest of the economy as far as the determination of the prices of the commodities produced in that sector and the determination of the endogenous distributive variable were concerned.

As a result, in such a system the technical autonomy of the basic sector meant that prices and the distributive variables were determined independently of the non-basic sector. To separate the basic sector from the non-basic sector we only needed to simultaneously rearrange the rows and columns of the technology matrix in such a way as to obtain zeros in the upper right-hand corner of matrix A. Commodities entering directly or indirectly in all methods of production formed the basic sector.

Therefore, to solve an economic problem (the simultaneous determination of relative prices and distributive variables with one degree of freedom) we were able to use a technical criterion, i.e., the indecomposability of the basic sector or the participation, direct or indirect, of a commodity in the production of all commodities.

Such a criterion cannot be applied in the general case of joint production for it is now in general impossible to state that a particular means of production enters the process of any particular commodity. This is for two reasons: first, a particular commodity may be produced by several processes; and, second, the contribution of any particular means of production used in a joint process cannot be attributed to any one of the several commodities produced jointly.

In such conditions any specific attribution is impossible, except in special cases. This helps to explain the difficulties and paradoxes we meet in the case of joint production. We shall now see that economic independence is no longer equivalent to technical autonomy as was the case with simple production. The processes constitute a kind of veil over the commodities but we shall see that by resorting to the basic system we shall be able to create a certain transparency of the economic system. In general an indecomposable system is not necessarily basic.[4]

We shall quickly address the case when system (A, B) is decomposable; as in simple production there is no difficulty in emphasising the basic and non-basic sectors. It is when (A, B) is indecomposable that some peculiarites may appear. Indeed, there may be a regular matrix M such that system (MA, MB) is decomposable and the indecomposable system (A, B) is then said to be non-basic. We will show this using a simple example and then we shall give a more general presentation. We will then be able to emphasise two sub-systems, one basic the other non-basic. Unlike the decomposable system, the partition of system (A, B) can be done in different ways, at least as far as the activities are concerned: depending on the partition of the system one activity in one part of the system may belong to the basic sub-system and in another part belong to a non-basic sub-system. However the distinction between basic and non-basic goods does not depend on the partition; still, we have to emphasise that the prices of the $(k-m)$ basic goods depend on their use (and production) in the m methods retained to form the non-basic sub-system.

Thus, a decomposable non-basic system appears to be a transition system that can exist only in a joint production context; moreover, it is the exact opposite of the simple production system where matrix $M^{-1}(r)$ is positive when the rate of profit is less than the maximum rate of profit; a decomposable non-basic system is the opposite extreme of simple production since, as we shall see, matrix $M^{-1}(r)$ cannot be positive.

4.2.1 Indecomposable and decomposable systems

Definition
Matrices A and B form a decomposable system if, and only if, there exists a permutation of their rows and columns such that A and B are simultaneously transformed into quasi-triangular matrices as shown below[5]

$$A = \begin{bmatrix} A_1^1 & 0 \\ A_2^1 & A_2^2 \end{bmatrix} \qquad B = \begin{bmatrix} B_1^1 & 0 \\ B_2^1 & B_2^2 \end{bmatrix}$$

with A_1^1 and B_1^1 being square matrices of the same dimension.[6]

The system of production just described is decomposable into two groups of processes, one of them (A_1^1, B_1^1) being technically autonomous from the rest of the economy. In these particular conditions the prices of the commodities produced and consumed by this group of processes (basic commodities) and the level of the endogenous distributive variable can be simultaneously determined independently of the prices of the other commodities.

The system of price equations is of the general form $(1 + r)Ap + wL = Bp$ and can be written as follows

$$p = \begin{bmatrix} p_1 \\ p_2 \end{bmatrix} \qquad L = \begin{bmatrix} L_1 \\ L_2 \end{bmatrix}$$

$$(1 + r) \begin{bmatrix} A_1^1 & 0 \\ A_2^1 & A_2^2 \end{bmatrix} \begin{bmatrix} p_1 \\ p_2 \end{bmatrix} + w \begin{bmatrix} L_1 \\ L_2 \end{bmatrix} = \begin{bmatrix} B_1^1 & 0 \\ B_2^1 & B_2^2 \end{bmatrix} \begin{bmatrix} p_1 \\ p_2 \end{bmatrix}$$

That is

$$(1 + r)A_1^1 p_1 + wL_1 = B_1^1 p_1$$
$$(1 + r)(A_2^1 p_1 + A_2^2 p_2) + wL_2 = B_2^1 p_1 + B_2^2 p_2$$

The first of the two systems is sufficient to determine vector p_1 and one of the distributive variables, given the other and given the numeraire.

The second system allows us to find vector p_2, once p_1 and the endogenous distributive variable have been determined. It thus appears as a non-basic system.

In short, when a system is decomposable it is easy to define it into a basic and a non-basic sector.

When a system (A, B) is not decomposable we may distinguish the basic sector subject to the condition that the technology matrices have certain collinearity properties that are even less restrictive than those previously required. It is thus possible to find a regular matrix M such that system (MA, MB) is decomposable. Then the indecomposable system (A, B) is said to be non-basic.

4.2.2 Indecomposable non-basic system

Example

To introduce the subject, let us consider a very simple example.[7] We have an economy with two processes of joint production defined by the following positive technology matrices

$$A = \begin{bmatrix} a_{11} & a_{12} \\ a_{21} & a_{22} \end{bmatrix} \qquad B = \begin{bmatrix} b_{11} & b_{12} \\ b_{21} & b_{22} \end{bmatrix}$$

It is obvious that system (A, B) is indecomposable. However, given certain assumptions of linear dependence in system $[A, B]$, we shall show that system $[A, B]$ although indecomposable is not necessarily basic.

$$[A, B] = \begin{bmatrix} a_{11} & a_{12} & b_{11} & b_{12} \\ a_{21} & a_{22} & b_{21} & b_{22} \end{bmatrix} \text{ is a } (2 \times 4) \text{ matrix}$$

Suppose that segment (a_{12}, b_{12}) belonging to the first process is linearly dependent on the corresponding segment of the second process, in other words there exists a scalar β such that[8]

$$[a_{12} \; b_{12}] = \beta [a_{22} \; b_{22}]$$

In these conditions, matrices A and B write

$$A = \begin{bmatrix} a_{11} & \beta a_{22} \\ a_{21} & a_{22} \end{bmatrix} \quad B = \begin{bmatrix} b_{11} & \beta b_{22} \\ b_{21} & b_{22} \end{bmatrix}$$

Thus we have the following price equations

$$p = \begin{bmatrix} p_1 \\ p_2 \end{bmatrix} \text{ and } L = \begin{bmatrix} l_1 \\ l_2 \end{bmatrix}$$

$$(1 + r) \begin{bmatrix} a_{11} & \beta a_{22} \\ a_{21} & a_{22} \end{bmatrix} \begin{bmatrix} p_1 \\ p_2 \end{bmatrix} + w \begin{bmatrix} l_1 \\ l_2 \end{bmatrix} = \begin{bmatrix} b_{11} & \beta b_{22} \\ b_{21} & b_{22} \end{bmatrix} \begin{bmatrix} p_1 \\ p_2 \end{bmatrix}$$

or

$$(1 + r)(a_{11} p_1 + \beta a_{22} p_2) + w l_1 = b_{11} p_1 + \beta b_{22} p_2$$
$$(1 + r)(a_{21} p_1 + a_{22} p_2) + w l_2 = b_{21} p_1 + b_{22} p_2$$

By using a linear combination of these two equations it is possible to find an equation with only three unknowns: p_1 and the distributive variables w and r. We only need to multiply the second equation by $(-\beta)$ and add up the two equations to eliminate p_2, hence

$$(1 + r)(a_{11} - \beta a_{21}) p_1 + w (l_1 - \beta l_2) = (b_{11} - \beta b_{21}) p_1$$

This equation shows that if we chose commodity 1 as a numeraire (with $p_1 = 1$) and assume that one of the distributive variables is given, the first commodity has every property of a basic commodity *vis-à-vis* the second commodity since we can determine the value of the endogenous distributive variable independently of p_2 (with p_1 fixed at 1). As for p_2, it can only be determined if p_1 and the endogenous distributive variable are known.

Note that we have obtained the preceding equation, which could be considered as a basic equation, by eliminating the second commodity simultaneously from both the means of production and the quantities produced, in the first equation for prices. This elimination is only possible because of the assumption of linear dependence between the two homologous segments of the methods of production. These segments have therefore disappeared from the 'basic equation'. At the same time, it is perfectly possible for some of the 'abstract quantities' to be negative (e.g., of the type $(a_{11} - \beta a_{21})$, $(b_{11} - \beta b_{21})$, $(l_1 - \beta l_2)$) and this of course cannot be related to any effective method of production. This is one of the apparent paradoxes of joint production (P.S. 56).

To conclude this example, it may be interesting to give another method for dealing with the problem, whose importance will become clear in the more general presentation given below. Let us construct a matrix[9]

$$M = \begin{bmatrix} 1 & -\beta \\ 0 & 1 \end{bmatrix}$$

which transforms A and B into quasi-triangular matrices given the assumption of linear dependence $(a_{12}, b_{12}) = \beta (a_{22}, b_{22})$[10]

$$MA = \begin{bmatrix} 1 & -\beta \\ 0 & 1 \end{bmatrix} \begin{bmatrix} a_{11} & a_{12} \\ a_{21} & a_{22} \end{bmatrix} = \begin{bmatrix} a_{11} - \beta a_{21} & 0 \\ a_{21} & a_{22} \end{bmatrix}$$

$$MB = \begin{bmatrix} 1 & -\beta \\ 0 & 1 \end{bmatrix} \begin{bmatrix} b_{11} & b_{12} \\ b_{21} & b_{22} \end{bmatrix} = \begin{bmatrix} b_{11} - \beta b_{21} & 0 \\ b_{21} & b_{22} \end{bmatrix}$$

and

$$\begin{bmatrix} 1 & -\beta \\ 0 & 1 \end{bmatrix} \begin{bmatrix} l_1 \\ l_2 \end{bmatrix} = \begin{bmatrix} l_1 - \beta l_2 \\ l_2 \end{bmatrix}$$

We have constructed a virtual system

$$(\bar{A}^1_1, \bar{B}^1_1, \bar{I}_1) = (a_{11} - \beta a_{21}, b_{11} - \beta b_{21}, l_1 - \beta l_2)$$

which appears as a basic system. While system (A, B) was technically indecomposable we have nonetheless been able to *create* a basic system within system (A, B) (given the assumption of linear dependence). We can generalise this procedure without difficulty by following a method proposed by Manara.

4.2.3 Indecomposable non-basic system. Generalisation[11]

Definition

A system (A, B) is called non-basic if there is a simultaneous permutation of the columns of A and B and a number m such that matrix $[A^2, B^2]$ composed of $m (1 \leq m \leq k - 1)$ last columns of A and B is of rank m.[12]

If m is the highest number having this property, the m goods associated to $[A^2, B^2]$ are non-basic.

Let us suppose that such a permutation has been made. System (A, B) which is non-basic by assumption, can then be written as follows

$k - m$ processes	A_1^1	A_1^2		B_1^1	B_1^2
m processes	A_2^1	A_2^2		B_2^1	B_2^2
	$k - m$	m		$k - m$	m

The $(k \times 2m)$ matrix $[A^2, B^2] = \begin{bmatrix} A_1^2 & B_1^2 \\ A_2^2 & B_2^2 \end{bmatrix}$ is of rank m.

It has m independent rows. Thus $(k - m)$ rows must be linear combinations of m others, assumed to be independent. If the last m rows of $[A^2, B^2]$ are independent we can then represent the first $(k - m)$ rows $[A_1^2, B_1^2]$ of $[A^2, B^2]$ as linear combinations of the last m rows $[A_2^2, B_2^2]$ taken as bases. Let $[A_1^2, B_1^2] = H[A_2^2, B_2^2]$ with H of dimension $(k - m, m)$.

By using Manara's procedure we can construct the following matrix

$$M = \begin{bmatrix} I_{k-m} & -H \\ 0 & I_m \end{bmatrix}$$

which transforms A and B into quasi-triangular matrices.[13]

$$MA = \begin{bmatrix} I_{k-m} & -H \\ 0 & I_m \end{bmatrix} = \begin{bmatrix} A_1^1 & A_1^2 \\ A_2^1 & A_2^2 \end{bmatrix} = \begin{bmatrix} A_1^1 - HA_2^1 & 0 \\ A_2^1 & A_2^2 \end{bmatrix}$$

$$MB = \begin{bmatrix} I_{k-m} & -H \\ 0 & I_m \end{bmatrix} = \begin{bmatrix} B_1^1 & B_1^2 \\ B_2^1 & B_2^2 \end{bmatrix} = \begin{bmatrix} B_1^1 - HB_2^1 & 0 \\ B_2^1 & B_2^2 \end{bmatrix}$$

The smallest among the systems of $([A_1^1 - HA_2^1], [B_1^1 - HB_2^1])$ type, i.e., the system of this type to which corresponds the greatest m, is called a *basic system*. If it is identical to (A, B), (A, B) will be said to be a basic system.

If we multiply the initial system by M we obtain

$$(1 + r)MAp + MLw = MBp$$

and therefore we have two sub-systems of equations

$$(1 + r)(A_1^1 - HA_2^1)p_1 + (L_1 - HL_2)w = (B_1^1 - HB_2^1)p_1$$
$$(1 + r)(A_2^1 p_1 + A_2^2 p_2) + L_2 w = B_2^1 p_1 + B_2^2 p_2$$

The first series of equations can be solved independently of the second. Of course, the two series together give the same results as the initial equations since the first are simply inferred from the second by a linear combination given by M.

4.2.4 Can a basic system be uniquely decomposable?

When system (A, B) is *non-basic* and has m non-basic goods and $k - m$ basic goods we can emphasise two sub-systems: a basic sub-system composed of the $(k - m)$ rows of matrices (MA, MB), that is $(A_1^1 - HA_2^1)$, $(B_1^1 - HB_2^1)$ and a non-basic sub-system composed of m rows (A_2, B_2) of matrices (MA, MB).

The decomposition of the non-basic system (A, B) into basic and non-basic systems *is not unique* when system (A, B) is indecomposable. Indeed, in this case matrix (A^2, B^2) of dimension $(k, 2m)$ is of rank m and has at least $m + 1$ non-zero rows. We can then choose m linearly independent rows among the k rows of matrix (A^2, B^2) in different ways. We thus obtain as many decompositions of system (A, B) into basic and non-basic systems. Therefore, if we have

$$A = \begin{bmatrix} 2 & 1 & 1 \\ 1 & 3 & 2 \\ 3 & 3 & 3 \end{bmatrix} \quad \text{and} \quad B = \begin{bmatrix} 4 & 0 & 2 \\ 0 & 5 & 4 \\ 2 & 2 & 6 \end{bmatrix}$$

Matrix $(A^2, B^2) = \begin{bmatrix} 1 & 2 \\ 2 & 4 \\ 3 & 6 \end{bmatrix}$ composed of the last columns of matrices A and B

is of rank 1 while matrix $(A^1, B^1) = \begin{bmatrix} 2 & 1 & 4 & 0 \\ 1 & 3 & 0 & 5 \\ 3 & 3 & 2 & 2 \end{bmatrix}$ composed of the first two

columns of A and B is of rank 3 greater than 2. As a result system (A, B) is *non-basic* and has *one* non-basic good, the third, while the first two are basic. In matrix (A^2, B^2) of rank 1, we can choose any of the three rows as a *base* and express the two other rows as 'linear combinations' of the row chosen as a base. Thus, using the notations of the preceding paragraph, we can write:

If $(A_2^2, B_2^2) = (3 \ 6)$ and $(A_1^2, B_1^2) = \begin{bmatrix} 1 & 2 \\ 2 & 4 \end{bmatrix} = \begin{bmatrix} 1/3 \\ 2/3 \end{bmatrix} (3 \ 6)$ which means that

$H_1 = \begin{bmatrix} 1/3 \\ 2/3 \end{bmatrix}$ and $M_1 = \begin{bmatrix} 1 & 0 & -1/3 \\ 0 & 1 & -2/3 \\ 0 & 0 & 1 \end{bmatrix}$ then we have

$$M_1A = \begin{bmatrix} 1 & 0 & 0 \\ -1 & 1 & 0 \\ 3 & 3 & 3 \end{bmatrix} \text{ and } M_1B = \begin{bmatrix} 10/3 & -2/3 & 0 \\ -2/3 & 11/3 & 0 \\ 2 & 2 & 6 \end{bmatrix}$$

If $(A_2^2, B_2^2) = (2 \ \ 4)$ and $(A_1^2, B_1^2) = \begin{bmatrix} 1 & 2 \\ 3 & 6 \end{bmatrix} = \begin{bmatrix} 1/2 \\ 3/2 \end{bmatrix} (2 \ \ 4)$ that is, $H_2 = \begin{bmatrix} 1/2 \\ 3/2 \end{bmatrix}$

and $M_2 = \begin{bmatrix} 1 & -1/2 & 0 \\ 0 & 1 & 0 \\ 0 & -3/2 & 1 \end{bmatrix}$; thus we have

$$M_2A = \begin{bmatrix} 3/2 & -1/2 & 0 \\ 1 & 3 & 2 \\ 3/2 & -3/2 & 0 \end{bmatrix} \text{ and } M_2B = \begin{bmatrix} 4 & -5/2 & 0 \\ 0 & 5 & 4 \\ 2 & -11/2 & 0 \end{bmatrix}$$

If $(A_2^2, B_2^2) = (1 \ \ 2)$ and $(A_1^2, B_1^2) = \begin{bmatrix} 2 & 4 \\ 3 & 6 \end{bmatrix} = \begin{bmatrix} 2 \\ 3 \end{bmatrix} (1 \ \ 2)$ which means that

$H_3 = \begin{bmatrix} 2 \\ 3 \end{bmatrix}$ and $M_3 = \begin{bmatrix} 1 & 0 & 0 \\ -2 & 1 & 0 \\ -3 & 0 & 1 \end{bmatrix}$ then we have

$$M_3A = \begin{bmatrix} 2 & 1 & 1 \\ -3 & 1 & 0 \\ -3 & 0 & 0 \end{bmatrix} \text{ and } M_3B = \begin{bmatrix} 4 & 0 & 2 \\ -8 & 5 & 0 \\ -10 & 2 & 0 \end{bmatrix}$$

In these three cases, we can see that the third good is a non-basic good in the sense that its price depends on the prices of both other goods, and of course on distribution, while the prices of the first two goods are obtained independently from the price of the third good. On the other hand, system (A, B) transformed into (MA, MB) can be broken down in three different ways into a basic sub-system and a non-basic sub-system. More precisely:

In $[M_1A, M_1B]$ the basic sub-system is composed of the first two rows of $[M_1A, M_1B]$, while the non-basic sub-system is composed of the third rows of $[M_1A, M_1B]$.

In $[M_2A, M_2B]$ the basic sub-system is composed of the first and the third rows of $[M_2A, M_2B]$ while the non-basic sub-system is composed of the second rows of $[M_2A, M_2B]$.

In $[M_3A, M_3B]$ the basic sub-system is composed of the last two rows of $[M_3A, M_3B]$ while the non-basic sub-system is composed of the first two rows of $[M_3A, M_3B]$.

Of course if system $[A, B]$ is *decomposable* it can be broken down *uniquely* into a basic sub-system (A_1^1, B_1^1) and a non-basic sub-system $[A_2, B_2]$ since matrix (A^2, B^2) of dimension $(k, 2m)$ is of rank m and has $k - m$ zero-rows.

Note that prices p_1 and p_2 are *independent* of the partition of system (A, B) into basic and non-basic sub-systems since they are in any case solutions to the following equation

$$(1+r)Ap + wL = Bp$$

We also note that the prices of the basic goods which are determined in the basic system, not only depend on A_1^1, B_1^1, L_1 but also on the conditions of use (A_2^1) and production (B_2^1) of the *basic goods in the non-basic sub-system* and of labour L_2 used in the non-basic sub-system.

4.2.5 Decomposable matrix associated with a non-basic system

It is not always easy to determine in a system (A, B) whether there exist m columns A^2 and B^2 of matrices A and B such that the matrix (A^2, B^2) is of rank m. However, when we have a square matrix we can quite quickly find out whether it is decomposable.

Let us now state and demonstrate two theorems establishing a link between the rank of matrix (A^2, B^2) and the decomposability of a square matrix of $(B - \mu A)^{-1} A$ type where μ is any number.

Theorem 1

A necessary and sufficient condition for system (A, B) to be basic is that there is a regular matrix M such that system (MA, MB) is decomposable.

Indeed, the condition is necessary since we have shown that if there are m columns A^2 and B^2 of matrices A and B such that the rank $[A^2, B^2] = m$, we can construct Manara's matrix

$$M = \begin{bmatrix} I & -H \\ 0 & I \end{bmatrix}$$

which is regular and such that matrices MA and MB are *quasi-triangular*.

The condition is sufficient for if system (MA, MB) is decomposable, we have

$$MA = \begin{bmatrix} \bar{A}_1^1 & 0 \\ \bar{A}_2^1 & \bar{A}_2^2 \end{bmatrix} \begin{matrix} k-m \\ m \end{matrix} \quad \text{and} \quad MB = \begin{bmatrix} \bar{B}_1^1 & 0 \\ \bar{B}_2^1 & \bar{B}_2^2 \end{bmatrix}$$
$$\begin{matrix} k-m & m \end{matrix}$$

and by writing $M^{-1} = [\bar{M}^1, \bar{M}^2]$ we obtain
$\quad\quad\quad\quad (k,k) \quad\ (k,m)$

$$[A^2, B^2] = M^{-1}[(MA)^2, (MB)^2] = [\bar{M}^2 \bar{A}_2^2, \bar{M}^2 \bar{B}_2^2] = \bar{M}^2[\bar{A}_2^2, \bar{B}_2^2]$$

and rank $[A^2, B^2] \leq$ rank $[\bar{A}_2^2, \bar{B}_2^2] = m$. Hence system (A, B) satisfies the definition of a non-basic system (see section 4.2.3 above).

Before stating the second theorem, let us first demonstrate the following proposition.

Proposition

Given the linear combination $X = B - \mu A$ of matrices A and B, system (A, X) is non-basic if and only if system (A, B) is non-basic. Furthermore, both systems have the same non-basic goods.

Indeed, if system (A, B) is non-basic there is a permutation of the columns of A and B and a number m such that the last columns A^2 and B^2 of A and B establish rank $[A^2, B^2] = m$.

Thus, rank $[A^2, X^2] = $ rank $[A^2, B^2 - \mu A^2] = $ rank $[A^2, B^2] = m$ and system $(A, X) = (A, B - \mu A)$ is non-basic and has the same m non-basic goods as system (A, B).

Similarly, if (A, X) is non-basic and rank $[A^2, X^2] = m$ after permutation of the columns of A and X. Since $B = X + \mu A$, then rank $[A^2, B^2] = $ rank $[A^2, X^2 - \mu A^2] = $ rank $[A^2, X^2] = m$ and system (A, B) is non-basic and has the same m non-basic goods as system (A, X).

Theorem 2

A necessary and sufficient condition for system (A, B) to be non-basic is that there exists a regular matrix $X = B - \mu A$ such that $X^{-1}A$ is decomposable. Further, systems (A, B) and $(X^{-1}A, I)$ have the same non-basic goods.

Indeed, the condition is necessary; since system (A, B) is non-basic, it is the same for system (A, X) and by theorem 1 there exists a regular matrix M such that system (MA, MX) is decomposable. Then, matrices MA and MX are *quasi-triangular* and it is the same for $(MX)^{-1}$ and $(MX)^{-1}MA = X^{-1}M^{-1}MA = X^{-1}A$, which means that matrix $X^{-1}A = (B - \mu A)^{-1}A$ is *decomposable*.

The condition is sufficient for if system $(X^{-1}A, I)$ is decomposable, by theorem 1, system $X(X^{-1}A, I) = (A, X)$ is non-basic and therefore system (A, B) is non-basic owing to the proposition above. Of course systems (A, B) and $(X^{-1}A, I)$ have the same non-basic goods since in all the linear transformations there are no permutations of the last m columns.

As a result, sytem (A, B)

is *basic* if matrix $X^{-1}A$ is *indecomposable*; in this case any matrix of (A^2, B^2) type and of dimension $(k, 2m)$ is of a rank at least equal to $m + 1$

is *non-basic* and has m non-basic goods if matrix

$$X^{-1}A = \begin{bmatrix} Z_1^1 & 0 \\ Z_2^1 & Z_2^2 \end{bmatrix} \begin{matrix} {\scriptstyle k-m} \\ {\scriptstyle m} \end{matrix}$$
$$\begin{matrix} {\scriptstyle k-m} & {\scriptstyle m} \end{matrix}$$

where $Z_2^1 \geq 0$ and Z_1^1 and Z_2^2 are indecomposable square matrices of orders $(k-m)$ and m. In that case there exists a matrix (A^2, B^2) of dimension $(k, 2m)$ and of rank m, and m is the highest integer for which we have this property.

has no non-basic goods if $X^{-1}A$ is totally decomposable; in this case if m is the highest integer such that matrix (A^2, B^2) of dimension $(k, 2m)$ is of rank m then matrix (A^1, B^1) composed of the first $(k-m)$ columns of A and B is of rank $(k-m)$.

Of course we assume that condition (N3) ensuring the existence of at least one rate of profit r, at which matrix $B-(1+r)A$ has an inverse, is established. Otherwise there would be no linear combination $X = B - \mu A$ that would be regular.

It is worth noting that:

if matrix B is regular we can choose $X = B$ and system (A, B) is basic or not depending on whether matrix $B^{-1}A$ is indecomposable.

if matrices A and B are singular but $(B-A)$ is regular, we can choose $X = B - A$ and system (A, B) is either basic or not depending on whether matrix $(B-A)^{-1} A$ is indecomposable.

Example

Let us revert to the previous model (A, B) where

$$A = \begin{bmatrix} 2 & 1 & 1 \\ 1 & 3 & 2 \\ 3 & 3 & 3 \end{bmatrix} \quad \text{and} \quad B = \begin{bmatrix} 4 & 0 & 2 \\ 0 & 5 & 4 \\ 2 & 2 & 6 \end{bmatrix}$$

Since matrix B is regular and

$$B^{-1} = \tfrac{1}{34} \begin{bmatrix} 11 & 2 & -5 \\ 4 & 10 & -8 \\ -5 & -4 & 10 \end{bmatrix}$$

we can calculate $B^{-1}A$ which is equal to

$$\tfrac{1}{34} \begin{bmatrix} 9 & 2 & 0 \\ -6 & 10 & 0 \\ 16 & 13 & 17 \end{bmatrix}$$

Matrix $B^{-1}A$ is really decomposable and here again, in model (A, B) the first two goods are basic while the last one is non-basic.

4.2.6 Transformation of matrix $X^{-1}A$ resulting from a permutation of the rows and columns of matrices A and B

If we simultaneously permutate the columns of A and B by post-multiplying them by a permutation matrix Q we transform A, B and X into AQ, BQ and XQ; thus we obtain

$$(XQ)^{-1}AQ = Q^{-1}X^{-1}AQ = Q'X^{-1}AQ$$

this means that the columns of matrix $X^{-1}A$ have undergone the same permutation as A's and B's and the same permutation has been performed on the rows of $X^{-1}A$. More particularly, if system (A, B) is *non-basic*, gathering non-basic goods in the last columns of matrices AQ and BQ transforms matrix $X^{-1}A = (B - \mu A)^{-1}A$ into

$$Q'X^{-1}A = \begin{bmatrix} Z_1^1 & 0 \\ Z_2^1 & Z_2^2 \end{bmatrix} \begin{matrix} (k-m) \\ m \end{matrix}$$
$$\begin{matrix} (k-m) & m \end{matrix}$$

Thus, the non-basic goods are in the last m columns of $Q'X^{-1}AQ$ and are 'produced' by the last m rows of $Q'X^{-1}AQ$.

If we simultaneously permutate the rows of matrices A and B by multiplying A and B by a permutation matrix P we transform A, B and X into

$$PA, PB, PX \text{ and } X^{-1}A \text{ into } (PX)^{-1}PA = X^{-1}P^{-1}PA = X^{-1}.I.A = X^{-1}A$$

which means that matrix $X^{-1}A$ remains invariant when we permutate the rows of matrices A and B; thus when system (A, B) is broken down into two sub-systems (basic and non-basic) we obtain the same equivalent system $(X^{-1}A, I)$ to determine prices.

   If we revert again to the non-basic decomposable model (A, B) analysed in the paragraphs above, we do find out that the three models transformed (M_1A, M_1B), (M_2A, M_2B), (M_3A, M_3B) are such that

$$(M_iB)^{-1}(M_iA) = B^{-1}M_i^{-1}M_iA = B^{-1}A \text{ with } i = 1, 2 \text{ or } 3$$

4.2.7 Characteristics of non-basic indecomposable systems

While in simple production any indecomposable system (A, I) is basic, we have shown that in joint production an *indecomposable* system (A, B) may be *non-basic*. We can show (see Bidard, 1982) that in such a system there is no rate of profit r at which matrix

$$[B - (1 + r)A]^{-1} \geq 0$$

To show this let us demonstrate the following theorem.

Theorem 3

Consider a non-basic system (A, B). If there exists a real number μ such that $X^{-1} = (B - \mu A)^{-1} \geq 0$ then system (A, B) is *decomposable*.

Indeed, let β be a real number such that the square matrix $Y = (B - \beta A)$ is regular and semi-positive. As system (A, B) is *non-basic* matrix $X^{-1}Y$ is *decomposable*, and if there are m non-basic goods, with

$$X^{-1} = \begin{bmatrix} \bar{X}_1^1 & \bar{X}_1^2 \\ \bar{X}_2^1 & \bar{X}_2^2 \end{bmatrix} \begin{matrix} (k-m) \\ m \end{matrix} \quad Y = \begin{bmatrix} Y_1^1 & Y_1^2 \\ Y_2^1 & Y_2^2 \end{bmatrix} \quad \text{and } X^{-1}Y = \begin{bmatrix} Z_1^1 & 0 \\ Z_2^1 & Z_2^2 \end{bmatrix}$$

$$\begin{matrix} (k-m) & m \end{matrix}$$

we have $\bar{X}_1^1 Y_1^1 + \bar{X}_1^2 Y_2^1 = 0$. Since matrices $\bar{X}_i^j \geq 0$ and $Y_i^j \geq 0$ owing to $X^{-1} \geq 0$ and $Y \geq 0$, we have

$$\bar{X}_1^1 Y_1^2 = 0 \text{ and } \bar{X}_1^2 Y_2^2 = 0$$

Since matrix Y is regular its last m columns $\begin{bmatrix} Y_1^2 \\ Y_2^2 \end{bmatrix}$ form a matrix of rank m and we can always rearrange its rows so that Y_2^2 is a regular matrix, thus what we assume here is

$$\bar{X}_1^2 Y_2^2 = 0 \text{ implies } \bar{X}_1^2 = 0$$

Hence X^{-1} is a quasi-triangular matrix as well as its inverse X. Since X^{-1} is regular, its first $(k-m)$ rows form the matrix $[\bar{X}_1^1, \bar{X}_1^2] = [\bar{X}_1^1 \ 0]$, it is of rank $(k-m)$; therefore matrix $\bar{X}_1^1$ is regular and

$$\bar{X}_1^1 Y_1^2 = 0 \text{ implies } Y_1^2 = 0$$

Thus, $X = \begin{bmatrix} X_1^1 & 0 \\ X_2^1 & X_2^2 \end{bmatrix}$ and $Y = \begin{bmatrix} Y_1^1 & 0 \\ Y_2^1 & Y_2^2 \end{bmatrix}$ and system (X, Y) is decomposable. Since matrices A and B are linear combinations of the quasi-triangular matrices X and Y, they are also quasi-triangular and system (A, B) is decomposable.

Corollary

If a system (A, B) is indecomposable and non-basic, there is no rate of profit r such that $[B - (1 + r)A]^{-1} \geq 0$.

Suffice to choose $\mu = (1 + r)$ in matrix $X = B - \mu A$. By theorem 3 if there exists r such that $[B - (1 + r)A]^{-1} \geq 0$ the system would necessarily be decomposable which is contrary to the corollary assumption according to which (A, B) is indecomposable.

Summary table

We assume that assumption (N3) is established, meaning that the rank of all matrices $[A^2 \; B^2]$ composed of m columns of A and B, associated with the same goods, is *greater than or equal to m*. Table 4.1 allows to determine the basic and non-basic goods of model $[A \; B]$ as a function of the rank of matrices $[A^2 \; B^2]$.

If matrix $X = A - \mu B$ is regular, table 4.2 summarises quite well the characteristics of matrix $X^{-1}A$.

Table 4.1.

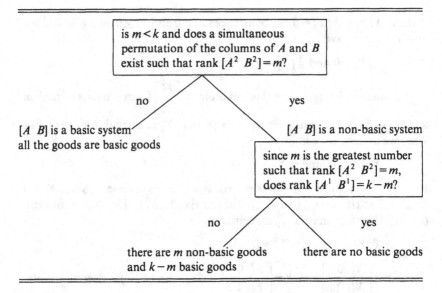

Table 4.2.

Matrix $X^{-1}A$	rank $[A^2, B^2]$	Model $[A \; B]$
indecomposable	$> m$	*basic*: every good is basic
decomposable[14]	$= m$ and rank $[A^1, B^1] > k - m$	*non-basic*: has m non-basic goods and $k - m$ basic goods
totally decomposable[15]	$= m$ and rank $[A^1, B^1] = k - m$	*non-basic*: has no basic goods

At this stage we have to remark that:

When system (A, B) is *non-basic* and has m non-basic goods, it can be decomposed into two sub-systems, namely, a basic sub-system with $(k-m)$ equations $[(A_1^1-HA_2^1),(B_1^1-HB_2^1)]$ and a non-basic sub-system with m equations (A_2, B_2).

The decomposition of the non-basic system (A, B) into a basic sub-system and a non-basic sub-system is *not unique* when system (A, B) is indecomposable, since matrix (A^2, B^2) of dimension $(k, 2m)$ is of rank m, we can choose in different ways m linearly independent rows that we can write (A_2^2, B_2^2); the corresponding sub-system $[(A_2^1, A_2^2),(B_2^1, B_2^2)]$ is a non-basic sub-system while sub-system $[(A_1^1-HA_2^1),(B_1^1-HB_2^1)]$ is basic.

Of course, if system (A, B) is decomposable it can be decomposed uniquely into a basic sub-system (A_1^1, B_1^1) and a non-basic sub-system (A_2, B_2).

The prices p_1 of the basic goods, that are determined in the basic sub-system not only depend on A_1^1, B_1^1 and L_1 but also on the conditions of use (A_2^1) and production (B_2^1) of the *basic goods in the non-basic sub-system* and on labour L_2 used in the non-basic sub-system.

Further, prices p_1 and p_2 do not depend on the decomposition of system (A, B) into basic and non-basic sub-systems, since they always are solutions to the following equation

$(1+r)Ap + wL = Bp$

We can determine the basic and non-basic goods in an indecomposable non-basic system (A, B); however, an activity may, according to the decomposition of the system into basic and non-basic systems, belong to the basic sub-system in one partition and to the non-basic sub-system in another.

4.3 Antibasic and non-antibasic systems

As far as the analysis of activities and relation $c(g)$ are concerned, moving from simple production to joint production creates similar difficulties to those springing from the analysis of prices and relation $w(r)$. Under simple production, we have already distinguished antibasic processes and non-antibasic processes when matrix A is decomposable. We shall directly contemplate the case where system (A, B) is indecomposable though non-antibasic, without reverting to the simple case, where in joint production system (A, B) is decomposable. We shall first define that kind of system and then we will define its various characteristics; the analysis has been considerably shortened for our aim is mainly to apply to activities the analysis that was used for prices.

4.3.1 Definition

A system (A, B) is said to be *non-antibasic* if there exists a simultaneous permutation of the *rows* of A and B and an integer n such that matrix $\begin{bmatrix} A_1 \\ B_1 \end{bmatrix}$, composed of the first n rows of A and B (where $1 \le n \le k-1$), is of rank n. If n is the greatest number having such a property, the n processes defined by $\begin{bmatrix} A_1 \\ B_1 \end{bmatrix}$ are *non-antibasic*.

Let us assume that the permutation has been done: by assumption, the non-antibasic system (A, B) can be represented in the following way

$$
A = \begin{array}{|c|c|}
\hline
A_1^1 & A_1^2 \\
\hline
A_2^1 & A_2^2 \\
\hline
\end{array}
\begin{array}{l} n \\ k-n \end{array}
\qquad
B = \begin{array}{|c|c|}
\hline
B_1^1 & B_1^2 \\
\hline
B_2^1 & B_2^2 \\
\hline
\end{array}
\begin{array}{l} n \\ k-n \end{array}
$$
$$
\quad\; n \quad\;\; k-n \qquad\qquad\quad n \quad\;\; k-n
$$

matrix $\begin{bmatrix} A_1 \\ B_1 \end{bmatrix} = \begin{bmatrix} A_1^1 & A_1^2 \\ B_1^1 & B_1^2 \end{bmatrix}$ of dimension $(2n, k)$ is of rank n.

Thus it has n independent columns and $(k-n)$ columns are linear combinations of the n other columns supposed to be independent. If the first n columns of matrix $\begin{bmatrix} A_1 \\ B_1 \end{bmatrix}$ are independent, we can represent the last $(k-n)$ columns of $\begin{bmatrix} A_1^2 \\ B_1^2 \end{bmatrix}$ of matrix $\begin{bmatrix} A_1 \\ B_1 \end{bmatrix}$ as linear combinations of the first n columns $\begin{bmatrix} A_1^1 \\ B_1^1 \end{bmatrix}$ which are a base. Thus we have $\begin{bmatrix} A_1^2 \\ B_1^2 \end{bmatrix} = \begin{bmatrix} A_1^1 \\ B_1^1 \end{bmatrix} H$, H being a matrix of dimension $(n, k-n)$. By using the regular matrix

$$
N = \begin{bmatrix} I_n & -H \\ 0 & I_{k-n} \end{bmatrix}
$$

we can transform matrices A and B into two quasi-triangular matrices

$$
AN = \begin{bmatrix} A_1^1 & A_1^2 \\ A_2^1 & A_2^2 \end{bmatrix} \begin{bmatrix} I_n & -H \\ 0 & I_{k-n} \end{bmatrix} = \begin{bmatrix} A_1^1 & A_1^2 - A_1^1 H \\ A_2^1 & A_2^2 - A_2^1 H \end{bmatrix} = \begin{bmatrix} A_1^1 & 0 \\ A_2^1 & A_2^2 - A_2^1 H \end{bmatrix}
$$

$$BN = \begin{bmatrix} B_1^1 & B_1^2 \\ B_2^1 & B_2^2 \end{bmatrix} \begin{bmatrix} I_n & -H \\ 0 & ;I_{k-n} \end{bmatrix} = \begin{bmatrix} B_1^1 & 0 \\ B_2^1 & B_2^2 - B_2^1 H \end{bmatrix}$$

The smallest of the systems of type $[(A_2^2 - A_2^1 H),(B_2^2 - B_2^1 H)]$, namely, the system of this type to which corresponds the greatest integer $k - n$, is called an *antibasic system*. If it is identical to (A, B), (A, B) is said to be antibasic.

Indeed, if we multiply the initial system by matrix N

$$(1 + g)yAN + cdN = yBN$$

we obtain two equation sub-systems

$$\begin{cases} (1+g)[y_1 A_1^1 + y_2 A_2^1]cd_1 = (1+g)[y_1 B_1^1 + y_2 B_2^1] \\ (1+g)y_2(A_2^2 - A_2^1 H) + c(d_2 - d_1 H) = (1+g)y_2(B_2^2 - B_2^1 H) \end{cases}$$

The second system is sufficient to determine vector y_2 and one of the distributive variables, given the other and given the numeraire of activity levels. As for the first system, it allows us to determine y_1 only if y_2 and the endogenous distributive variable are known. Both series of equations give the same results as the initial equations since the first are simply deduced from the second by a linear combination defined by the regular matrix N.

4.3.2 Characteristics of the indecomposable and non-antibasic systems

Let us now state three theorems which link the rank of matrix $\begin{bmatrix} A_1 \\ B_1 \end{bmatrix}$ and the decomposability of a square matrix AX^{-1} where $X = B - \mu A$.

Theorem 1'
A necessary and sufficient condition for system (A, B) to be non-antibasic is the existence of a regular matrix N such that system (AN, BN) is decomposable.

Proposition
Given matrix $X = B - \mu A$, system (A, X) is non-antibasic if and only if system (A, B) is non-antibasic. Furthermore, both systems have the same non-antibasic processes.

Theorem 2'
A necessary and sufficient condition for system (A, B) to be non-antibasic is the existence of a regular matrix $X = B - \mu A$ such that matrix AX^{-1} is decomposable. Furthermore, systems (A, B) and (AX^{-1}, I) have the same non-antibasic processes.

Theorem 3′
Let (A, B) be a non-antibasic system. If there exists a real number μ such that $X^{-1} = (B - \mu A)^{-1} \geq 0$, sytem (A, B) is thus decomposable.

Corollary
If a system (A, B) is indecomposable and non-antibasic there is no rate of growth g such that $[B - (1 + g)A]^{-1} \geq 0$ (theorems 1′, 2′ and 3′ respectively demonstrate as theorems 1, 2 and 3).

Summary table
We assume that requirement (N3′) is established, that is, the rank of any matrix $\begin{bmatrix} A_1 \\ B_1 \end{bmatrix}$ composed of n rows of A and B, corresponding to the same n processes, is greater than or equal to n. Table 4.3 allows us to determine the antibasic and non-antibasic processes of model $[A, B]$ as a

Table 4.3.

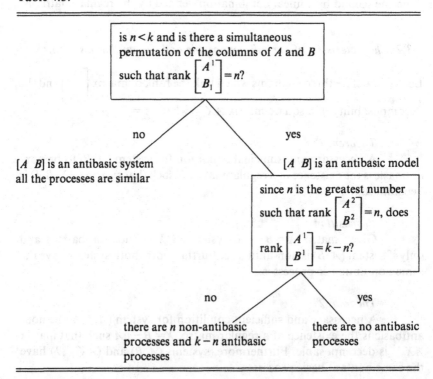

is $n < k$ and is there a simultaneous permutation of the columns of A and B such that rank $\begin{bmatrix} A^1 \\ B_1 \end{bmatrix} = n$?

no — $[A \ B]$ is an antibasic system all the processes are similar

yes — $[A \ B]$ is an antibasic model

since n is the greatest number such that rank $\begin{bmatrix} A^2 \\ B^2 \end{bmatrix} = n$, does rank $\begin{bmatrix} A^1 \\ B^1 \end{bmatrix} = k - n$?

no — there are n non-antibasic processes and $k - n$ antibasic processes

yes — there are no antibasic processes

Table 4.4.

matrix $X^{-1}A$	rank $\begin{bmatrix} A^1 \\ B^1 \end{bmatrix}$	model $[A, B]$
indecomposable	$> n$	*antibasic*: all the processes are antibasic.
decomposable[16]	$= n$ and rank $\begin{bmatrix} A^2 \\ B^2 \end{bmatrix} > k - n$	*non-antibasic*: has n non-antibasic processes and $k - n$ antibasic processes.
totally decomposable[17]	$= n$ and rank $\begin{bmatrix} A^2 \\ B^2 \end{bmatrix} = k - n$	*non-antibasic*: has no antibasic processes

function of the ranks of matrices $\begin{bmatrix} A_1 \\ B_1 \end{bmatrix}$.

If matrix $X = B - \mu A$ is regular, we obtain table 4.4 as a function of the characteristics of matrix AX^{-1}.

4.4 Various partitions of an indecomposable system

It is worth noting that when a model (A, B) is *indecomposable* it can be:
basic and antibasic
basic and non-antibasic
non-basic and antibasic
non-basic and non-antibasic.

Indeed, we have already shown that the indecomposable model (A, B) can be basic or non-basic depending on whether the square matrix $(B - \mu A)^{-1} A$ is indecomposable or not. On the other hand, it is antibasic or non-antibasic depending on whether the square matrix $A(B - \mu A)^{-1}$ is indecomposable or not (see table 4.5).

Table 4.5. *Nature of the indecomposable model (A, B)*

$A(B - \mu A)^{-1}$ $(B - \mu A)^{-1}A$	indecomposable	decomposable
indecomposable	basic and antibasic	non-basic and antibasic
decomposable	basic and non-antibasic	non-basic and non-antibasic

The following examples illustrate the last three cases.

The indecomposable model (A, B) where

$$A = \begin{bmatrix} 3 & 1 & 1 \\ 2 & 4 & 1 \\ 3 & 1 & 3 \end{bmatrix} \qquad B = \begin{bmatrix} 8 & 3 & 3 \\ 1 & 9 & 6 \\ 1 & 5 & 7 \end{bmatrix}$$

is *non-basic* for $B^{-1}A = \frac{1}{249} \begin{bmatrix} 60 & 0 & 0 \\ -32 & 166 & -83 \\ 121 & -83 & 166 \end{bmatrix}$ is decomposable. But it is

antibasic for $AB^{-1} = \frac{1}{249} \begin{bmatrix} 95 & -2 & 3 \\ 58 & 163 & 129 \\ 86 & 76 & 135 \end{bmatrix}$ is indecomposable.

Note that the matrix, of dimension 3×4, composed of the juxtaposition

of the last two columns of A and B, namely $[A^2, B^2] = \begin{bmatrix} 1 & 1 & 3 & 3 \\ 4 & 1 & 9 & 6 \\ 1 & 3 & 5 & 7 \end{bmatrix}$ is of rank 2

since the first row equals the sum of 2/11 times the second row and 3/11 times the third row.

If we consider model (A', B'), where A' and B' are the transpose of matrices A and B of the previous model, we have an indecomposable model that is *basic and non-antibasic.*

Finally, the indecomposable model (A, B) where

$$A = \begin{bmatrix} 2 & 1 & 1 \\ 1 & 3 & 2 \\ 2 & 1 & 3 \end{bmatrix} \text{ and } B = \begin{bmatrix} 4 & 0 & 2 \\ 0 & 5 & 4 \\ 4 & 2 & 6 \end{bmatrix}$$

is *non-basic* for $B^{-1}A = \frac{1}{12} \begin{bmatrix} 7 & 6 & 0 \\ 4 & 12 & 0 \\ -2 & -6 & 6 \end{bmatrix}$ is decomposable and *non-antibasic*

since $AB^{-1} = \frac{-1}{24} \begin{bmatrix} 20 & 8 & 12 \\ 15 & 18 & -19 \\ 0 & 0 & 12 \end{bmatrix}$ is decomposable.

In these three cases we know that by theorems 3 and 3' there is no rate of profit r such that $M^{-1}(r) = [B - (1+r)A]^{-1} \geq 0$.

For an indecomposable model (A, B) to have at least a rate of profit r such that $M^{-1}(r) = [B - (1+r)A]^{-1} > 0$ the model must be basic and antibasic.

The theorem[18] below specifies the conditions of existence of r such that $M^{-1}(r) > 0$.

Theorem 4

Let (A, B) be a *basic* and *antibasic* joint production system with a maximum rate of profit $R > 0$ and such that there exist vectors $q \geq 0$, $\bar{p} \geq 0$ establishing

$$q[B - (1 + R)A] = 0, \; [B - (1 + R)A]\bar{p} = 0, \text{ and rank } [B - (1 + r)A] = k - 1$$

There is then an interval $[R_0 \; R[$ such that matrix $M^{-1}(r) = [B - (1 + R)A]^{-1} > 0$ for $r \in [R_0 \; R[$, R is the simple root of $[B - (1 + r)A] = 0$, $q > 0$ and $\bar{p} > 0$.

In such conditions, for $g \in [R_0 \; R[$, all the commodities are separately producible and all the activities are necessary whatever the structure of the final demand.

When R_0 is negative, all the properties of simple production are established in the model.

Mathematical appendix

Let us now demonstrate that condition (N3′), stated below, has to be established so that at least one real number r exists such that matrix $B - (1 + r)A$ is regular.

Condition (N3′)

There exists no integer m where $1 \leq m \leq k$, such that after permutation of the columns of A and B, matrix $[A^2, B^2]$ of dimension $(k, 2m)$ composed of the last m columns of A and B is of a rank p *strictly less than m*.

Condition (N3′) springs from the following theorem.

Theorem

If after permutation of the columns of A and B there exists a name m such that matrix $[A^2, B^2]$ of dimension $(k, 2m)$ composed of the last m columns of A and B is of rank p strictly less than m, all linear combinations $\mu A + \lambda B$ of matrices A and B are *singular*.

Indeed, after permutation and decomposition of A and B, we have $A = [A^1, A^2]$ and $B = [B^1, B^2]$. As a result

$$\underset{(k,k) \; (k,m)}{} \qquad \underset{(k,k) \; (k,m)}{}$$

$$\mu A + \lambda B = [\mu A^1 + \lambda B^1, \mu A^2 + \lambda B^2]$$

and the rank of matrix $\mu A + \lambda B$ is at most equal to the sum of the ranks of matrices $\mu A^1 + \lambda B^1$ and $\mu A^2 + \lambda B^2$. But the rank of $\mu A^1 + \lambda B^1$ is at most equal to $k - m$ and that of $\mu A^2 + \lambda B^2$ is at most equal to p since $[A^2, B^2]$ is of rank p. The rank of $\mu A + \lambda B$ is thus less than $k - m + p < k - m + m = k$ since $p < m$ and the square matrix of order k, $\mu A + \lambda B$ which is of a rank strictly less than k is *singular* whatever the numbers μ and λ.

Corollary

If there exists a real number r such that $B - (1 + r)A$ is *regular* and if rank $\begin{bmatrix} A_1^1 & A_1^2 \\ A_2^1 & A_2^2 \end{bmatrix} \leq m$ then rank $\begin{bmatrix} A_1^1 & A_1^2 \\ A_2^1 & A_2^2 \end{bmatrix} = m$. Indeed if rank $\begin{bmatrix} A_1^1 & A_1^2 \\ A_2^1 & A_2^2 \end{bmatrix} < m$, owing to the previous theorem, when we choose $\lambda = 1$ and $\mu = -(1 + r)$, matrix $\mu A + \lambda B = B - (1 + r)A$ is *non-regular*, which is at variance with the assumption.

Note that we can replace condition (N3′) by condition (N3″) stated below.

Condition (N3″)

There exists no integer n where $1 \leq n \leq k$ such that after permutation of the rows of A and B matrix $\begin{bmatrix} A_1 \\ B_1 \end{bmatrix}$ of dimension $(2n, k)$ composed of the first n rows of A and B is of *rank p strictly less than n*.

Note that if matrix B (or A) is *regular*, condition (N3′) is always established since any matrix B^2 composed of the m columns of B is of rank m and thus rank $[A^2, B^2] > $ rank $(B^2) = m$.

More particularly, in *simple* production $B = 1$ is regular and condition (N3) always holds.

5   Standards and blocking goods

5.1 Seeking the invariant standard of value

Economists' search for an 'invariant standard of value' is similar to the search for the philosopher's stone. We know that the issue was addressed by Ricardo in section VI of *The Principles of Political Economy and Taxation*, entitled 'On an invariable measure of value', which specifies the topic of research and what is at stake.

When commodities varied in relative value it would be desirable to have the means of ascertaining which of them fell and which rose in real value, and this could be effected only by comparing them one after another with some invariable standard measure of value, which would itself be subject to none of the fluctuations to which commodities are exposed.

He also adds that even if we do not take into account a possible variation in prices due to alterations in production conditions, we have to take into account those due to changes in distribution. Since, to determine prices we need to choose a given quantity of a given commodity as a numeraire, it is quite impossible to know, when distribution varies, what part of the variation in prices is due to the commodity in question and what part is due to the commodity chosen as a numeraire. Hence the following proposition:

If, then, I may suppose myself to be possessed of a standard so nearly approaching to an invariable one, the advantage is that I shall be enabled to speak of the variations of other things without embarassing myself on every occasion with the consideration of the possible alteration in the value of the medium in which price and value are estimated.

In the following lines, Ricardo assumes that gold is the 'invariable' commodity, though he underlines . . . 'I fully allow that money made of gold is subject to most of the variations of other things'.

Does the standard-commodity constructed by Sraffa (P.S., chapter 4) in *Production of Commodities by Means of Commodities* have the properties sought for by Ricardo? Is there a commodity i (or a basket of commodities $y = (y_1, y_2, \ldots, y_i, \ldots, y_k) \geq 0$) such that its price ($p_i$ or yp depending on the assumption retained) remains invariant with variations in distribution? Are both these questions identical?

The issue deserves to be addressed all the more since in the introduction of Ricardo's *Works and Correspondence*, Sraffa writes:

The search for what has been called the 'chimera of an invariable standard of value' preoccupied Ricardo to the end of his life. However, the problem which mainly interested him was not of finding an actual commodity which would accurately measure the value of corn and silver at different times and place; but rather of finding the conditions which a commodity would have to satisfy in order to be invariable in value. (Sraffa, 1970, p. xli).

We shall show that *a specific commodity can have all the properties of an invariable standard provided we choose a proper numeraire.* The purpose of this chapter is to give a precise definition of what might be an 'invariant standard of value' and show how it can be constructed. We shall first reason within a very simple context of an indecomposable model with circulating capital, about which Sraffa's propositions will have to be specified owing to a recent controversy (see Burmeister 1980, Malinvaud 1981, Flaschel 1986, Schefold 1986).

Then we shall address the cases of decomposable systems, on the one hand, and systems taking into account joint production, on the other hand, moving away from Sraffa's position. More particularly, we shall show that the search for an 'invariable standard of value' refers to von Neumann model; the price standard – which exists in any case – can be constructed from the activity and price system characterised as a 'blocking system'. These cases being further developed, we shall start with the indecomposable system with single-product industries and circulating capital.

5.1.1 Indecomposable system with single-product industries and circulating capital

In order to answer these questions, we shall start with Sraffa's simple production model with circulating capital described by the triple (A, I, L).

Prices p are determined with the usual notations

$$p = (1 + r)Ap + wL \tag{1}$$

The price normalisation equation writes

$$u(I - A)p = 1 \tag{2}$$

with $u = (u_1, u_2, \ldots, u_i, \ldots, u_k) \geq 0$ and $uL = 1$.

Note that first, Sraffa normalises the price system by the condition $e(I-A)p=1$; in other words, he chooses a specific numeraire where $e=(1,1,\ldots,1)$ represents the activity vector showing the effective operation of the system in question. The treatment that we suggest here is more general.

Further, we know that if $u=q$ defined by $q=(1+R)qA$ (where R is the maximum rate of profit of the system) the wage–profit curve $w(r)$ becomes linear. If the system is regular,[1] this numeraire is the only one ensuring linearity.

How can a 'fixed-value commodity' be determined when distribution varies?

From (1) and (2), we obtain

$$1=u(I-A)p(r)=ruAp+wuL=ruAp+w \tag{2'}$$

When w decreases from 1 to 0, r increases from 0 to the maximum rate of profit R. A variation dr of the rate of profit causes a variation dw of the wage $w(r)$ and a variation dp of the price vector $p(r)$. We obtain dp by differentiating both members of equation (1); thus we have

$$dp=(1+r)d(Ap)+Apdr+Ldw \tag{3}$$

The price of a composite commodity $y=(y_1,y_2,\ldots,y_i,\ldots,y_k)\geq0$ is equal to $yp(r)$ and when the rate of profit varies by dr, the price of the composite commodity y undergoes a variation $d(yp)=yd(p)$. For the composite commodity to have an invariant value when distribution varies, $yp(r)$ needs and only needs to remain constant when r moves from 0 to R, meaning that the differential $d(yp)$ is zero, or

$$\begin{aligned}0=d(yp)&=ydp\\&=(1+r)d(yAp)+yApdr+yLdw\end{aligned} \tag{4}$$

for any $r\in[0\ R]$.

Expression (4) is of the form $(1+r)X+Y=0$. Suffice that $X=0$ and $Y=0$ or:

(a) $d(yAp)=0$ for all $r\in[0\ R]$.
(b) $yAp.dr+yL.dw=0$ for all $r\in[0\ R]$.

Condition (a) means that the input value yAp of commodity y must, as yp, be constant when r varies from 0 to R. As a result, the ratio yAp/yp also remains constant at $r\in[0\ R]$. If we write this constant α, we obtain the following condition

$$\frac{yAp}{yp}=\alpha \tag{5}$$

or

$$yAp = \alpha yp$$

or

$$y[\alpha I - A]p = 0 \text{ for all } r \in [0 \quad R] \tag{5'}$$

In the assumption retained here, where model $[A, I, L]$ is regular, condition (5') is established if and only if

$$y[\alpha I - A] = 0 \text{ or } \alpha y = yA \tag{6}$$

that is, if α is an eigenvalue of the square matrix A and y is an eigenvector corresponding to α. Since matrix A is taken to be *indecomposable*, as $y \geq 0$, α is the dominant eigenvalue $\alpha(A)$ of matrix A and $y > 0$.

As vector y is defined up to the multiplication by scalars, we can choose vector q that is homothetic to y and such that $qL = 1$.

Thus, vector $q > 0$ defined by

$$qA = \alpha q \tag{7}$$

and

$$qL = 1 \tag{8}$$

establishes (a) which is the first condition for commodity q to have an invariant value.

Note that commodity q satisties Sraffa's recurrence condition, since

$$\frac{qA^{i+1}p}{qA^i p} = \frac{\alpha^{i+1}qp}{\alpha^i qp} = \alpha = \frac{1}{1+R} \text{ at all } r \in [0 \quad R] \text{ and } i = 0,1,2,\dots$$

Condition (b) must also be satisfied by commodity y, that is

$$yApdr + yLdw = 0 \text{ for all } r \in [0 \quad R].$$

Since commodity q is homothetic to y which also satisfies $qL = 1$, condition (b) becomes

$$qAp.dr + qL.dw = qAp.dr + dw = 0$$

that is

$$w' = \frac{dw}{dr} = -qAp \text{ at all } r \in [0 \quad R]$$

which means that since, by condition (a), qAp is constant, the derivative w' of w in relation to r has to be constant, i.e., the wage–profit relation must be linear. However, as previously stated, when the model is regular this requires a specific numeraire $u = q$, that is

$$q(I-A)p(r)=1 \tag{2''}$$

In such conditions, by pre-multiplying both terms of equation (1) by vector q, we obtain

$$qp=(1+r)qAp+wqL=(1+r)qAp+w=qAp+rqAp+w \tag{9}$$

hence

$$qp-qAp=rqAp+w$$

and

$$rqAp+w=q(I-A)p=1 \text{ for all } r\in[0 \;\; R]$$

More particularly, at $r=R$, we have $w=0$. Hence $RqAp=1$ thus $qAp=1/R$ and

$$qp=\frac{qAp}{\alpha}=(1+R)\,qAp=\frac{(1+R)}{R}$$

Therefore, in model (A,I,L) the composite commodity q defined by (7) and (8) is the commodity sought for, the invariant value of which is equal to $(1+R)/R$ provided the numeraire retained is $q(I-A)$.

Note Since $rqAp=1-w$ and $qAp=\frac{1}{R}$, we have $\frac{r}{R}=1-w$.

This implies that if $w\to 0$, $\frac{r}{R}\to 1$ and $r\to R$, all prices being positive.

Properties of the standard
We can write that the standard q establishes the following relation

$$\frac{qp}{qAp}=\frac{qp}{\alpha qp}=\frac{1}{\alpha}=1+R \qquad \forall r\in[0 \;\; R] \tag{10}$$

which means that when distribution varies the ratio of outputs (qp) to inputs (qAp) remains invariant and equals $1+R$.

Thus we understand why Sraffa refers to the standard as a balanced commodity.

Further, since $qAp=\frac{1}{R}$ when $qL=1$ for all $r\in[0 \;\; R]$, we have

$$\frac{qL}{qAp}=R \qquad \forall r\in[0 \;\; R] \tag{11}$$

This means that the labour/means of production ratio is independent of distribution and equal to R in the activity producing commodity q.

Furthermore, from relation (11) we deduce that, for any integer n

$$\frac{qA^nL}{qA^{n+1}p}=\frac{\alpha^nqL}{\alpha^nqAp}=\frac{qL}{qAL}=R \qquad \forall r\in[0 \ \ R] \qquad (12)$$

This means that the labour/means of production ratio is independent of distribution and equal to R in all the successive layers of means of production in the activity producing commodity q. We revert here to the recurrence condition emphasised by Sraffa (P.S. 21) in *Production of Commodities by Means of Commodities*.

Finally we establish

$$\frac{w}{q(I-A)p}=1-\frac{r}{R} \qquad \forall r\in[0 \ \ R] \qquad (13)$$

which means that the wage expressed in terms of the numeraire $q(I-A)$ is the equation line

$$w=1-\frac{r}{R}$$

Note   If the wage is advanced, then we know that the wage–profit curve is an equilateral hyperbola (see chapter 2).

We have shown that, at a given r, prices were the same whether wages are advanced or paid on surplus; as a result, for a given model $[A,I,L]$ commodity q is a standard even if the wage is advanced.

As an illustration, let us determine the standard commodity in the concrete system contemplated by Sraffa. Such a system only includes basic industries respectively producing iron, coal and wheat, in the following way:

90 tons iron + 120 tons coal + 60 quarters wheat $+\frac{3}{16}$ labour →
180 tons iron

50 tons iron + 125 tons coal + 150 quarters wheat $+\frac{5}{16}$ labour →
450 tons coal

40 tons iron + 40 tons coal + 200 quarters wheat $+\frac{8}{16}$ labour →
480 quarters wheat

Totals = 180 tons   285 tons   410 quarters

By taking as a standard for each of the three goods the quantity produced of each good, we obtain the price equations

$$p=(1+r)Ap+wL$$

where

$$A = \begin{bmatrix} \frac{1}{2} & \frac{12}{45} & \frac{1}{8} \\ \frac{5}{18} & \frac{5}{18} & \frac{5}{16} \\ \frac{2}{9} & \frac{4}{45} & \frac{5}{12} \end{bmatrix} \text{ and } L = \begin{bmatrix} \frac{3}{16} \\ \frac{5}{16} \\ \frac{8}{16} \end{bmatrix}$$

The dominant eigenvalue $\alpha = 1/(1 + R)$ of matrix A is 5/6 which corresponds to a maximum rate of profit $R = 20\%$. The left-hand-side eigenvector q corresponding to the dominant eigenvalue 5/6 is $q = (1 \ 3/5 \ 3/4)$, which means that the standard composite commodity includes (up to the multiplication by scalars) one unit of iron, 3/5 units of coal and 3/4 units of wheat, that is to say, 180 tons of iron, $3/5 \times 450 = 270$ tons of coal and $3/4 \times 480 = 360$ quarters of wheat or 1 ton of iron, 1.5 tons of coal and 2 quarters of wheat.

As the standard commodity is defined up to the multiplication by scalars, only its structure is known, while the level of the basket, of this structure, is not. To show this explicitly, suffice to write the level of the standard commodity as μ times the previous structure, with μ being any scalar

$$q = \mu(1 \tfrac{3}{5} \tfrac{3}{4}) = (\mu \ \tfrac{3}{5}\mu \ \tfrac{3}{4}\mu)$$

It is possible to choose μ, i.e., to normalize vector q by condition $qL = 1$ which gives

$$1 = \mu[1 \tfrac{3}{5} \tfrac{3}{4}] \begin{bmatrix} \frac{3}{16} \\ \frac{5}{16} \\ \frac{8}{16} \end{bmatrix} = \mu[\tfrac{3}{16} + \tfrac{3}{5} \cdot \tfrac{5}{16} + \tfrac{3}{4} \cdot \tfrac{8}{16}] = \tfrac{3}{4}\mu$$

from which we obtain $\mu = \tfrac{4}{3}$ and $q = \tfrac{4}{3} \tfrac{4}{5} 1$.

The standard commodity (whose structure *and* level are now fixed) includes 4/3 units of iron, 4/5 units of coal, 1 unit of wheat, that is, $4/3 \times 180 = 240$ tons of iron, $4/5 \times 450 = 360$ tons of coal and 480 quarters of wheat. We can easily check that the standard system is the following:

120 tons iron + 160 tons coal + 80 quarters wheat + $\tfrac{4}{16}$ labour →
240 tons iron

40 tons iron + 100 tons coal + 120 quarters wheat + $\tfrac{4}{16}$ labour →
360 tons coal

40 tons iron + 40 tons coal + 200 quarters wheat + $\tfrac{8}{16}$ labour →
480 quarters wheat

Totals = 200 tons   300 tons   400 quarters   16/16

It is, as Sraffa termed it (P.S. 26), the *Standard net product* and the *Standard national income* made up with 40 tons of iron, 60 tons of coal and 80 quarters of wheat, which will help normalise prices, with the value of the Standard national income set equal to 1 in order to ensure the linearity of the wage–profit relation.

In the *Standard system* defined by Sraffa as 'the set of equations (or of industries), taken in the proportions that produce the Standard commodity', the proportion in which the various commodities are produced are equal to those in which they enter the aggregate means of production; the standard system consumes 200 tons of iron, 300 tons of coal, 480 quarters of wheat; the percentage of excess quantity produced over the quantity used up in production is the same for every commodity; it is here equal to 20% and corresponds to the maximum rate of profit R.

In short, the standard commodity is $q = (240\ 360\ 480)$, with $q(I - A) = (40\ 60\ 80)$ being the numeraire chosen to express prices and wages.

5.1.2 What happens when the system is decomposable?

In a decomposable system, there may be several homothetic commodities of type $q_i = (1 + R_i)q_i A$ with $q_i \geq 0$. We write q the positive eigenvector corresponding to α, the dominant eigenvalue of A.

Let us revert to Sraffa's beans example

$$A = \begin{bmatrix} 20/23 & 0 \\ a_{21} & 10/11 \end{bmatrix}$$

has two eigenvalues $\alpha = 10/11$ and $\alpha_2 = 20/23$.

To the dominant eigenvalue $\alpha = 10/11$ corresponds q, the eigenvector on the left such that $qA = \alpha q$; we can see that it is strictly positive and equal to $q = \lambda\,(25, 3a_{21}, 1) > 0$ if we choose $\lambda > 0$.

If we choose $q(I - A)$ such that $qL = 1$, as the numeraire of prices, the wage–profit relation $w = 1 - r/0.10$ is linear and intersects points $(r = 0, w = 1)$ and $(r = 0.10, w = 0)$;

To the dominant eigenvalue $\alpha_2 = 20/23$ corresponds q^2, the eigenvector on the left such that $q^2 A = (20/23)q^2$; we can see that $q^2 A = (20/23)q^2$ with $q^2 = \lambda(1,0) \geq 0$ when we choose $\lambda > 0$. If we choose vector $q^2(I - A)$ such that $q^2 L = 1$, as the numeraire to express prices, the wage–profit curve is linear and intersects points $(r = 0, w = 1)$ and $(r = 0.15, w = 0)$.

Let us now contemplate the following three-sector model

$$A = \begin{bmatrix} 0.4 & 0 & 0 \\ 0.1 & 0.5 & 0 \\ 0.1 & 0.1 & 0.6 \end{bmatrix}$$

$\alpha = 0.6$ is the dominant eigenvalue of A to which corresponds the strictly positive eigenvector $q = (1 \ 1 \ 1)$; to the other eigenvalues α_2 and α_3 (which is the eigenvalue of the basic sector) respectively correspond the eigenvectors $q^2 = (1 \ 1 \ 0)$ and $q^3 = (1 \ 0 \ 0)$. We can thus define three homothetic commodities with a common property; with a proper normalisation of the price system, that is $q_i(I - A)p = 1$ (with $q_i L = 1$), they allow us to obtain a linear w/r relation, that is, $q = 1 - r/R_i$. Thus in this example, we would have $R_1 = 1/4$, $R_2 = 3/7$, $R_3 = 3/2$.

Among these homothetic commodities, only one has the required properties to construct a price standard. Indeed, the price standard commodity must meet the following condition: $w \to 0$, $r \to R$ with $p \geq 0$ at $r \in [0 \ R]$, while this is not true[2] at $r > R_h = \min R_i$.

Recall that the dominant eigenvalue of the decomposable matrix A is equal to the dominant eigenvalue of one of the square matrices A_{hh} located on 'the main diagonal'. Matrix A_{hh} represents the use of the goods with the lowest growth rate in their own production and characterises the 'blocking goods' of the system.

Therefore, among the R_is, characterising each of the homothetic commodities, we shall retain the lowest R, written R_h, which as a consequence will be determined from a matrix A_{hh}, representing the 'blocking' goods; $\alpha_h(A_{hh})$ is the dominant eigenvalue of system A.

Since $q_h = (1 + R_h)q_h A_{hh} \geq 0$, the price standard q_h includes, on the one hand, all the commodities making up the blocking sector and, on the other hand, all the commodities directly or indirectly used in the sector (and more particularly basic commodities).

In Sraffa's beans example, the 'standard' includes the 'blocking' good, namely beans, and the good used to produce the blocking good, namely the basic good. Thus, in this case, Sraffa's suggestion consisting of only considering the basic sector leads to a mistake. In the beans example, it is surely possible to define a 'homothetic commodity' including only the basic good and associated with the rate of profit $R_2 = 15\%$, but such a 'homothetic commodity' is not the price standard sought because it is not defined from the maximum rate of profit R, which here amounts to 10%.

Thus, the composition of the standard provides us with major information. We already know that the use of the standard allows to confer a certain transparency to the system; as any homothetic commodity, it allows us to make the wage–profit relation linear: further, it is a price standard true to the definition previously given. Finally, its composition is determined from the peculiar category of 'blocking' goods that we have just defined as those determining the maximum rate of profit (and growth) of the system.

While in an indecomposable system, the basic and blocking goods are the same, when the system is decomposable the blocking goods may differ from the basic goods. That is the case of Sraffa's beans example.

Note that there are blocking goods even if there are no basic goods. If the system is totally decomposable, the blocking goods are defined from the eigenvector corresponding to the dominant eigenvalue of the blocking sector A_{hh}. It is only in the peculiar case when $\alpha_i(A_{ii}) = 0 \ \forall i$ that there are no blocking goods.

Consequently, the price standard, which is unique, has to be considered as composed of blocking goods (and not basic goods), and of goods directly or indirectly entering their production.

Should the system be indecomposable, the blocking and basic sectors are the same.

If the system is totally decomposable, there are no basic goods, however there always is a blocking sector.

The blocking sector determines the critical proportion, and thus the maximum rate of profit as well. The basic sector allows us to calculate the prices of basic commodities, independently of the prices of the non-basic goods, at any positive rate of profit that is less than the maximum rate of profit. The price standard necessarily includes the commodities which determine the blocking sector and therefore, if this is the case, the 'beans' and the commodities directly or indirectly entering their production.[3]

5.1.3 Joint products

The problem of the construction of the standard in joint production reveals many difficulties, some of which we shall briefly recall in the following pages, throwing a new light on the argument.

While contemplating the problem, Sraffa notes that some multipliers entering its construction may become negative (see P.S. chapter 8). And he adds:

Thus a Standard commodity which includes both positive and negative quantities can be adopted as money of account without too great a stretch of the imagination provided that the unit is conceived as representing, like a share in a company, a fraction of each asset and of each liability, the latter in the shape of an obligation to deliver without payment certain quantities of particular commodities (section 56).

However, such a point of view cannot be accepted; of course, there is no objection if some of the multipliers are zero or negative (some q_i of vector q). However, choosing a commodity qB or $q(B-A)$ including negative quantities as a numeraire is out of question. For, under this hypothesis, and since prices p vary with distribution, qBp or $q(B-A)p$ could be zero at some values of r and thus of p as well; therefore, the expression of prices in terms of such a zero commodity could not be defined. Such a commodity could not be true to its purpose, namely providing an invariant standard of value.

Difficulties abound: for example, Manara has shown that the standard ratio may not be determined; some examples also show that the possibility of having several homothetic commodities associated to distinct R_i can be dismissed.

We have shown that in any square production model there always exists a standard ratio R and a standard system. It is possible to define a commodity q which will serve as an invariant standard of value (provided the price system is normalised by $q(I-A)p=1...$).

The ratio $\frac{p_i}{qp}$ varies with distribution, but such variations are only due to the variations of p_i. The commodity qp is the standard commodity of value sought for.

If we consider a decomposable simple production model, there may be several homothetic commodities associated to distinct standard ratios R_i, but only the homothetic commodity associated to the smallest standard ratio R is the price standard. Non-basic goods may be included in the standard commodity, since they are blocking or they enter the production of blocking goods.

In joint production, we can show that, provided free goods are allocated zero prices in von Neumann's solution at a profit rate R equal to the standard ratio, we can always find a composite commodity that is homothetic for economic goods and meets the requirements of the standard commodity.

5.1.4 Irregular systems and plurality of standards

We know that when the labour profile matrix $K=[L, AL, A^2L, ..., A^{k-1}L]$ is of rank $m<k$, model $[A, I, L]$ is irregular. Then, we have shown that

$$N[K]=N[p(r)]=N[\hat{p}(r)] \tag{6}$$

which means that for all vector z of the kernel of K, we have

$$zK=0 \Leftrightarrow zp(r)=0 \Leftrightarrow z\hat{p})(r)=0.$$

More particularly, we have

$$zA^nL=0 \text{ for } n=0,1,2... \tag{4}$$

that is

$$z.A^n \in N(K) \text{ and } zA^n \in N[p(r)] \text{ for } n=0,1,2... \tag{10}$$

and all $z \in N(K)$ establishes

$$z[\alpha I - A]p(r) = 0 \text{ for any } \alpha \in R \tag{11}$$

Linearisation of the wage–profit relation

Let us consider an irregular model $[A, I, L]$ where the input matrix is indecomposable. We know that the standard $q(I-A)$ makes the wage–profit relation linear (see, chapter 2, section 2.3.3).

Let us show that if $z \in N[K]$ any price standard $v(I-A)$, where $v = q + vz \geq 0$ with $vL = 1$, makes the $w - r$ relation linear.

Indeed, since we have:

$$\frac{w}{q(I-A)p} = 1 - \frac{r}{R} \text{ for } q \text{ defined by } qA = \alpha q \text{ and } qL = 1.$$

$v(I-A)p(r) = q(I-A)p(r) + vz(I-A)p(r) = q(I-A)p(r)$ by (11) as a result, for any $z \in N[K]$ such that $v = q + vz \geq 0$

$$\frac{w}{v(I-A)p} = \frac{w}{q(I-A)p} = 1 - \frac{r}{R}$$

Thus the standard $q(I-A)$ is no longer the only one ensuring the linearity of the $w - r$ relation when K is not of full rank; in that case, any standard $v(I-A)$ where $v = q + vz \geq 0$, makes the relation $w - r$ linear.

Standards

In chapter 1, we have shown that for all $r \in [0\ R]$, a commodity y had an invariant price $yp(r)$ if it established the following conditions:
(a) $d(yAp) = 0$ for all $r \in [0\ R]$.
(b) $yAp.dr + yL.dw = 0$ for all $r \in [0\ R]$.

Relation (b) means that $\dfrac{dw}{dr}$ must be constant, i.e., relation $w - r$ must be linear.

Therefore, we have to choose as a numeraire the standard $v(I-A)$ where $v = q + vz \geq 0$ with q establishing $qA = \alpha q$ and $qL = 1$ and $z \in N[K]$.

Relation (a) leads to the following condition

$$y[\alpha I - A]p(r) = 0 \text{ for all } r \in [0\ R] \tag{5'}$$

which is established if we choose

$$y = q + \mu z \tag{12}$$

where $z \in N[K]$.

Then we do have

$$y[\alpha I - Ap(r)] = [q + \mu z][\alpha I - A]p(r)$$

$$= q[\alpha I - A]p(r) + \mu z(\alpha I - A)p(r) = 0$$

since $q(\alpha I - A) = 0$ because $\alpha q = qA$ and $z(\alpha I - A)p(r) = 0$ by (11).

Note that when K is of rank $m < k$, its kernel includes non-zero vectors and as a result the invariant standard of value is no longer unique; in addition to vector q, any vector $y = q + \mu z \geq 0$ where $z \in N[K]$ is a standard.

Number of linearly independent standards

If matrix K is of *rank m* the kernel $N[K]$ is a vector sub-space of R^k the *dimension of which is $k - m$*. Thus, every *base* of $N[K]$ includes $(k - m)$ vectors $z_1, z_2, \ldots, z_h, \ldots, z_{k-m}$ and we can always find constants $\mu_1, \ldots, m_h, \ldots, m_{k-m}$ such that the $(k - m)$ vectors $u_h = q + \mu_h z_h$ are semipositive. By the Miyao theorem, $u_1, u_2, \ldots, u_{k-m}$ are $(k - m)$ standards of $[A, I, L]$ which are linearly independent since $z_1, z_2, \ldots, z_{k-m}$ form a base of $N[K]$. Further, since $qK = [qL, qAL, \ldots, qA^{k-1}L] = [1, \alpha, \ldots, \alpha^{k-1}] \neq 0$ the standard q does not belong to $N[K]$ and thus is linearly independent of vectors $z_1, \ldots, z_h, \ldots, z_{k-m}$.

As a result, when matrix K is of *rank m*, system $[A, I, L]$ possesses $k - m + 1$ *independent standards*: Sraffa's standard q, and the $k - m$ standards $u_1, u_h, \ldots, u_{k-m}$ that we call *Miyao's standards*.

Uniqueness of Sraffa's standard   Sraffa's standard commodity q is the only standard (up to the multiplication by scalars) of model $[A, I, L]$ if and only if matrix A is indecomposable and matrix K is of full rank.

Indeed, if rank $(K) = k$, kernel $N(K)$ is of dimension $k - k = 0$. Thus we have $N[K] = \{0\}$ and by the Miyao theorem, model $[A, I, L]$ has only one standard, namely q.

Similarly, if q is the only standard of model $[A, I, L]$ by the Miyao theorem, we have $N[K] = \{0\}$ and rank $(K) = k$.

Standards when matrix K is of rank 1   If rank $(K) = 1$, the kernel $N(K)$ is of rank $k - 1$ and the system $[A, I, L]$ possesses $k - 1 + 1 = k$ independent standards that is to say, every commodity $u \geq 0$ such that $uL = 1$ is a standard.

5.2 Duality and standards

Our purpose is to show that it is possible to contemplate the construction of a standard in the dual system, that of quantities and activity levels.

What is the meaning of such a standard? How is it to be constructed? What are its characteristics? What is its composition?

We shall first specify some assumptions and notations and then we will address the topic within the context of an indecomposable system and then of a decomposable system. Our reasoning will be limited to the case of a system with single-product industries and circulating capital.

5.2.1 System of activity levels and 'virtual good'

Let us now contemplate the problem of accumulation in model $[A, I, L, \bar{d}]$ by seeking for the activity level vector y, allowing for the same growth rate g for all goods and a consumption withdrawn from surplus which remains homothetic to a vector $\bar{d}$,[4]

The activity level vector $y(g)$ of model $[A, I, L, \bar{d}]$ satisfies the equation:

$$y = (1+g)yA + c\bar{d} \tag{1}$$

This equation is completed by a normalisation condition to which we shall revert.

The components y_i vary when the distribution between accumulation and consumption in the surplus varies. (Note that if we write e^i the column

vector $\begin{bmatrix} 0 \\ \vdots \\ 1 \\ \vdots \\ 0 \end{bmatrix}$ the component y_i, which is the level of the ith activity also

measures the gross production $y.e^i$ of the ith good.)

In fact, when the accumulation/consumption distribution varies, the activity level vector $y(g)$ of model $[A, I, L, \bar{d}]$ is altered and the ratios y_i/y_j of any activities i and j do not remain constant when g varies.

As y_i can be interpreted as the gross production of goods i, we can see that in general, the gross production ratios of goods i to goods j are altered when g varies. As the denominator as well as the numerator of y_i/y_j vary, it is quite impossible to determine, when accumulation varies, what part of the change is due to the commodity in question and what part is due to the commodity that has been used in the normalisation condition of the activity system.

Here, a problem parallel to the invariant standard of value appears, namely the problem of finding the 'invarant standard of activity levels' or, which comes down to the same, the problem of finding a real or virtual *commodity* whose gross production remains invariant when distribution varies.

In order to specify the notion of 'virtual commodities', we first have to distinguish activity level, technical coefficient, and quantity. Just as when we multiply a volume by a specific weight (density) we obtain a weight, when we multiply an activity level by a technical coefficient, we obtain a quantity.

Of course, when in simple production, the technical coefficient b_{ii} (density) is equal to 1, when it is multiplied by an activity level y_i (volume), the quantity $y_i.1 = y_i$ is obtained. In this equality, the term y_i on the left-hand side stands for an activity level, while y_i on the right-hand side represents a quantity: the same number (y_i) represents two different things.

However, a column $b^i = \begin{bmatrix} b_{1i} \\ b_{ii} \\ b_{ki} \end{bmatrix}$ of the output matrix B, which in simple

production is $b^i = \begin{bmatrix} 0 \\ 1 \\ 0 \end{bmatrix}$, has technical coefficients as components. Thus,

if we make the scalar product of the activity level row vector $y = (y_1, \ldots, y_i, \ldots, y_k)$ by the column vector b^1 we obtain a quantity $yb^i = y_1 b_{1i} + \ldots + y_i b_{ii} + \ldots + y_k b_{ki}$, since it is the sum of the terms $y_i b_{ii}$ which are quantities (the product of an activity level y_i by a technical coefficient b_{ii}). In simple production, $yb^i = 0 + \ldots + y_i.1 + \ldots + 0 = y_i$.

If model $[A, B, I, L]$ operates at the level $y = (y_1, \ldots, y_i, \ldots, y_k)$, the quantities $ya^i = y_1 a_{1i} + \ldots + y_i a_{ii} + \ldots + y_k a_{ki}$ and $yb^i = y_i$ represent the quantities of good i respectively used and produced. Each of the pairs $[a^1 \; b^1], \ldots, [a^i \; b^i], \ldots, [a^k \; b^k]$, represents a (real) good which is used and produced by model $[A, B, L]$.

By extension, a pair of column vectors of order k, $[h \; z]$ can define a new commodity or a 'virtual commodity' whose input and output technical coefficients are respectively

$$h = \begin{bmatrix} h^1 \\ h^i \\ h^k \end{bmatrix} \quad z = \begin{bmatrix} z^1 \\ z^i \\ z^k \end{bmatrix}$$

The produced quantity of that good would be $yz = y_1 z_1 + \ldots + y_i z_i + \ldots + y_k z_k$ and the quantity used would be yh.

A 'virtual commodity' is not a 'composite commodity' but *dual to a composite commodity*: while a composite commodity can be compared to an activity or to a pair of rows of matrices A and B, with components representing quantities of several goods, a 'virtual commodity' can be assimilated to a pair of columns of matrices A and B, with components representing technical coefficients of a same good.

5.2.2 Indecomposable system with single-product industries and circulating capital

Let $[A, I, L, \bar{d}]$ be a model where the input matrix A is *indecomposable*. We assume that:

the growth rate is uniform for *all means of production* and is equal to g, with g included between 0 and $G = R = (1 - \alpha(A))/\alpha(A)$;

when g grows from 0 to G, the consumption withdrawn from surplus decreases but remains homothetic to $\bar{d}$. We write $c(g)\bar{d}$ where $c(g)$ is the *consumption level* which then decreases from 1 to 0;

returns are constant.

The activity level vector $y(g)$ of model $[A, I, L, d]$ establishes the following equation

$$y = (1 + g)yA + c\bar{d} \qquad (1)$$

Actually, this matrix equation is a system with k equations and $k + 2$ unknowns: the k activity levels $y_1, y_2, \ldots, y_i, \ldots, y_k$, the growth rate g, and the consumption level c. As returns are constant, vector y is defined up to the multiplication by scalars and the $k + 2$ unknowns are totally determined if we normalise activity levels and if one of the distributive variables c or g is defined exogenously.

We can normalise activity levels by writing

$$y(g)(I - A)v = 1 \qquad (2)$$

where $v \geq 0$ such that $\bar{d}v = 1$.

owing to (1) and (2), we obtain

$$1 = y(g)(I - A)v = gyAv + c\bar{d}v = gyAv + c \qquad (2')$$

and when c decreases from 1 to 0, g decreases from 0 to the maximum rate of growth G.

The level y_i of the ith activity stands for the gross production of the ith good by the model; it also appears as the scalar product of the activity level vector y by vector $e^i = (0, 0, \ldots, 1, \ldots, 0)$ representing the quantities of good i produced by each of the k activities.

Vector v, which serves as a standard for activity levels, can be interpreted as a vector whose components are the quantities of a 'virtual' commodity produced by each of the k activities of the model so that the net production $y(I - a)v$ is equal to 1.

Instead of vector v, we can choose the eigenvector $\bar{p}$ on the right of matrix A corresponding to the dominant eigenvalue $\alpha(A)$ and defined as follows

$$A\bar{p} = \alpha(A)\bar{p} \quad \text{and} \quad \bar{d}\bar{p} = 1 \qquad (3)$$

or

$$\bar{p} = (1 + G)A\bar{p} \tag{4}$$

thus we have

$$y(g)\bar{p} = (1 + G)y(g)A\bar{p} \tag{5}$$

for all g included between 0 and G and the new activity level standard

$$y(g)(I - A)\bar{p} = 1 \tag{6}$$

makes the consumption–accumulation relation linear since (2') gives

$$1 = y(I - A)\bar{p} = gyA\bar{p} + c = g/G + c$$

as we deduce from (5):

$$1 = y(I - A)\bar{p} = GyA\bar{p}$$

where $yA\bar{p} = 1/G$.

Further, if the model is d – regular,[5] the standard $y(I - A)\bar{p} = 1$ is the only standard, up to the multiplication by scalars, which makes consumption and accumulation linear, i.e., $c(g) = 1 - g/G$ and consequently makes the derivative $dc/dg = -1/G$ constant.

5.2.3 Definition of a good whose gross production remains invariant when the accumulation–consumption distribution varies

Let us revert to the activity level system of model $[A, I, L, \bar{d}]$.

When the accumulation–consumption distribution varies, the activity level vector $y(g)$ of model $[A, I, L, \bar{d}]$ which establishes the equation, is altered and the ratios y_i/y_j of the levels of any activities i and j do not remain constant.

Let us show that a real or virtual commodity exists, such that its gross production remains invariant when distribution varies. Recall that the gross production of a 'virtual' commodity z is by definition the scalar product of yz where y establishes equation (1).

We can choose a *temporary standard*, represented by a vector $v \geq 0$, to express activity levels $y(g)$ and consumption $c(g)$ when the growth rate g is exogenous.

A variation dg of the growth rate causes a variation dc of consumption $c(g)$ and a variation dy of the activity level vector $y(g)$.

We obtain dy by differentiating both members of equation (1) and we have

$$dy = (1 + g)d(yA) + yA dg + \bar{d}.dc \tag{10}$$

the gross production of a virtual commodity $z = [z_1, \ldots, z_i, \ldots, z_k]$ being equal to $y(g)z$; when the growth rate undergoes a variation dg, the gross production of the virtual commodity z undergoes a variation $d[yz] = d[y]z$.

For the virtual commodity z to have an *invariant gross production* when accumulation changes, $y(g)z$ needs and only needs to remain constant when g varies from 0 to G, i.e., the differential $d[yz]$ must be *identically* zero or

$$0 = d[yz] = dy.z = (1+g)d[yAz] + yAzdg + \bar{d}zdc \qquad (11)$$

for all $g \in [0\ G]$.

Since the identity (11) must be established for all g, the following conditions are sufficient:

(a) $d[yAz] = 0$ \qquad for all $g \in [0\ G]$.

(b) $yAzdg + \bar{d}zdc = 0$ \qquad for all $g \in [0\ G]$.

Condition (a) means that the consumption yAz of the virtual commodity z as an input must, just as the gross production of commodity yz, be constant when g varies from 0 to G. As a result the ratio yAz/yz also remains constant when $g \in [0\ G]$. If we call that constant μ, we obtain a first necessary condition

$$yAz/yz = \mu \qquad (12)$$

or

$$yAz = \mu yz$$

or

$$y[\mu\ I - A]z = 0 \qquad \text{for all } g \in [0\ G] \qquad (12')$$

If model $[A, I, L, \bar{d}]$ is $\bar{d}$-regular, condition (12') is established if and only if

$$[\mu\ I - A]z = 0 \quad \text{or} \quad \mu z = Az \qquad (13)$$

that is, if μ is the eigenvalue of the square matrix A and z is the corresponding eigenvector on the right. Since matrix A is indecomposable and $z \geq 0$, μ is the dominant eigenvalue $\alpha(A)$ of matrix A and $z > 0$.

Vector z being defined up to the multiplication by scalars, we can choose vector $\bar{p}$ that is homothetic to z and such that $\bar{d}\bar{p} = 1$.

Thus vector $\bar{p} > 0$ defined by

$$A\bar{p} = a(A)\bar{p} \qquad (14)$$

and

$$\bar{d}\bar{p} = 1 \qquad (15)$$

establishes condition (a) which ensures an invariant gross production of the virtual good $\bar{p}$ when the accumulation–consumption distribution varies.

Now let us turn to condition (b)

$$yAzdg + \bar{d}zdc = 0 \qquad \text{for all } g \in [0 \ G]$$

and since commodity $\bar{p}$ is homothetic to z and also establishes $\bar{d}\bar{p} = 1$, condition (b) becomes

$$yA\bar{p}dg + \bar{d}\bar{p}dc = 0 \quad \text{or} \quad yA\bar{p}dg + dc = 0$$

that is

$$c' = dc/dg = -yA\bar{p} \qquad \text{for all } g \in [0 \ G]$$

Since by condition (a) $yA\bar{p}$ is constant, this means that the derivative c' of c in relation to g must be constant, in other words, the accumulation–consumption relation must be linear. But this is possible only if the activity level and consumption standard is homothetic to the eigenvector on the right $\bar{p}$.

As $(I - A)\bar{p} = (1 - \alpha(A))\bar{p}$ is homothetic to $\bar{p}$, we can choose it as a standard and write

$$y(g)(I - A)\bar{p} = 1 \tag{2''}$$

In these conditions, by post-multiplying both terms of equation (1) by vector $\bar{p}$, we obtain

$$y\bar{p} = (1 + g)yA\bar{p} + c\bar{d}\bar{p} = (1 + g)yA\bar{p} + c = yA\bar{p} + gyA\bar{p} + c \tag{16}$$

hence

$$y\bar{p} - yA\bar{p} = gyA\bar{p} + c$$

and

$$gyA\bar{p} + c = y(I - A)\bar{p} = 1 \qquad \text{for all } g \in [0 \ G].$$

More particularly, for $g = G$, we have $c = 0$, hence $GyA\bar{p} = 1$, that is

$$yA\bar{p} = 1/G \qquad y\bar{p} = yA\bar{p}/\alpha(A) = (1 + G)yA\bar{p} = (1 + G)/G$$

Thus, in model $[A, I, L, \bar{d}]$, the virtual commodity $\bar{p}$ defined by (14) and (15) has a *quantity-invariant gross production* if the activity level standard is $y(I - A)\bar{p} = 1$

Note 1 If model $[A, I, L, \bar{d}]$ is not $\bar{d}$-regular, there exist m independent virtual goods whose gross productions are invariant. They are represented by the vectors

$$s^j = \bar{p} + h^j > 0$$

where $y(g)h^j = 0$ and j varies from 1 to m.

If we normalise activity levels by $(I - A)u^j$ where u^j is also a semi-positive vector of type $\bar{p} + h^j$ (which can be equal to or different from s^j), all commodities ys^j are invariant standards of activity levels.

When $\bar{d}$ is an eigenvector to the left of matrix A, the model is of course irregular and all the commodities have quantity-invariant gross productions. In this case, $dy = 0$ when g varies from 0 to G.

Note 2   In joint production, we only need to apply the same reasoning as the one used in section 5.1.3 for the price standard.

If $p^*(R)$ is the von Neumann solution of model $[A, B, L]$, the activity level standard is $\bar{p} = p^*(R)$, which only applies the activities used in the Von Neumann solution.

5.2.4 What happens when the system is decomposable?

When model $[A, I, L, \bar{d}]$ is decomposable, the activity levels y_i are non-negative only if g, the growth rate of the economy, is less than

$$G = R = (1 - \alpha(A))/\alpha(A).$$

We know that G, the maximum growth rate of the economy, is the blocking commodities', which are characterised by a sub-matrix $A(h, h)$ whose dominant eigenvalue $\alpha(A(h, h))$ is equal to $\alpha(A)$.

In these conditions, it appears that when $g \to G$, $c \to 0$ with $y > 0$.

Note that in a *decomposable* system, there may exist *several homothetic virtual commodities* of type $\bar{p}^j = (1 + G_j)A$ with $\bar{p}^j \geq 0$. We write $\bar{p}$ the non-negative eigenvector on the right corresponding to the dominant eigenvalue $\alpha(A)$ of A such that $\bar{d}\bar{p} = 1$.

Among the homothetic virtual commodities, only one has the properties of the invariant standard of activity levels; It is the one which corresponds to the dominant eigenvalue of matrix A, that is to the blocking goods' maximum growth rate G, which is the lowest of the G_js.

Indeed, it is the only one for which $c \to 0$ when $g \to G$ with $y > 0$.

Therefore, the *activity level standard* is a virtual good which is used (and produced) by the blocking sector and the activities directly or indirectly using blocking goods.

It is worth noting that blocking commodities play a vital role in the determination of prices and activity levels of the decomposable model $[A, I, L, \bar{d}]$. They determine the model's maximum rate of profit R and maximum growth rate G and consequently the price and activity level standards.

Further, the price standard includes the blocking commodities and the goods directly or indirectly entering their production while the activity level standard is a virtual commodity which is used (and produced) by the activities which directly or indirectly use blocking commodities.

6 Labour values and the problem of transformation

The debate over 'transformation' is not purely theoretical; it is not only concerned with the problem of the transformation of labour values into prices of production, but also with Marx's definition of the rate of profit.[1] However, the current theory of production prices shows that they are determined simultaneously with profit and thus are independent of labour values. The famous formula given by Marx as the definition and the basis to calculate the average rate of profit is therefore wrong (except in specific cases). It is possible, however, to enhance the relation (that is different from Marx's) between a properly defined rate of profit and the rate of exploitation.

We shall thoroughly analyse the (peculiar and therefore unimportant) cases for which Marx's formulation is revealed to be correct. We shall also emphasise the fact that Marx's presentation can be analysed as the starting point of an iteration, which, provided it is completed, comes close to the current theory of production prices.

We shall also have to revert to the case of the decomposability of production structures: according to some hypotheses, 'luxury' goods, or more precisely non-basic goods, may be produced in such conditions that the mere existence of a production price system is questioned. A certain number of paradoxes may also be emphasised in the case of joint production; as a result, the labour value theory, which is concerned neither with natural resources nor with non-reproducible goods cannot be applied to non-separately reproducible goods. Finally, we shall give more precise details on the relation between capitalists's consumption and accumulation.

6.1 Marx's analysis: formal presentation

In the very first pages of *Capital*, Marx points out that a commodity's 'magnitude of value' is measured 'by the quantity of the value-creating substance, the labour, contained in the article' (I, 38). Here, we only deal with the values of commodities reproducible by social labour, thus excluding works of art and land. Further, we assume that these commodities are useful otherwise they would have no value: 'nothing can have *value*, without being an object of utility' (I, 41). Finally, in the calculations we need to take into account not only direct labour but also indirect labour, the value transmitted by the use of the means of production in the production process: indeed, Marx specifies: 'The quantity of labour expended in the production of the consumed article, forms a portion of the quantity of labour necessary to produce the new use-value' (I, 200).

Thus, we shall use the hypothesis and the notations previously stated in the developments dealing with systems with single-product industries and circulating capital; a_{ij} then stands for the quantity of good j used to produce one unit of good i and l_i denotes the quantity of direct labour necessary to produce one unit of the same good (as previously, we assume that there is only one category of workers). The technology structure of the economy is thus summarised in the technology matrix A and the column vector L of needs in direct labour.

Let $\Lambda = \begin{bmatrix} \lambda_1 \\ \vdots \\ \lambda_2 \\ \vdots \\ \lambda_k \end{bmatrix}$ be the column vector of the various commodities' labour

values; since to produce one unit of good i, intermediate consumptions denoted by vector $a_i = (a_{i1}, a_{i2}, \ldots, a_{ij}, \ldots, a_{ik})$, are needed as well as a quantity of direct labour l_i, the labour value, the quantity of direct and indirect labour λ_i of one unit of good i is determined by

$$\lambda_i = a_{i1}\lambda_1 + a_{i2}\lambda_2 + \ldots + a_{ij}\lambda_j + \ldots + a_{ik}\lambda_k + l_i$$
$$\lambda_i = a_i\Lambda + l_i \quad \text{for } i = 1, 2, \ldots, k$$

This is therefore a system with k equations (there are as many equations as there are activities and thus an equal number of commodities) which writes

$$\Lambda = A\Lambda + L$$

hence $(I - A)\Lambda = L$ and if $(I - A)$ is regular

$$\Lambda = (I - A)^{-1}L$$

To show that the labour value represents the direct and indirect labour contained in a commodity, we shall use a method inspired by Sraffa's subsystem methods (see Appendix A in *Production of Commodities by Means of Commodities*).

We know that at $g=0$, the production of a net surplus of commodities $d=(d_1,d_2,\ldots,d_k)$ requires the use of the activity-level vector y which establishes the equation $y=yA+d$. More particularly, the production of one unit of the ith good, that is to say the net surplus $d=e_i=(0,\ldots,1,\ldots,0)$ with all its components being zeros except for the ith which equals 1, requires the use of vector y_i such that $y_i=y_iA+e_i$, that is, $y_i=e_i(I-A)^{-1}$ (if $\det(I-A)\neq0$).

The quantity of direct or indirect labour used by the previous system to produce one unit of good i is thus given by

$$y_iL=e_i(I-A)^{-1}L=e_i\Lambda=\lambda_i$$

A commodity's labour value λ_i does represent the quantity of direct and indirect labour necessary to produce one unit of that commodity.

The labour value vector[2] is strictly positive if matrix A is indecomposable (indeed, in that case matrix $(I-A)^{-1}$ is strictly positive); if matrix A is decomposable, some labour values may be zeros if the labour vector is semi-positive, for matrix $(I-A)^{-1}$ is semi-positive. Since the usual hypothesis holds that every activity uses labour, then labour values are positive whether matrix A is decomposable or not.

$d=(d_1,d_2,\ldots,d_i,\ldots,d_k)\geq0$ denotes the basket of consumption goods a worker can buy in the considered society with the wage he receives as a payment for each unit of labour provided (days or hours). Thus d represents the mode of satisfying workers' wants; we know that for Marx 'the number and extent of ... necessary wants, as also the modes of satisfying them, are themselves the product of historical development, and depend therefore to a great extent on the degree of civilisation of a country' (I, 171).

Labour power is a commodity which according to Marx has the virtue of being a source of exchange value. 'The value of labour is determined as in the case of every other commodity, by the labour time necessary for the production ... the value of labour power is the value of the means of subsistence necessary for the maintenance of the labourer' (I, 170–1). Thus, the value of labour power (or variable capital) consisting in the supply of one unit of labour and therefore in the creation of a unit of new exchange value, is represented by the value of the commodities allowing the maintenance and replacement of the labour power $\Sigma\lambda_id_i=d\Lambda$; the surplus value withdrawn by the capitalist is the difference between the value created by the labourer (unity by assumption) and the value of the labour power; hence the expression of the rate of surplus value or exploitation rate, the ratio of the surplus value to the value of variable capital

$$e=\frac{1-d\Lambda}{d\Lambda}$$

From which we obtain: $1 = (1 + e)d\Lambda$ and the new formulation of the commodity's value

$$\lambda_i = a_i\Lambda + l_i = a_i\Lambda + l_i 1 = a_i\Lambda + l_i(1 + e)d\Lambda$$
$$\lambda_i = a_i\Lambda + l_i d\Lambda + el_i d\Lambda$$

The commodity's value is thus the sum of
(a) the value of constant capital entering its production $a_i\Lambda$;
(b) the value of variable capital entering its production $l_i d\Lambda$;
(c) and the resulting surplus value $el_i d\Lambda$.
Hence the following expression of the system of values

$$\Lambda = A\Lambda + L(1 + e)d\Lambda = A\Lambda + Ld\Lambda + eLd\Lambda$$

Let $y = [y_1, y_2, \ldots, y_k]$ be the vector of activity levels and under simple production $yI = y$ be the vector of the produced quantities of each good. We have

$$y\Lambda = yA\Lambda + yLd\Lambda + eyLd\Lambda$$

with $y\Lambda$ = the aggregate value of all produced commodities,

$yA\Lambda$ = the aggregate value of the means of production used, that is to say the total constant capital expressed in terms of value,

$yLd\Lambda$ = the total variable capital expressed in terms of value,

$eyLd\Lambda$ = the total surplus value.

Hence the rate of profit r defined by Marx as the ratio of the total surplus value to the total capital advanced by the capitalists

$$r = \frac{eyLd\Lambda}{yLd\Lambda + yA\Lambda} = \frac{e}{1 + k}$$

where $k = \dfrac{yA\Lambda}{yLd\Lambda}$ is the organic composition of capital.

It is this average rate of profit applied to the total capital advanced in each industry, which will allow us to determine prices of production p, hence

$$p = (1 + r)(A\Lambda + Ld\Lambda)$$

Note
In this chapter, the price vector p and the rate of profit r are defined by the previous system and have nothing to do with the notations used in the developments about Sraffa's system.

It is worth emphasising that in the solution given by Marx of which we have been reminded in the summary above:
(a) The determination of prices requires previous knowledge of the values that appear in their mere expression; they thus appear as values which

have been transformed, or altered. Compared to the production price system that we have addressed in the previous chapters, Marx's production prices show a significant difference: they are not defined up to the multiplication by scalars and there is no need to ponder on the normalisation condition; indeed, they are directly defined on the basis of labour values, that is to say as the sum of direct and indirect labour, with the rate of profit redistributing so to speak the aggregate surplus value to the benefit of industries with a relatively high organic composition and to the detriment of those with a relatively low organic composition.

(b) The rate of profit is also defined on the basis of the system of values; it is indeed the ratio of the aggregate surplus value to the total capital advanced by the capitalists, or in other words the ratio of two quantities expressed in terms of values.

(c) By construction the total profit equals the aggregate surplus value; indeed owing to the equation defining the rate of profit r we can see that the aggregate profit (defined by Marx as the product of the rate of profit r by the total value of the advanced capital: $yA\Lambda + yLd\Lambda$) equals the aggregate surplus value $eyLd\Lambda$

$$r(yA\Lambda + yLd\Lambda) = eyLd\Lambda$$

(d) The sum of prices equals the sum of values, this means, as indicated in the arithmetical example developed by Marx, that the set of produced commodities represented by the gross production vector y has the same value whether one uses it to assess either Marx's production price system p or the content in direct and indirect labour; in short the labour value system. This reads clearly in the following lines: 'the sum of the prices of production of all commodities produced in society – the totality of all branches of production – is equal to the sum of their values' (Marx, III, 159).

Indeed, by premultiplying the column vector of prices previously defined by the row vector of quantities y, we obtain

$$yp = (1+r)y(A\Lambda + Ld\Lambda) = yA\Lambda + Ld\Lambda + r(yA\Lambda + yLd\Lambda)$$

Owing to the previous results, we can replace the last term of the expression above, which represents the aggregate profit, by the aggregate surplus value, hence

$$yp = yA\Lambda + yLd\Lambda + eyLd\Lambda = y(A\Lambda + Ld\Lambda + eLd\Lambda)$$

And since $\Lambda = A\Lambda + Ld\Lambda + eLd\Lambda$, the sum of prices equals the sum of values $yp = y\Lambda$.

6.2 Reformulation

6.2.1 Simultaneous determination of the rate of profit $R^* \neq r$ and the production prices

Marx himself was aware of the 'approximate' character of his solution. In the third volume of *Capital* he says:

We had originally assumed that the cost-price of a commodity equalled the value of the commodities consumed in its production. But for the buyer the price of production of a specific commodity is its cost-price, and may thus pass as cost-price into the prices of other commodities. (III, 162)

And later he adds:

It is necessary to remember this modified significance of the cost-price, and to bear in mind that there is always the possibility of an error if the cost-price of a commodity in any particular sphere is identified with the value of the means of production consumed by it.

But having pointed out this possibility of error Marx immediately adds: 'our present analysis does not necessitate a closer examination of this point' (III, 162). However, the contemporary analysis shows that production prices are determined simultaneously with the average rate of profit, which enters the production price of a commodity since it is assessed in terms of prices and not of value. Hence the new expression of the production price system denoted by p^*

$$p^* = (1 + R^*)(Ap^* + Lw)$$

R^* is the rate of profit taken to be uniform, w the level of real wages allowing to buy worker consumption goods assessed in terms of production prices, that is: $w = \Sigma d_i p_i^* = dp^*$

The production price system can also be written

$$p^* = (1 + R^*)(Ap^* + Ldp^*) = (1 + R^*)(A + Ld)p^*$$

Let A^* be the 'socio-technological' matrix obtained from the technology matrix A and vectors d and L

$$A^* = A + Ld \quad \text{or} \quad a_{ij}^* = a_{ij} + l_i d_j$$

We obtain

$$\boxed{p^* = (1 + R^*)A^* p^*} \Leftrightarrow A^* p^* = \frac{1}{1 + R^*} p^*$$

Thus p^* appears as the eigenvector corresponding to the dominant eigenvalue $\alpha^* = 1/(1 + R^*)$ of matrix A^*; by the Perron–Frobenius theorem,

p^* is strictly positive if A^* is indecomposable and semi-positive if A^* is decomposable. Vector p^* always exists and, unlike the price vector p defined by Marx, it is defined up to the multiplication by scalars; it may (and must) be normalised by a condition of the following type: $up^* = 1$ where $u = (u_1, u_2, \ldots, u_k) \geq 0$. Therefore, such production prices are not transformed values.

The rate of profit $R^* = (1 - \alpha^*)/\alpha^*$ *is thus obtained only on the basis of the production system and defined simultaneously with all its prices* while in the system contemplated by Marx, the rate of profit was determined prior to prices p. Further, *the rate of profit* R^* *is* (generally) *different from the rate of profit* r *defined by Marx*

$$R^* \neq r = \frac{m}{c+v} = \frac{e}{1+k}$$

Although calculating R^* does not imply the use of the system of values where the rate of exploitation is defined, we may however underline the relation between the rate of profit R^* and the rate of exploitation e. Further, it is worth re-examining the status of the equalities emphasised by Marx, of the aggregate surplus value and the aggregate profit, on the one hand, and of the sum of prices and the sum of values, on the other hand.

6.2.2 Relation between the rate of profit R^* and the rate of exploitation e

Whatever the level of outputs and thus of activities (y) characterising the economy in question, it is always possible to define the production structure, a (unique) linear combination of activities q^* such that q^*, the eigenvector on the left corresponding to the dominant eigenvalue $\alpha^* = 1/(1+R^*)$ of matrix A^*, is strictly positive when A^* is indecomposable and semi-positive when A^* is decomposable

$$\alpha^* q^* = q^* A^* \Leftrightarrow q^* = (1 + R^*)q^* A^*$$

hence $q^*(I - A^*) = R^* q^* A^*$ where R^* is the rate of profit defined by

$$\alpha^* p^* = A^* p^* \Leftrightarrow p^* = (1 + R^*)A^* p^*$$

By multiplying both members of the equality defining q^* by the vector of values Λ, we obtain

$$q^*(I - A^*)\Lambda = R^* q^* A^* \Lambda$$

hence

$$R^* = \frac{q^*(I - A^*)\Lambda}{q^* A^* \Lambda} = \frac{eq^* Ld\Lambda}{q^* A\Lambda + q^* Ld\Lambda}.$$

We have thus constructed an abstract system characterised by the same technical data (A and L are identical) and the same level of workers consumption as the real system (d is the same). The only difference lies in the fact that activity levels (and thus here production levels) are not defined by vector y any more but by vector q^*.

Vector q^* is by construction a linear combination of activities allowing a balanced growth, that is homothetic to the system. $q^*l=q^*$ stands for a peculiar composite commodity that we shall characterise as a balanced commodity or a commodity that is homothetic to the socio-technological matrix. To be produced, such a commodity uses means of production q^*A whose value, the content in direct and indirect labour, is $q^*A\Lambda$; further, it uses a labour power q^*L whose value is $q^*Ld\Lambda$. By defining k^* $= q^*A\Lambda/q^*Ld\Lambda$ as the organic composition of the homothetic commodity q^*, we obtain

$$R^* = \frac{eq^*Ld\Lambda}{q^*A\Lambda + q^*Ld\Lambda} = \frac{e}{\dfrac{q^*A\Lambda}{q^*Ld\Lambda} + 1}$$

or $\boxed{R^* = \dfrac{e}{1+k^*}}$ with $k^* = \dfrac{q^*A\Lambda}{q^*Ld\Lambda}$.

We have thus established a *relation between the rate of profit R^** (simultaneously determined with the set of production prices) and *the rate of exploitation e*; while the (mistaken) relation given by Marx $r=e/(1+k)$ implied the use of the social or average organic composition $k = yA\Lambda/yLd\Lambda$, the formulation above implies the use of the organic composition of the homothetic commodity k^*.

It may be worthwhile reverting to another difference: *in Marx's analysis, the formulation of r was also a determination of the rate of profit*; it is quite different here: *calculating R^* does not necessarily imply the use of the system of values*.

6.2.3 Normalisation of the price system

The system of transformation of values into production prices elaborated by Marx emphasises the *equality of the sum of prices and the sum of values*, on the one hand, and the *equality of the aggregate profit and the aggregate surplus value*, on the other hand. But, when the system of production prices is written in a consistent manner (inputs and outputs are both evaluated in terms of production prices), *there is no logical reason why these equalities should be true in general*.

Indeed

$$\Lambda = A\Lambda + L$$
$$p^* = (1 + R^*)A^*p^*$$

These are two distinct systems of valuation. The first, the system of 'value', represents labour content, i.e., absolute values, while the price system determines relative prices, defined up to the multiplication by scalars. *(Relative) prices and (absolute) values cannot be compared; they are incommensurable a priori.*

They may be made commensurable however; this implies the use of *the normalisation condition of the price system.* Instead of writing $up^* = 1$ as usual, which consists in using the price of the composite commodity $u = (u_1, u_2, \ldots, u_k)$ as the numeraire, we could write $up^* = u\Lambda$; thus the price of a certain basket of commodities is set equal to its own value. This, which is always possible as the normalisation condition of the price system, as a result makes prices and values commensurable since prices are thus expressed in terms of labour.

But we may also set $yp^* = y\Lambda$ as the normalisation condition: this means that the valuation of the set of commodities produced in terms of production prices is *by assumption* equal to the labour value of that very set, in other words, *by assumption, the sum of prices equals the sum of values.* While the equality of the aggregate profit and the aggregate surplus value cannot in general be established.

Indeed, consider the following system of values

$$\Lambda = A\Lambda + L = A\Lambda + (1 + e)Ld\Lambda$$

the aggregate surplus value is then defined by

$$eyLd\Lambda = y\Lambda - yA\Lambda - yLd\Lambda = y\Lambda - y(A + Ld)\Lambda$$
$$= y\Lambda - yA^*\Lambda = y(I - A^*)\Lambda$$

Since the system of prices writes $p^* = (1 + R^*)A^*p^*$, we have: $yp^* = (1 + R^*)yA^*p^*$ and the aggregate profit is $R^*yA^*p^* = yp^* - yA^*p^* = y(I - A^*)p^*$. By using the normalisation condition $yp^* = y\Lambda$, it appears clearly that the aggregate profit cannot equal the total surplus value since (at least in general) $yA^*p^* \neq yA^*\Lambda$.

Remark

We could however use another normalisation condition for prices, namely: $y(I - A^*)p^* = y(I - A^*)\Lambda$; this would mean that *by assumption the aggregate profit is set equal to the total surplus value.*

In that case we can easily show, at least in general, that the equality of the 'sum of prices' and the 'sum of values' does not hold. Indeed

$$y(I - A^*)\Lambda = y\Lambda - yA^*\Lambda = eyLd\Lambda$$
$$y(I - A^*)p^* = yp^* - yA^*p^* = R^*yA^*p^*$$

It is clear that the normalisation condition 'aggregate profit equals aggregate surplus-value' entails $yp^* = y\Lambda$ only if $yA^*p^* = yA^*\Lambda$, and there is no reason for the latter to be satisfied.

It is therefore always possible to obtain either the *aggregate profit/ aggregate surplus value equality*, or the *sum of prices/sum of values equality*. Both are *alternative normalisation conditions* that we can always choose and which have no specific meaning per se.

However, *in general both equalities* (which correspond to different normalisation conditions for production prices) *cannot be simultaneously established*. But, as we shall see, in some cases they are.

6.3 Peculiar cases when Marx's statement holds

The rate of profit r defined by Marx writes

$$r = \frac{y(I - A^*)\Lambda}{yA^*\Lambda}$$

The system of production prices p^* defined by $p^* = (1 + R^*)A^*p^*$ can be completed by the normalisation condition $yp^* = y\Lambda$ which also implies that the sum of production prices equals the sum of values.

Thus we have

$$R^* = \frac{y(I - A^*)p^*}{yA^*p^*}$$

Marx's theory holds if and only if

$$R^* = r \text{ or } \frac{y(I - A^*)\Lambda}{yA^*\Lambda} = R^*$$

Indeed, owing to the normalisation condition for prices $yp^* = y\Lambda$, it is clear that $r = R^* \Leftrightarrow y(I - A^*)\Lambda = y(I - A^*)p^*$ (the aggregate surplus value equals the aggregate profit).

The condition $R^* = y(I - A^*)\Lambda/yA^*\Lambda$ can write

$$y[I - (1 + R^*)A^*]\Lambda = 0$$

which *defines the set of cases when Marx's theory holds*.

Two cases deserve a closer look owing to their simplicity.

6.3.1 1st case: the golden rule of accumulation

The production vector y is the eigenvector on the left of matrix A^*, taken to be indecomposable

$$y \equiv q^* = (1 + R^*)q^* A^*$$

This[3] may refer to a very peculiar behaviour hypothesis of the capitalists who accumulate the whole surplus value or surplus; their final consumption is zero; on the other hand, workers consume the whole of their salaries. But we may also suppose that workers' savings exactly compensate for capitalists' consumption so that we have $G^* = R^*$. Obviously, 'transformation' is achieved here

$$y \equiv q^* \Rightarrow y [I - (1 + R^*)A^*]\Lambda = 0$$

owing to the mere definition of q^*.

It is worth noting that the configuration contemplated by Samuelson (1971) is only an alternative to this one. Indeed, he assumes that 'In this case every one of the departments happens to use the various raw materials and machine services in the same proportions that society produces them in toto.' Further, it is to be assumed that 'the minimum-subsistence budget is a market basket of goods that comes in those same relative proportions as the goods are used as inputs in production'.

6.3.2 2nd case: identity of the organic compositions of the various sectors

The (symmetric) case to the previous one is that with the vector of values being the eigenvector (on the right) of matrix A^*; we shall show that this case does correspond to the case of identity of the organic compositions.

Let us first demonstrate that L and Λ are homothetic. The definition equation of values $\Lambda = A\Lambda + L$ can be written

$$\Lambda = A\Lambda + Ld\Lambda + L - Ld\Lambda = A^*\Lambda + L(1 - d\Lambda)$$

Owing to the assumption $\alpha^*\Lambda = A^*\Lambda$, we have

$$\Lambda = \alpha^*\Lambda + L(1 - d\Lambda)$$

as α^* and $d\Lambda$ are scalars, we have

$$L = \frac{(1 - \alpha^*)\Lambda}{1 - d\Lambda}$$

Vectors L and Λ are thus homothetic. Consequently: $\alpha^*\Lambda = A^*\Lambda \Rightarrow a^*L = A^*L = (A + Ld)L$ and $L(\alpha^* - dL) = AL$; therefore L is the eigenvector corresponding to the dominant eigenvalue $\alpha = \alpha^* - dL$ of matrix A. Similarly, $A\Lambda = \alpha L$ and thus, $\forall i$

$$a_i \Lambda = a l_i = \frac{\alpha}{1 - \alpha} l_i$$

since $L = \Lambda - A\Lambda = \Lambda - \alpha\Lambda = (1\alpha)\Lambda$.

Thus we have

$$\frac{a_i \Lambda}{l_i} = \frac{\alpha}{1 - \alpha} \forall i \text{ and } k_i = \frac{a_i \Lambda}{l_i d\Lambda} = \frac{\alpha}{1 - \alpha} = k$$

Thus, if $\alpha^* \Lambda = A^* \Lambda$, $k_i = k$ and the transformation is achieved since $\alpha^* p^* = A^* p^*$ and owing to the normalisation condition, production prices equal values. (We can show without any difficulty that $k_i = k \Rightarrow \alpha^* \Lambda = A^* \Lambda$.) These two cases are not the only ones ensuring the transformation. The latter is achieved every time $y[I - (1 + R^*)A^*]\Lambda = 0$, or by writing

$$b = [I - (1 + R^*)A^*]\Lambda$$

when $yb = 0$ which implies the *orthogonality of vectors y and b*.[4]

Example

Consider an economy which produces and uses three commodities;[5] by assumption we have

$$A = \begin{bmatrix} 0.5 & 0.3 & 0 \\ 0 & 0.2 & 0.2 \\ 0.1 & 0.3 & 0.6 \end{bmatrix} \qquad L = \begin{bmatrix} 0.2 \\ 0.4 \\ 0.4 \end{bmatrix} \qquad d = [0.2 \ 0 \ 0]$$

From which we obtain

$$\Lambda = \begin{bmatrix} 1 \\ 1 \\ 2 \end{bmatrix} \qquad A^* = \begin{bmatrix} 0.54 & 0.3 & 0 \\ 0.08 & 0.2 & 0.2 \\ 0.18 & 0.3 & 0.6 \end{bmatrix} \qquad \alpha^* = 0.8 \Leftrightarrow R^* = 0.25$$

The transformation condition writes: $y[I - (1 + R^*)A^*]\Lambda = 0$, that is: $-0.05 y_1 + 0.15 y_2 - 0.10 y_3 = 0$. We can see that the condition is met for $y = q^* = (1, 1, 1)$ but also for $y = (5, 3, 2)$. The example is economically relevant for $y(I - A^*) = (1.7 \ 0.3 \ 0.2) > 0$.

The previous condition results in that all vectors $y > 0$ of the hyper plane orthogonal to vector $b = [I - (1 + R^*)A^*]\Lambda$ represent the activity levels enabling transformation.

Thus, in order to achieve transformation in the sense of Marx, vectors y representing activity levels need and only need to belong to the cone $C = \{y \mid yb = 0 \text{ and } y > 0\}$. Further, if it is required that the production of each good is at least equal to its intermediate consumption by the whole system, y must establish the constraint $y(I-A^*)\geq 0$ and belong to a cone $C_a=\{y|yb=0 \text{ and } y(I-A^*)\geq 0\}$ which is included in cone C.

6.4 Marx's solution: an incomplete iteration(?)

A number of authors have recently shown that it is possible to move from values to production prices by stating Marx's procedure in general terms and deducing the prices of values.[6] The Marxian theory appears as the starting point of a series of iterations which, completed and stated properly, leads to the contemporary formulation of production prices.

There is indeed, in a way, a 'passage', a transformation of values into production prices. But, this is achieved only by means of an infinite series of iterations; on the other hand, it is worth noting that the transformation of the aggregate surplus value into aggregate profit is not achieved in Marx's way of thinking; if the equality of the sum of prices and the sum of values is indeed established, the equality of the aggregate profit and the aggregate surplus-value does not in general hold. As for the rate of profit which appears at the end of the series of iterations, it is of course the rate of profit R^* associated to the dominant eigenvalue of matrix A^* but not the rate of profit r defined by Marx.

We shall first demonstrate how the transformation of values into production prices is carried out before showing that in general the two equalities characterising the transformation in the sense of Marx do not hold. We shall then ponder on the economic meaning of such a procedure.

6.4.1 From values to production prices

In what follows, we shall denote the socio-technological matrix by C to lighten notations. Thus, let $C=A+Ld$ the dominant eigenvalue of which is denoted by α^*. The other notations do not change. $p_1, p_2, \ldots, p_i, \ldots, p_n$ are column vectors of production prices with k components. We write $p_0=\Lambda$. With these notations, table 6.1 can easily be understood.

From the system of values $\Lambda(=p_0)$ and the level of gross production, we can deduce the rate of profit defined by Marx (and written here r_1) as the ratio of the aggregate surplus value ($eyLd\Lambda=y\Lambda-yC\Lambda$) to the aggregate value of advanced capital (constant capital $yAA+yLd\Lambda=y(A+Ld)\Lambda$ $=yC\Lambda$). By applying such a rate of profit to the values consumed in the process of production for each commodity, we can determine the system of production prices written p_1 as defined by Marx.

Marx stopped the procedure of transformation at this stage. But the table shows that the iteration procedure can be continued. From the system of prices p_1, the ratio of the value of the surplus produced ($y-yC$)p_1

Table 6.1.

$$\Lambda = A\Lambda + L$$

$$\Downarrow$$

$$r_1 = \frac{y\Lambda - yC\Lambda}{yC\Lambda} = \frac{y\Lambda}{yC\Lambda} - 1$$

$$\Downarrow$$

$$p_1 = (1 + r_1)C\Lambda$$

$$\Downarrow$$

$$r_2 = \frac{yp_1 - yCp_1}{yCp_1} = \frac{yp_1}{yCp_1} - 1 = \frac{(1 + r_1)yC\Lambda}{(1 + r_1)yC.C\Lambda} - 1$$

$$\Downarrow$$

$$r_2 = \frac{yC\Lambda}{yC^2\Lambda} - 1$$

$$\Downarrow$$

$$p_2 = (1 + r_2)Cp_1 = (1 + r_2)(1 + r_1)C.C\Lambda = (1 + r_2)(1 + r_1)C^2\Lambda$$

$$\Downarrow$$

$$r_3 = \frac{yp_2 - yCp_2}{yCp_2} = \frac{yp_2}{yCp_2} - 1$$

$$\Downarrow$$

$$r_3 = \frac{yC^2\Lambda}{yC^3\Lambda} - 1$$

$$\Downarrow$$

$$p_3 = (1 + r_3)Cp_2 = (1 + r_3)(1 + r_2)(1 + r_1)C^3\Lambda$$

$$\Downarrow$$

$$r_4 = \ldots = \frac{yC^3\Lambda}{yC^4\Lambda} - 1$$

$$\Downarrow$$

$$p_{n-1} = (1 + r_{n-1})(1 + r_{n-2})\ldots(1 + r_{n-i})\ldots(1 + r_1)C^{n-1}\Lambda$$

$$\Downarrow$$

$$r_n = \frac{yp_{n-1} - yCp_{n-1}}{yCp_{n-1}} = \frac{yp_{n-1}}{yCp_{n-1}} - 1$$

$$\Downarrow$$

$$r_n = \frac{yC^{n-1}\Lambda}{yC^n\Lambda} - 1$$

$= yp_1 - yCp_1$ to the value of the means of production used yCp_1 allows one to define an average rate of profit r_2 that can be expressed in terms of labour values $\Lambda(=p_0)$ owing to the expression of p_1. The rate of profit r_2 allows us in turn to define a second series of production prices denoted by p_2 which puts an end to the second wave of iterations.

From this new system of prices, we then define an average rate of profit r_3, the ratio of the value of surplus (expressed in terms of p_2) to the aggregate value of advanced capital (also calculated in terms of p_2); r_3 can also be expressed in terms of labour values Λ and the iteration can be continued.

At the nth iteration, we obtain

$$1+r_n = \frac{yC^{n-1}\Lambda}{yC^n\Lambda}$$

But a matrix C^n is represented by a linear matrix combination of α_j^n's where the α_js are eigenvalues

$$C^n = a_1^n M_1 + a_2^n M_2 + \ldots + a_j^n M_j + \ldots + a_k^n M_k$$

where matrices M_j, independent of n, only depend on the eigenvectors of matrix C.

If the modulus of one of the eigenvalues is strictly greater than the modulus of the others, the following formula shows that it imposes its quality behaviour on C^n. If for example $|a_1| > |a_j| \forall j = 2\ldots, k$, suffice to write when $n \to +\infty$

$$\lim \left[\frac{C}{\alpha_1}\right]^n \Rightarrow M_1 \text{ for } \left[\frac{\alpha_j}{\alpha_1}\right]^n \to 0$$

and thus $C^n \to a_1^n M_1$ for n sufficiently large.

As a result for n sufficiently large

$$1+r_n \to \frac{\alpha_1^{n-1} y M_1 \Lambda}{\alpha_1^n y M_1 \Lambda}$$

Since $y M_1 \Lambda$ is a scalar and the dominant eigenvalue of matrix C is denoted by α^*, we have

$$1+r_n \to \frac{1}{\alpha^*} = 1 + R^*$$

The iteration is thus convergent. *For a great number of iterations we do obtain from the values the rate of profit R^* such that*

$$\frac{1}{\alpha^*} = 1 + R^*$$

Furthermore, the price vector of the nth iteration establishes

$$p_n = (1+r_1)(1+r_2)\ldots(1+r_n)C^n\Lambda$$
$$= \frac{y\Lambda}{yC\Lambda} \cdot \frac{yC\Lambda}{yC^2\Lambda} \cdots \frac{yC^{n-1}\Lambda}{yC^n\Lambda} C^n\Lambda$$

that is: $p_n = \dfrac{y\Lambda}{yC^n\Lambda} C^n\Lambda$.

We know that when $n \to +\infty$, $C^n \to a^{*n}M^*$ where α^* is the dominant eigenvalue of C and M^* is a square matrix of order k defined on the basis of the eigenvectors of C associated to the dominant eigenvalue.

We have

$$M^* = p^*q^* \text{ with } Cp^* = \alpha^* p^* \text{ and } q^*C = \alpha^* q^*$$

Thus when $n \to +\infty$, $C^n \to \alpha^{*n}M^*$ and $p_n \to \dfrac{y\Lambda}{yM^*\Lambda} . M^*\Lambda$.

Let us show that this limit is the eigenvector p^* of C. Indeed

$$C. \frac{y\Lambda}{yM^*\Lambda} . M^*\Lambda = \frac{y\Lambda}{yM^*\Lambda} CM^*\Lambda = \frac{y\Lambda}{yM^*\Lambda} Cp^*q^*\Lambda$$

and since $Cp^* = \alpha^* p^*$ and $M^* = p^*q^*$

$$C. \frac{y\Lambda}{yM^*\Lambda} . M^*\Lambda = \frac{y\Lambda}{yM^*\Lambda} \alpha^* p^* q^*\Lambda = \frac{y\Lambda}{yM^*\Lambda} \alpha^* M^*\Lambda$$

$$C\left[\frac{y\Lambda}{yM^*\Lambda} . M^*\Lambda \right] = \alpha^* \left[\frac{y\Lambda}{yM^*\Lambda} M^*\Lambda \right]$$

This means that the expression within brackets is the eigenvector of C associated to the dominant eigenvalue α^* that is to say p^* (up to a multiplication constant).

The iteration is indeed convergent. When n tends towards infinity, the equation $p_n = (1 + r_n)Cp_{n-1}$ becomes

$$p^* = (1 + R^*)Cp^* = (1 + R^*)(A + Ld)p^*$$

6.4.2 Aggregate profit and surplus value

As Shaikh (1977) puts it, the 'correct' production prices can be calculated on the basis of values *in the way suggested by Marx himself in the transformation procedure.* However we must not be misled by such a conclusion: if we do obtain production prices p^* from labour values, the aggregate profit is not equal to the aggregate surplus value.

Of course, at each stage the equality of the sum of prices and the sum of values is maintained. Indeed, taking into account the definitions given in the previous table, we have $p_1 = (1 + r_1)C\Lambda$ and therefore $yp_1 = (1 + r_1)yC\Lambda$

since $r_1 = \dfrac{y\Lambda}{yC\Lambda} - 1$ then $yp_1 \dfrac{y\Lambda}{yC\Lambda} yC\Lambda = y\Lambda$.

Further, whatever n

$$p_n = (1 + r_n)Cp_{n-1}$$
$$yp_n = (1 + r_n)yCp_{n-1}$$

and as

$$r_n = \frac{yp_{n-1}}{yCp_{n-1}} - 1$$

we have

$$yp_n = \frac{yp_{n-1}}{yCp_{n-1}} yCp_{n-1}$$
$$yp_n = yp_{n-1} = \ldots = y\Lambda$$

On the other hand, *the equality: aggregate profit = aggregate surplus value is not ensured* any more from the second iteration. At the first iteration (contemplated by Marx), we do have

aggregate profit $= r_1 yC\Lambda = y\Lambda - yC\Lambda =$ aggregate surplus value.

But, at the second iteration, the aggregate profit is

$$r_2 yCp_1 = yp_1 - yCp_1$$

As $yp_1 = y\Lambda$, we have

$$r_2 yCp_1 = y\Lambda - yCp_1 \neq y\Lambda - yC\Lambda$$

and since, allowing for exceptions, $yCp_1 \neq yC\Lambda$.

At the nth iteration, the aggregate profit is

$$r_n yCp_{n-1} = yp_{n-1} - yCp_{n-1}$$
$$= y\Lambda - yCp_{n-1} \neq y\Lambda - yC\Lambda \text{ for } yCp_{n-1} \neq yC\Lambda$$

It is only in the peculiar case previously mentioned that the aggregate profit equals the aggregate surplus value: indeed, activity levels y must allow us to establish the condition: $y[I - (1 + R^*)A^*]\Lambda = 0$.

6.4.3 *Economic meaning of the contemplated procedure*

Here, the aim is briefly to analyse the transformation procedure, and more particularly its economic content. We know that Marx was far from being clear concerning the concrete process allowing the rate of profit r to be imposed on all the capitalists. It is in fact quite impossible to make the transformation process lie on the competition of capital: such a competition would indeed lead the capitalists to give up the sectors with a high organic composition (with little surplus value to be retrieved) and to concentrate on sectors with a low organic composition. For the transformation process contemplated by Marx to work actually, there must be a central (planning) office which calculates the rate of profit r_1 on the basis of the system of values, and then $r_2, r_3, \ldots, r_n$ and indicates their levels to capitalists so that they can set their production prices.

The change from values to production prices is thus purely formal; further, allowing for exceptions, it does not ensure the 'transformation' in the sense of Marx: one of these peculiar cases is of course when the growth rate equals the rate of profit.

6.5 Non-basic goods and luxury goods

If the socio-technological matrix A^* is decomposable, we can, by permutation of its rows and columns, clearly emphasise the $(k-m)$ basic goods and the m non-basic goods. Basic goods not only include the goods which directly or indirectly enter the production of all other goods but also the consumption goods necessary for the replacement of the labour power. We have

$$A^* = \begin{bmatrix} A^{*1}_1 & 0 \\ A^{*1}_2 & A^{*2}_2 \end{bmatrix} \begin{matrix} (k-m) \\ (m) \end{matrix}$$
$$\quad (k-m) \quad (m)$$

Let p_1^* and p_2^* be the price vectors of the basic and non-basic sectors respectively. Owing to the fact that $p^* = (1+R^*)A^*p^*$, we have

$$p^* = \begin{bmatrix} p_1^* \\ p_2^* \end{bmatrix} = (1+R^*) \begin{bmatrix} A^{*1}_1 & 0 \\ A^{*1}_2 & A^{*2}_2 \end{bmatrix} \begin{bmatrix} p_1^* \\ p_2^* \end{bmatrix}$$

$$\begin{cases} p_1^* = (1+R^*)A^{*1}_1 p_1^* \\ p_2^* = (1+R^*)(A^{*1}_2 p_1^* + A^{*2}_2 p_2^*) \end{cases}$$

As seen earlier (chapter 3, 1), two cases have to be distinguished.

6.5.1 The dominant eigenvalue is determined by the basic sector

Let $\alpha^*(A^*) = \alpha^*(A^{*1}_1)$: this is the thesis spelt out by L. von Bortkiewicz (1907) and resumed by Sweezy (1942): the production conditions of luxury goods have no influence on the determination of the aggregate rate of profit.

However, such a thesis has to be specified and qualified: it is perfectly correct if we stick to the definition of luxury goods given by Marx in the second volume of *Capital*. In the analysis of reproduction, Marx opposes Department I which produces 'means of production' and Department II which produces 'articles of consumption'. Within Department II, he distinguishes two sub-divisions

(a) 'articles of consumption, which enter into the consumption of the working-class, and ... also form a portion of the consumption of the capitalist class.'

(b) 'articles of *luxury*, which enter into the consumption of only the capitalist class and can therefore be exchanged only for spent surplus value, which never falls to the share of the labourer' (II, 407).

By definition, such 'articles of luxury' are pure consumption goods in the sense that they cannot enter their own production, or the production of other luxury goods; since they are never used as means of production, matrix A^{*2}_2 is zero and Bortkiewicz's thesis holds perfectly. It does in fact, as soon as $\alpha^*(A^*) = \alpha^*(A^{*1}_1) > \alpha^*(A^{*2}_2)$. But it is questioned when non-basic goods are used in an 'abnormally high' proportion in their own production. Let us now consider this case.

6.5.2 The dominant eigenvalue is determined by the non-basic sector

Let $\alpha^*(A^*) = \alpha^*(A^{*2}_2) > \alpha^*_1(A^{*1}_1)$. It is thus the case when non-basic goods enter their own production in an 'abnormaly high' proportion, as in Sraffa's 'beans' example.

Consider the following production model with three goods: a production good, a workers' consumption good, a luxury good. Wage being advanced, the production conditions are the following

$$A = \begin{bmatrix} 0.4 & 0 & 0 \\ 0.1 & 0.1 & 0 \\ 0.1 & 0 & 0.6 \end{bmatrix} \qquad L = \begin{bmatrix} 2 \\ 2 \\ 1 \end{bmatrix} \qquad d = [0 \; 0.1 \; 0]$$

Hence $Ld = \begin{bmatrix} 0 & 0.2 & 0 \\ 0 & 0.2 & 0 \\ 0 & 0.1 & 0 \end{bmatrix}$ and $A^* = A + Ld = \begin{bmatrix} 0.4 & 0.2 & 0 \\ 0.1 & 0.3 & 0 \\ 0.1 & 0.1 & 0.6 \end{bmatrix}$.

In this model the dominant eigenvalue of the basic sector $\alpha^*(A^{*1}_1) = 0.5$ is less than the non-basic sector's: $\alpha^*(A^{*2}_2) = 0.6$.

We know that the price system p^*_1 associated to the dominant eigenvalue of the basic sector $\alpha^*_1(A^{*1}_1) = 0.5 \Leftrightarrow R^*_1 = 1$ has components of opposite signs (see chapter 3, section 3.1) and we can check that $p^*_1 = \begin{bmatrix} 2 \\ 1 \\ -3 \end{bmatrix}$.

Let us now contemplate the price system associated to the dominant eigenvalue of system: $\alpha^*(A^*) = \alpha^*(A_2^{*2}) = 0.6$. It is vector $p^* = \begin{bmatrix} 0 \\ 0 \\ 1 \end{bmatrix}$.

Both basic commodities are available at zero price even though they are not overabundant.

Therefore the relative price between these two basic goods cannot be calculated for the value $R^* = 0.6$.

It would be the same for a model with $k - m$ basic goods and m non-basic goods which, as in the previous example, would fix the maximum rate of profit of the system. The prices of the $k - m$ basic goods associated to the maximum rate of profit would all be zeros and the exchange ratios of these $k - m$ goods could not be calculated.

This rules out the possibility for the uniform rate of profit to be, in Marx's example, fixed by the production conditions of the non-basic goods; as a matter of fact the prices of the m non-basic goods expressed in terms of a basket of $k - m$ basic goods would be infinite which should normally lead to a zero demand for these goods and thus cause the non-basic sector to disappear.

6.6 Joint production and negative values

The joint production hypothesis with one activity producing several economic goods, shows a certain number of problems and difficulties. One of the first emphasised was the possibility of having negative labour values (P.S. 70). More recently Steedman (1975) has pointed out an additional paradox: it may happen that the average rate of profit is positive while workers are not exploited, which is impossible in the case usually contemplated of single-product industries and circulating capital. Morishima (1974) has consequently developed an alternative theory of labour values using a treatment in inequality terms while the usual approach uses equalities. It seems to us that the inequality treatment should be rejected and the traditional approach kept; let us note however, that the mere existence of negative labour values is necessarily excluded in the case of separately reproducible goods.[7]

6.6.1 One difficulty: labour values may be negative

If we assume that wages are 'advanced', the system of production prices is, with the usual notations

$$Bp = (1 + r)(Ap + Lw)$$

By setting $w = 1$, which comes down to defining 'wage prices'

$$\hat{p} = B\hat{p} = (1 + r)(A\hat{p} + L)$$

In the case of single-product industries with circulating capital, we have $B = I$ where I is the unit matrix of outputs of dimension $k \times k$; if the rate of profit is zero ($r = 0$) wage prices $\hat{p}(0)$ are then defined by

$$I\hat{p}(0) = \hat{p}(0) = A\hat{p}(0) + L$$

and

$$(I - A)\hat{p}(0) = L$$

When matrix A is productive, i.e., when there is a surplus in goods (which mathematically corresponds to the case when the dominant eigenvalue of matrix A taken to be indecomposable is less than unity), matrix $(I - A)$ has an inverse $(I - A)^{-1}$ that is strictly positive; the system of $\hat{p}(0)$s then defines the quantities of direct and indirect labour included, 'labour values' denoted by Λ which are strictly positive

$$\hat{p}(0) = (I - A)^{-1}L > 0 \text{ with } \hat{p}(0) = \Lambda$$

The problem is quite different under joint production where wage prices $\hat{p}(0)$, corresponding to a zero rate of profit, are then

$$B\hat{p}(0) = A\hat{p}(0) + L$$

or

$$(B - A)\hat{p}(0) = L$$

and if $\det(B - A) \neq 0$ then $\hat{p}(0) = (B - A)^{-1}L$.

But, there is no reason for $(B - A)^{-1}$ to be strictly positive contrary to the case of single-product industries with circulating capital where the system only needs to be productive for $(I - A)^{-1}$ to be positive. Therefore, it may happen that negative components appear in vector $\hat{p}(0)$.

Is it possible then to keep on assimilating prices $\hat{p}(0)$ and values Λ as in simple production? If yes, then what is the meaning of negative 'labour values'?

In this connection it is worth noting that the evaluation of labour values in joint production entails some methodology problems even if negative labour values do not result from calculations. The fact is that the labour absorbed by a production process has to be distributed among the various commodities produced. Such a distribution cannot be arbitrary: in the square joint production system in question, a process produces several commodities and one commodity is produced by several processes. The distribution problem has to take into account this kind of interdependence, and in some cases, there will be no solutions unless some commodities are given negative labour values.

In the case of single-product industries with circulating capital, the notion of labour values, the content in labour, does not pose such problems since a process produces only one commodity and transfers to it the entire direct and indirect labour needed for its production. In such a situation, commodities appear as depositories of value, crystals of human labour in the abstract as Marx puts it. It is such a transparency in the activity system that disappears under joint production.

The meaning of negative labour values has been clearly specified by Sraffa in paragraphs 69 and 70 of *Production of Commodities by Means of Commodities*:

we are driven to the conclusion that in the actual situation, with profits at a perfectly normal rate of, say, 6%, that commodity is in fact being produced by a *negative* quantity of labour.

This looks at first as if it were a freak result of abstraction-mongering that can have no correspondence in reality. But if ... we suppose that the quantity of such a commodity entering the net product of the system is *increased* (the other components being kept unchanged), we shall find that as a result the aggregate quantity of labour employed by society has indeed been *diminished.*[8]

This can be illustrated with an example due to Steedman (1975) presenting an economy with two goods and two production processes. The first combines five units of good (1) and one unit of labour to produce six units of good (1) and one unit of good (2); the second process uses ten units of good (2) and one unit of labour to produce three units of good (1) and twelve units of good (2). With the usual notations, we have

$$A = \begin{bmatrix} 5 & 0 \\ 0 & 10 \end{bmatrix} \qquad L = \begin{bmatrix} 1 \\ 1 \end{bmatrix} \qquad B = \begin{bmatrix} 6 & 1 \\ 3 & 12 \end{bmatrix}$$

Let $\Lambda = \begin{bmatrix} \lambda_1 \\ \lambda_2 \end{bmatrix}$ be the vector of labour values defined by $B\Lambda = A\Lambda + L$.

We obtain

$$\begin{cases} 6\lambda_1 + \lambda_2 = 5\lambda_1 + 1 \\ 3\lambda_1 + 12\lambda_2 = 10\lambda_2 + 1 \end{cases}$$

hence

$$\lambda_1 = -1 \text{ and } \lambda_2 = 2$$

The labour value of good (1) is indeed negative. And paradoxically, *the average* (or general) *rate of profit may be positive even though the rate of surplus value* (or rate of exploitation) *is negative*. If, with the usual notations, $d = (1/2\ 5/6)$, the value of the labour power would be $v = dA = 7/6$; the surplus value, the difference between the value produced by the unit labour power and the value of that very labour power is thus negative ($-1/6$); the rate of surplus value, the ratio of the surplus value to the value of the labour power, is also negative $(-1/6)/(7/6) = -1/7$.

Production prices are determined simultaneously with the rate of profit R^*: we have $Bp^* = (1 + R^*)(A + Ld)p^*$; we check that $p_1^*/p_2^* = 0.161 > 0$ and $R^* = 14.38\% > 0$. Thus, we can see with that example that under joint production, *the whole set of production prices and the rate of profit R^* may be positive in spite of a negative[9] rate of exploitation*.

6.6.2 An alternative definition of value?

Morishima's position spelt out in a number of works[10] consists mainly in developing what is to be called an alternative theory of labour-values. The author considers indeed that the solutions developed by Steedman (1975) were not relevant:

However, as far as his example is concerned, the values Steedman obtained have nothing to do with the labour values of commodities (i.e. the Marxian values), because the latter should be non-negative by definition, while the former contain negative ones. In fact, as we all know, the value of a commodity is defined as the amount of human labour expended directly or indirectly for its production. It should be non-negative. How can we exert, or expend, a negative amount of labour? Whatever can be meant by a negative amount of labour? (Morishima and Catephores (1978), p. 32)

How is the value of a commodity to be defined or redefined? Morishima and Catephores point out that apart from the two (equivalent) definitions of value given in *Capital*, Marx gives a third definition of value; they base their argument on a quotation from *The Poverty of Philosophy* by Marx: 'It is important to insist upon this point, that, what determines value is not the time in which a thing has been produced, but the minimum time in which it is susceptible of being produced, and this minimum is demonstrated by competition.'

It is on the basis of this argument that they suggest giving up the traditional definition and redefine value, they write:

In order to obtain, as solutions, true values of commodities rather than pseudo-values, we have to weaken the input–output equations into inequalities so as to allow for excess supply, because we may reach aimed net outputs in an efficient way by simply discarding appropriate units of outputs of those commodities which are overproduced because of joint production. (Morishima and Catephores, p. 33)

In order to specify the authors' approach, we shall briefly use the previous example, used by them in a different respect. Let us consider a problem to minimise the total amount of labour that is required to produce a net output $z = (8, 7)$. The vector of activity levels must satisfy

$$yB \geq yA + z \quad \text{with} \quad y \geq 0$$

Owing to matrices A and B previously used, we have

$$(y_1, y_2) \begin{bmatrix} 6 & 1 \\ 3 & 12 \end{bmatrix} = (y_1, y_2) \begin{bmatrix} 5 & 0 \\ 0 & 10 \end{bmatrix} + (8 \ \ 7) \text{ with } y \geq 0$$

that is to say

$$\begin{cases} 6y_1 + 3y_2 \geq 5y_1 + 8 \\ y_1 + 12y_2 \geq 10y_2 + 7 \end{cases}$$

$$\begin{cases} y_1 + 3y_2 - 8 \geq 0 \\ y_1 + 2y_2 - 7 \geq 0 \end{cases}$$

with $y_1 \geq 0$ and $y_2 \geq 0$.

The total quantity of labour used is $N = yL = y_1 . 1 + y_2 . 1 = y_1 + y_2$ which is minimised, subject to the previous constraint for $y_1 = 0$ and $y_2 = 7/2$.

Thus, we shall allocate $7/2$ units of labour to the second process (the first is not used) and obtain a net excess supply of the first good $(3 - 0).7/2 = 21/2 > 8$. We shall then have an excess supply of the first good that we only need to discard. On the other hand, the output of the second good perfectly satisfies demand $(12 - 10).7/2 = 7$. The second good is thus an economic good, while the first, by the von Neumann rule, becomes a free good.

Morishima and Catephores add that the minimised labour level does not vary 'even though net outputs are increased from $(8, 7)$ to $(9, 7)$. In the same way, we find that the minimum amount of labour increases by 0.5 when the net outputs change from $(8, 7)$ to $(8, 8)$. It is apparent that these efficient employment multipliers, 0 for commodity 1 and 0.5 for commodity 2 at $(8, 7)$, are different from the Steedman values, -1 and 2, respectively' (Morishima and Catephores, p. 34) (figure 6.1).

Thus, Morishima and Catephores wish to define the value of a commodity on the basis of optimal employment multipliers. The labour value is then here the minimum quantity of labour needed for its production. Such a definition of 'optimal values' or 'true values' allows us to confer general validity to 'the Fundamental Marxian Theorem which is of decisive importance to Marxian economics' (Morishima and Catephores (1978), p. 38).

In spite of the intrinsic importance of such an argument, reformulating in

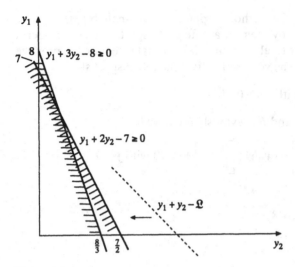

Figure 6.1

terms of optimal values does not seem relevant to define labour values in the sense of Marx. Not only because they are not additive, as emphasised by Morishima himself, but also for a much more important reason.

The set of activities retained, the technique springing from the minimisation of aggregate employment and which allows to determine 'optimal values', the so-called 'true values', may be totally different from the set of activities, or the technique, determining the rate of profit R^* and the system of production prices.[11] Thus, in the treatment of the example due to Steedman, the paradox emphasised by the latter disappeared because the problem has been removed.

The so-called optimal solution consists in pretending that the first activity was abandoned by only using the second; we are thus led to reasoning within a pseudo-system which has nothing to do with the system we are analysing, which, by assumption, is made up of two activities and not just one.

6.6.3 Do negative values reveal the inefficiency of the technique used?

The appearance of negative values does indeed show a certain inefficiency of the technique used for some values of r; at $r = R^*$, methods or processes are used with some of them being dominated or inefficient at $r = 0$.

The example due to Steedman is in this connection perfectly clear: the net surplus of the first process amounts to (1 1) while that of the second is much greater (3 2). We have at $r = 0$

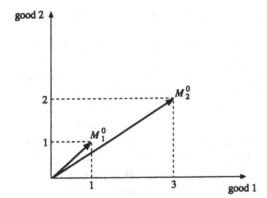

Figure 6.2

$$[B - A] = \begin{bmatrix} 1 & 1 \\ 3 & 2 \end{bmatrix}$$

As $l_1 = l_2 = l$ it is clear that the second process dominates, outclasses the first, which appears clearly in figure 6.2 where at $r = g = 0$, the line of consumption possibilities $M_1^\circ M_2^\circ$ has a positive slope which equals a negative price ratio[12] (see chapter 1).

As a matter of fact, we may recall that at the going rate of wages, the set of prices (and the rate of profit) are positive: we have $p_1^*/p_2^* = 0.161 > 0$ and $R^* = 14.038\%$. Negative values only show that at a rate of profit $r = 0$, production prices would be negative and the choice of methods should be reconsidered.

As emphasised by Sraffa in section 70 of *Production of Commodities by Means of Commodities*, *no paradox appears at the ruling rate of profit*.

In a golden rule context, we could add that the system in question would be inefficient under simple production (at $r = g = 0$) and would remain so as long as the rhythm of accumulation does not reach a threshold R_0; beyond that threshold (see Abraham-Frois and Berrebi, 1984b) all prices and wages are positive up to the maximum rate of profit; which explains why there may be negative values along with positive production prices; in that case and subject to additional conditions, there may be simultaneously a positive rate of profit and (in spite of) a negative exploitation rate.

6.6.4 Labour values and separately reproducible goods

We know that the theory of labour values is not concerned with natural resources, land and more generally the 'commodities, the value of which is determined by scarcity alone' (Ricardo, 1984, chapter 1). Such goods have a price but no value.

But among reproducible goods, we still have to determine which are separately reproducible and which are not. Separately reproducible goods are those which are separately reproducible at $g=0$. All goods are separately reproducible if $(B-A)^{-1}>0$. It is worth noting however, that even if goods are not separately reproducible, all labour-values may be positive: if $(B-A)^{-1}$ is not greater than 0 it does not necessarily imply that $\Lambda=(B-A)^{-1}$ is not greater than zero; and even if some values are negative, this by no means implies that the rate of surplus value $(e=(1-d\Lambda)/d\Lambda)$ is also negative while the rate of profit is simultaneously positive.

However, such difficulties vanish away if we assume $(B-A)^{-1}>0$; therefore, *Marx's analysis carried out under simple production may, in the case of joint products, be extended to the case of separately reproducible goods.* This also means that natural resources, scarce goods but also non-separately reproducible goods must be discarded of the field of labour values.

6.7 Consumption and accumulation

In Marx's analysis, workers' consumption is fixed (at a given instant) and integrated to the model's socio-technological matrix, with the rate of wages ensuring by assumption the reproduction of labour power. The capitalists who take over the entire surplus (assuming that there are no rents) allocate the latter to consumption or accumulation as they wish. If we assume that the capitalist consumption structure is fixed and represented by vector δ, and if we write ξ the level of such a consumption, i.e., the number of consumption baskets δ, then the activity system writes (for simplicity's sake,[13] we limit ourselves to simple production):

$$y=(1+g)yA^*+\xi\delta$$

We know (see chapter 5) that if the level of consumption is measured in terms of standard commodity of activity levels, the relation between the level of consumption and the rhythm of accumulation (g) is linear. However, the production price vector p^*, defined by $(1+R^*)A^*p^*$, is nothing but the vector defining the virtual commodity of activity levels of matrix (A^*).

By writing $y(I-A^*)p^*=1$, which comes down to assuming that the value of the net surplus is taken to be equal to unity whatever the activity structure, the *capitalist consumption level*, defined as a fraction of the (constant) value of the net surplus, is a *linear* (and decreasing) *function of the rhythm of accumulation*

$$\xi = 1 - \frac{g}{G^*}$$

In a golden rule context $\xi = 0$ and if the system is indecomposable $g = G^* = R^*$.

7   Switch in methods of production

Up to now the analysis of production-price systems has been carried out within a context of 'square' systems, assuming that the number of methods of production was equal to the number of economic goods. We shall relax this restrictive assumption in the present chapter: let us now suppose that, to produce one of the commodities, we may choose among several methods of production. What choice criteria shall we use, and what will be the consequences of such a choice?

We shall first address the problem using systems with single-product industries and circulating capital, or for short, 'simple production systems'. Then we shall develop the specific problems that arise in joint production systems, more particularly the problem of the life span and depreciation of machines. Finally, we will analyse the relationship between linear programming and the production price theory.

Prior to this, we shall put the emphasis on the importance of distinguishing the truncation of the system and the choice of methods of production, the latter being based on a production cost minimisation criterion.

7.1 Truncation of the system and choice of methods of production

We have already remarked that in 'simple' production, Sraffa (1960) carried out his analysis directly within a square system, 'as if' the problem of choosing a method of production did not exist or had been solved earlier. In the beginning of chapter 7 dealing with 'joint production', it is stated as a necessary rule, so to speak, that 'the number of processes is to be brought to equality with the number of commodities so that the prices may be determined'.

In fact the problem of the number of methods of production used, and thus the problems of the choice of or the switch in methods of production does not arise in the same way depending on whether we are in a context of 'simple' production or 'joint' production. In simple production, since each

176

method produces, by assumption one commodity, there must be at least k methods to produce k goods; hence the problem of choosing among methods of production because one cannot be eliminated without another being chosen (according to a criterion we shall revert to). On the other hand, in joint production, since one method may produce several goods, producing k goods does not necessarily require the use of k methods: one method may be suppressed without being replaced by another, since the production of the various goods is ensured by the other existing methods; though the system is square, it is not in the same sense as earlier. Therefore, it is necessary to distinguish between the mere suppression of methods of production (this is the problem of 'truncation') and the substitution of methods of production.

7.1.1 Suppression of a method

In joint production, the suppression of a method may emerge for two reasons: the first is the impossibility to perfectly satisfy demand, the second is the domination of one method over another which leads to negative prices.

The impossibility of perfectly satisfying demand has already been analysed in chapter 1; it results in the use of only one method of production, and the good the supply of which exceeds needs is available at zero price. Of course, both goods keep on being produced by the unique method of production used. This is however a 'square' system, with one method producing only one economic good, the other being a free good. The rule that allows the determination of prices is the equality of the number of methods of production and the number of *economic* goods.

Further, Sraffa notes that 'only those methods of production are practicable which, in the conditions actually prevailing (i.e., at the given wage or at the given rate of profits) do not involve other than positive prices' (P.S. 50). The emergence of negative prices reveals the inefficiency of the system due to an improper choice of methods of production.

Let us briefly revert to the diagrammatic approach of a system with the two goods and two activities previously used (figure 7.1).

In a golden rule situation, we know that the price ratio is equal to the opposite of the consumption possibilities line slope or the system's efficiency frontier. In the case contemplated above, the efficiency frontier springing from the simultaneous use of methods M_i and M_j (at a given g and with $l_i = l_j = l$) would be increasing, which means that one of the prices would be negative. In this example, it is clear that method M_j dominates method M_i, since both components of the net g-product vector are greater. The inefficiency revealed by negative prices must lead to the suppression of

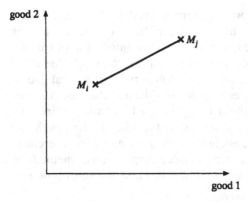

Figure 7.1

the dominated method. As a result, the number of economic goods must be reduced since demand cannot be perfectly satisfied (it is the comparison of the demand structure and the net production structure of the activity used which will allow us to determine which is the economic good and which is the free good).

7.1.2 Choice of methods

The problem of substitution, of choice of methods of production, only arises for those which allow to simultaneously satisfy the same structure of wants. Such a condition does not apply in 'simple' production, where the final demand can be satisfied by any combination of methods producing the various goods.

How is the choice of methods satisfying the same needs to be determined? – by the minimisation of production costs. This is indeed, the criterion 'naturally' retained by Sraffa when he addresses (P.S., chapter 12) the problem of switch in methods of production using the simplest case with the commodity in question being a '*non-basic* good' (italics not in Sraffa): 'At any given level of the general rate of profits (taken as the independent variable), the method that produces at a lower price is *of course*[1] the most profitable of the two for a producer who builds a new plant' (P.S. 92).

In section 93, Sraffa adds: 'If the product is a basic one, the problem is complicated by the circumstance that each of the two alternative methods of producing it implies a distinct economic system, with a distinct maximum rate of profit'.

Thus, there are $(k + 1)$ methods of production to produce k goods, which means that to produce one good we can choose between two methods of production. Consequently, we can construct two distinct production systems, denoted by I and II, by using the first or the second method and compare their respective 'cheapness'. Sraffa adds (we shall revert to this): 'It can however be shown[2] that, while the extent of the cheapness of one method of production relatively to the other will vary according as the comparison is carried out in system I or in system II, the *order* of the two methods as to cheapness must be the same in the two systems' (section 93).

Therefore Sraffa's criterion is perfectly clear: the purpose is to minimise the costs of production of the commodity in question taking into account the going price system (and distributive variable).[3]

Such a criterion is to be related to von Neumann's analysis. In the first pages of his article, he writes: 'There may be more technically possible processes of production than goods and for this reason "counting of equations", is of no avail. The problem is rather to establish which processes will actually be used and which not (being "unprofitable")' (von Neumann, 1945–6, p. 1). And further 'in equilibrium no profit[4] can be made on any process P_i .... If there is a loss, however, i.e. if P_i is unprofitable, then P_i will not be used' (p. 3) Champernowne comments upon this is the following: 'Profitability rule – Only those processes will be used which, with the actual prices and rate of interest, yield zero profits after payment of interest. These processes will be the most profitable ones available' (Champernowne, 1945–6, p. 13).

It is that profitability rule which is thoroughly commented on and used by Morishima (1969) in *Theory of Economic Growth* (especially in pages 101, 137 and 150). It is a choice criterion of methods of production whose principle is identical to the one used by Sraffa. One difference is that in von Neumann's model, the wage paid on surplus is zero. The second difference lies in that von Neumann, Champernowne (and Morishima) deal with an interest rate while Sraffa's analysis refers to a uniform rate of profit: using one method or the other does not pose any kind of problem. Therefore, the equivalence of the criteria is not questioned.[5]

We shall call a *cost minimising system* (c.m.s, for short) a system with such prices that none of the methods can make excess profits at the going rate of profit and level of wage.

Such a definition which goes without saying in simple production has to be stated in joint production.[6] In this case, indeed, it is not always possible to define a good's cost of production, since one method can produce more than one good and one good can be produced by more than one method. But however 'excess profit' is specific to each activity and can be defined even in joint production.

In formal notation, let (a_i, b_i, l_i) be a method of production where a_i and b_i are the input and output vectors respectively and l_i is the quantity of direct (homogeneous) labour necessary for the activity to operate. If vector p and the scalars r and w are such that $[b_i - (1+r)a_i]p > wl_i$, then method (a_i, b_i, l_i) makes excess profits at the considered values of p, w and r. On the contrary if $[b_i - (1+r)a_i]p < wl_i$, then method (a_i, b_i, l_i) has a lower profitability at the values of p, w, r and would require a subsidy to operate.

In other words, system $[A_k, B_k, L_k]$ minimises costs of production at a rate of profit r if and only if

$$[B_h - (1+r)A_h]p_k \leqq w_k L_h \text{ for all } h \in H$$

where H is the set of available methods of production, and p_k and w_k are determined by

$$\begin{cases} [B_k - (1+r)A_k]p_k = w_k L_k \\ up_k = 1 \end{cases}$$

7.2 Single-product industries and circulating capital

In the case of 'simple production', we shall show that the minimisation of costs (at a given r) leads to the maximisation of wages and that both criteria are strictly equivalent, though only the first makes sense in an economy that is not centrally regulated. We shall deduce from this that the minimisation of costs is independent of the system of production in which it takes place, thus demonstrating Sraffa's previously stated proposition. It will also appear, provided a golden rule situation prevails, that minimising costs comes down to maximising consumption per unit of labour (at a given $r = g$). We shall specify the evolution of relative prices and the change in employment due to a switch in methods of production. Finally, we shall revert to the hypothesis of advanced wage and Marx's analysis under the light of Okishio's theorem.

6.2.1 Cost minimisation and wage maximisation

Let us compare two production systems (A_k, I, L_k) and (A_h, I, L_h) with $r = \bar{r} < \min (R_k, R_h)$, R_k and R_h being the maximum rates of profit of both systems of production. Prices are normalised by the condition $up_k = up_h = 1$ and $w_k(r)$ and $w_h(r)$ are the wage–profit curves of each system.

Let us show[7] that system (k) minimises costs of production (with $r = \bar{r}$) if and only if $w_k(\bar{r}) \geq w_h(\bar{r})$.

The production price system (k) denoted by p_k, where the wage w_k appears, is defined by

$$p_k = (1+\bar{r})A_k p_k + w_k L_k \text{ with } up_k = 1$$

from which we obtain,

$$[I-(1+\bar{r})A_k]p_k = w_k L_k$$
$$p_k = w_k[I-(1+\bar{r})A_k]^{-1}L_k$$

Owing to the price normalisation condition, we have

$$1 = up_k = w_k u[I-(1+\bar{r})A_k]^{-1}L_k$$

$$w_k = \frac{1}{u[I-(1+\bar{r})A_k]^{-1}L_k}$$

Similarly, given the exogenous rate of profit $\bar{r}$, the price production system (h) denoted by p_h, where wage w_h appears, is defined by

$$p_h = (1+\bar{r})A_h p_h + w_h L_h \text{ with } up_h = 1$$

From which we obtain

$$w_h = \frac{1}{u[I-(1+\bar{r})A_h]^{-1}L_h}$$

If system k minimises costs of production, we have by definition

$$[I-(1+\bar{r})A_h]p_k \leq w_k L_h$$

Hence, since $[I-(1+\bar{r})A_h]$ has an inverse which is strictly positive at $r < R_h$

$$p_k \leq w_k[I-(1+\bar{r})A_h]^{-1}L_h$$

or also, by premultiplying both sides of the inequality above by $u \geq 0$

$$up_k \leq w_k u[I-(1+\bar{r})A_h]^{-1}L_h$$

Owing to the normalisation condition already mentioned, $up_k = 1$, and the above expression of w_h, we have

$$1 \leq w_k \frac{1}{w_h} \quad \text{that is, } w_h \leq w_k \quad \text{since } w_h > 0$$

We shall prove the converse by reducing it to the absurd and show that if $w_h \leq w_k$, it is impossible for system (h) to be cost minimising. Indeed, if so it were and owing to the definition previously given of the c.m.s, we would have

$$[I-(1+\bar{r})A_k]p_h \leq w_h L_h$$

and by pre-multiplying both sides of this inequality by $u[I-(1+\bar{r})A_k]^{-1}$

$$up_h \leq w_h u[I-(1+\bar{r})A_k]^{-1}L_k = \frac{w_h}{w_k}$$

and owing to the normalisation condition $up_h = 1$, this would mean that $w_h \geq w_k$, which is at variance with the hypothesis retained.

Therefore, in a system with single-product industries and circulating capital, system (A_k, I, L_k) is cost minimising if and only if, at the considered exogenous rate of profit $\bar{r}$, $w_k(\bar{r}) \geq w_h(\bar{r})$ for all $h \in H$, where H is the set of available methods of production.

Thus the choice criterion of techniques is not the maximisation of w at a given r; the choice of techniques, of methods of production, lies in the minimisation of costs (r given) which (in the context of single-product industries and circulating capital retained) is equivalent to the maximisation of w at a given r.

Remarks

(1) The previous developments justify and demonstrate Sraffa's propositions stated earlier, namely, 'the order of the two methods as to cheapness must be the same in the two systems' even if 'the extent of cheapness of one method of production relatively to the other will vary according as the comparison is carried out in system I or in system II'. The systems compared have been denoted by (h) and (k).

(2) If the previous inequality between $w_h(\bar{r})$ and $w_k(\bar{r})$ is strict: $w_k > w_h$, system (k) is the only cost minimising system. If, however, at the considered exogenous rate of profit $\bar{r}$, $w_k = w_h$, systems (h) and (k) are compatible; in that case we can make sure that prices in system (h) and (k) are equal. Such situations are usually called 'switching points'; note that there is no reason that we should rule out the possibility of 're-switching': it only means that systems (k) and (h) are 'compatible' at several values of r.

(3) The previous demonstration has been done for any semi-positive numeraire of prices u; thus, *the domination of a technique over another is independent of the numeraire*: at $r = \bar{r}$, $w_k > w_h \forall u \geq 0$. Similarly, *the existence of switching points is independent of the retained numeraire*: for $r = \bar{r}$, $w_k = w_h \forall u \geq 0$ (see Pasinetti, 1977 and Berrebi, 1982). Of course, these properties are valid only in the context retained, namely a system with single-product industries and circulating capital; we shall see that in joint production this is not the case.

(4) In the *golden rule hypothesis, the minimisation of production costs is equivalent to the maximisation of consumption per unit of labour.*

We have already seen (chapter 1) that $r = g \Rightarrow w(r) \equiv c(g)$.[8] Since the minimisation of costs ensures the maximisation of w, at a given r, then if $r = g$, the maximisation of c at a given g is ensured.

The non-respect of the golden rule may lead to inefficient choices as shown in figure 7.2, where two systems of production are compared; for both of them, curves $c(g)$ and $w(r)$ are identical owing to the retained

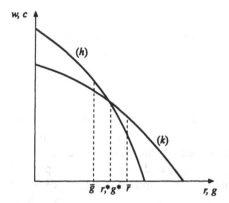

Figure 7.2

normalisation of the price system. Note that according to the line retained, system (h) is better when g (or r) is less than g^* (or r^*); however, system (k) must be used at values of g (and of r) greater than $g^* - r^*$, which is the value corresponding to the switching point. But, owing to the equilibrium condition on the goods market and the relation springing from it between r and g (that is, $r = g/s_p$ assuming that capitalists' propensity to save is $s_p > 0$ and where workers consume the totality of their wages) in some cases it may happen that $g < g^*$ and simultaneously $r > r^*$ (it is the situation contemplated in figure 7.2). In such condititons it would be suitable to choose system (h) to obtain the maximum level of consumption: at $g = \bar{g}c_h > c_k$. But, system (k) dominates (h) at $r = \bar{r} = \bar{g}/s_p$: $w_k > w_h$. Therefore, the system chosen on the basis of the price system does not ensure a maximum level of consumption if $r \neq g$. Respecting the golden rule ensures efficient choices.

7.2.2 The evolution of relative prices

Let us now examine the evolution of relative prices following a switch in methods of production. For simplicity, assume that the switch in methods of production concerns wheat which is the kth good in the system. We write

$$A = \begin{bmatrix} \bar{A} & a_b \\ a^b & a_{bb} \end{bmatrix} \quad L = \begin{bmatrix} \bar{L} \\ l_b \end{bmatrix} \quad P = \begin{bmatrix} \bar{p} \\ p_b \end{bmatrix} \quad u = [\bar{u} \; u_b]$$

The production price system writes

$$(1 + r)Ap + wL = p$$

to which we add the normalisation equation of prices: $up = 1$. From the previous system, we obtain

$$(1+r)(\bar{A}\bar{p}+a^b p_b)+w\bar{L}=\bar{p} \tag{I}$$

By calculating $\bar{p}$ as a function of w, p_b and r in (I) and by adding this value to the normalisation equation $1=up=\bar{u}\bar{p}+u_b p_b$, we obtain

$$p_b = \frac{1-w\bar{u}[I-(1+r)\bar{A}]^{-1}\bar{L}}{u_b+\bar{u}[I-(1+r)\bar{A}]^{-1}(1+r)a^b}$$

Since $\bar{u}[I-(1+r)\bar{A}]^{-1}\bar{L}>0$ and $u_b+\bar{u}[I-(1+r)\bar{A}]^{-1}(1+r)a^b>0$ owing to $[I-(1+r)\bar{A}]^{-1}>0$, p_b is a decreasing function of w if $\bar{u}\geq 0$. Thus, *any switch in methods of production* which minimises the production costs of this good causes (at a given r) an increase in wages and a decrease in the price of the good in question.[9] If, at the contemplated value r of the rate of profit both production systems are compatible ($w_k=w_h$), i.e., at the 'switching point', the price of the good is the same; both systems are 'compatible'.

Similarly, we can calculate p_b as a function of $\bar{p}$ in the normalisation equation and add this value in the matrix equation (I). We obtain

$$\bar{p}=\left[I-(1+r)\left(\bar{A}-\frac{a^b\,\bar{u}}{u_b}\right)\right]^{-1}\left[w\bar{L}+(1+r)\frac{a^b}{u_b}\right]$$

where we assume $u_b\neq 0$, that is to say, 'wheat' enters the composition of the commodity chosen as a numeraire.

Since $[I-(1+r)(\bar{A}-a^b\,\bar{u}/u_b)]^{-1}>0$ and $\bar{L}>0$, the price vector $\bar{p}$ is an *increasing* function of w. Therefore, any change in the methods of production of a good leading to a decrease in its production costs, leads to an increase[10] in the relative price of the other goods whose methods of production have not been changed. If the production systems are compatible, prices are equal.

Note that if we choose wheat as a numeraire, we have

$$u=[\bar{u}\ u_b]=[0\ 1]$$
$$p_b=1 \text{ and } \bar{p}=[I-(1+r)\bar{A}]^{-1}[w\bar{L}+(1+r)a^b]$$

Thus, when we choose as a numeraire the good whose production costs have been decreased owing to a switch in methods, the wage and the prices of the other goods must increase; they remain constant if the switch in methods of production has not caused any decrease in costs.

7.2.3 The evolution of employment

Let (A_h,I,L_h) be an economic system in which emerges a net surplus of commodities $z\geq 0$. If we write $\varLambda_h$, the vector of direct and indirect quantities of labour necessary to produce each good (see chapter 6), we have

$$\Lambda_h = (I - A_h)^{-1} L_h \frac{p_h(0)}{w_h}$$

Thus, the total labour required to produce z is $N_h = z\Lambda_h$.

Let us consider a switch in methods of production such that the new system is now (A_k, I, L_k). We write Λ_k the vector of direct and indirect quantities of labour required to produce each good $\Lambda_k = (I - A)^{-1} L_k = p_k(0)/w_k$ and the total quantity of labour necessary to produce z, is then

$$N_k = z\Lambda_k.$$

Now we can compare N_k and N_h quite easily, and enhance the evolution of employment following a switch in methods of production. As a matter of fact we can point out that:

(1) *It is not because a production system reduces the costs of production that it also decreases employment.* We know indeed that if system (A_k, I, L_k) minimises the costs of production at a given rate of profit $r = \bar{r}$, it is not necessarily true at another value of r and more particularly when $r = 0$. However, as stated above, the direct and indirect quantities of labour required to produce the commodities are nothing else but wage prices corresponding to $r = 0$. It is therefore quite possible for system (k) to be cost minimising at a rate of profit $r = \bar{r}$, without its substitution to system (h) causing any decrease in employment (system (h) only needs to be cost minimising when $r = 0$).

(2) *The evolution of employment is independent of the net surplus of commodities z produced by the contemplated economic system.* Indeed, we

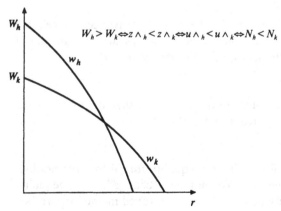

Figure 7.3

have just seen that to analyse the evolution of employment, we had to compare both systems or techniques, at $r = 0$: the question is to compare $zp_h(0)/w_h$ and $zp_k(0)/w_k$ or, which comes down to the same, $w_h/zp_h(0)$ and $w_k/zp_k(0)$, or also w_h and w_k at $r = 0$ with $zp_h(0) = zp_k(0) = 1$; thus, z plays the role of the numeraire of prices and we have already seen that the domination of a technique over another is independent of the numeraire z. Therefore, when system (h) employs more workers than system (k) to produce z, it will be the same for any other semi-positive vector u.

If we use the diagrammatic presentation, the comparison of $w_h(r)$ and $w_k(r)$ at $r = 0$, that is to say on the vertical axis, allows us to characterise the evolution of employment following a switch in methods and therefore in techniques.

7.2.4 Advanced wage and Marx's analysis: the Okishio theorem

If the wage is advanced, the rate of profit R^* (chapter 6) is a function of the dominant eigenvalue α^* of the socio-technological matrix A^* $R^* = (1 - \alpha^*)/\alpha^*$. Okishio (1961) has studied the consequences of an innovation on the average rate of profit R^*; he has notably demonstrated the following propositions: *At a given real wage level, a cost-decreasing innovation cannot cause a decrease in the general rate of profit.* More precisely, he comes to the following conclusions:

(1) If the industry is one where the new technique is a non-basic industry, then the general rate of profit is not influenced at all;
(2) if the industry introducing the new technique is one of the basic industries then the general rate of profit *necessarily* rises. (Okishio, article quoted p. 91)

Here, we shall limit ourselves to showing that if the socio-technological matrix is indecomposable, the innovation, that decreases costs of production, makes the average rate of profit increase.

With the usual notations and in the case of 'advanced wage', the production prices p^* are defined at the same time as the average rate of profit R^* on the basis of the socio-technological matrix A^*:

$$(1 + R^*)A^* p^* = p^*$$

Let A_i^* be the new socio-technological matrix that differs from the previous one by one activity; from prices p^* we obtain

$$(1 + R^*)A_i^* p^* \leq p^*$$

This is a vector inequality with strict equality for all the commodities whose methods of production have not been changed. The inequality concerns the ith commodity produced by an improved method of production and which is less costly on the basis of the going prices p^*.

Let $q_i^* = (1 + R_i^*)q_i^* A_i^*$ be the eigenvector corresponding to the dominant eigenvalue of A_i^*. By pre-multiplying the previous inequality by q_i^*, we obtain the following strict inequality between scalars

$$(1 + R^*)q_i^* A_i^* p^* < q_i^* p^* = (1 + R_i^*)q_i^* A_i^* p^*$$

and as, $q_i^* A_i^* p^* > 0$,

$$R^* < R_i^*$$

Therefore, at a given real wage level, any technical improvement which decreases the cost of production of a basic good, causes an increase in the rate of profit.

7.3 Joint production: new problems

Difficulties arise in reference to the system with single-product industries and circulating capital. The hypothesis of single product industries (and circulating capital) leads to a certain number of simplifications which disappear in joint production.

Demand or the satisfaction of wants, does not seem to play any role in the determination of production prices. It is no doubt because the emphasis is put on the presentation of systems with single-product industries and circulating capital, in which (with the usual condition of profitability) it is always possible to satisfy wants and thus to meet demand. This is not necessarily the case in joint production systems (see chapter 1), which is not without consequences for switches in methods of production, the choice of methods and the minimisation of production costs.

Another difference between simple and joint production systems is that comparing the wage–profit curves is not necessarily relevant; the system which ensures the minimisation of costs does not always coincide with the one allowing to pay the highest wages at the going rate of profit.

Here again, respecting the golden rule of accumulation allows us to make efficient choices: indeed, production systems have to satisfy the same needs and establish the golden rule.

We shall also see that identifying the method of production to be eliminated poses specific problems that did not arise in simple production. Further, there may be negative prices which is a sign of inefficiency in the system; however, they can be corrected by truncation.

7.3.1 Satisfying demand

A brief footnote by Sraffa in the beginning of chapter 7 in *Production of Commodities by Means of Commodities* shows that he was quite aware of

Table 7.1.

	input			output	
	good 1	good 2	labour	good 1	good 2
method 1	0	1	1	$\frac{3}{2}$	3
method 2	$\frac{3}{8}$	1	2	$\frac{9}{8}$	6
method 2'	1	0	2	$\frac{9}{2}$	3

the problem even though he never explicitly addressed it; nor did he use the term demand, preferring to talk about 'proportions ... in which they [the commodities] are required for use'. The full quotation is:

Incidentally, considering that the proportions in which the two commodities are produced by any one method will in general be different from those in which they are required for use, the existence of two methods of producing them in different proportions will be necessary for obtaining the required proportion of the two products through an appropriate combination of the two methods. (P.S. 50, footnote 2)

But, when the role of demand is ignored, the price system may present nonsensical phenomena, as shown in the following example.

Consider an economy with two goods and three methods of production whose characteristics are shown in table 7.1.[11]

We assume $r = 0$ and $u_1 = u_2 = 1$.

The simultaneous use of methods (1) and (2) defines system (k) where we have

$$w^k = \tfrac{24}{13} \qquad p_1^k = \tfrac{4}{13} \qquad p_2^k = \tfrac{9}{13}$$

The simultaneous use of methods (1) and (2') defines system (h) where we have

$$w^h = \tfrac{5}{3} \qquad p_1^h = \tfrac{2}{3} \qquad p_2^h = \tfrac{1}{3}$$

We have here two possible production price systems and each of them ensures the minimisation of production costs: this is the case for system (k): at the prices of (k), method (2') shows a negative surplus; indeed (since $r = 0$), the cost of production $p_1^k + 2w^k = 4/13 + 2.4/13 = 52/13$ is greater than the value of production $(9/2)p_1^k + 3p_2^k = 9/2.4/13 + 3.9/13 = 45/13$.

System (h) also ensures the minimisation of costs: at the prices of (h) method (2) shows a negative surplus; indeed, the cost of production

Table 7.2.

	inputs			outputs	
	good 1	good 2	labour	good 1	good 2
method 1	0.5	0.5	1	1	2
method 2	0	3	1	3	0
method 2′	0	0.5	1	1	0

(at $r=0$), $(3/8)p_1^h + p_2^h + 2w^h = 3/8.2/3 + 1/3 + 2.5/3 = 94/24$ is greater than the value of production $(9/8)p_1^h + 6p_2^h = 9/8.2/3 + 6.1/3 = 66/24$.

We have here two possible systems of production prices, which are different, incompatible and both simultaneously minimise production costs.

However, if we normalise activity levels so that each method of production uses one unit of labour, when the system is at a stationary state, the net product matrix of the three methods writes

$$[B-A] = \begin{bmatrix} \frac{3}{2} & 2 \\ \frac{6}{16} & \frac{5}{2} \\ \frac{7}{4} & \frac{3}{2} \end{bmatrix}$$

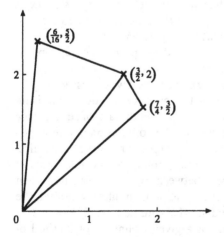

Figure 7.4

Figure 7.4 shows the net products of the three methods; it appears that systems (k) and (h) respectively composed of methods $(1, 2)$ and $(1, 2')$ do not satisfy the same needs (except in the specific case when $d = (3/2, 2)$). According to the structure of demand, we shall choose one of the two systems without being concerned with the minimisation of costs.

7.3.2 *The irrelevance of comparing the wage–profit curves*

Comparing $w(r)$ curves is not necessarily relevant any more: indeed, the system ensuring the minimisation of costs does not always coincide with the one pay the highest wages at the considered rate of profit.

Let us use Salvadori's example (1984, p. 183) of a production system with two commodities and three methods of production, characterised as shown in table 7.2.

System (k) is defined by the simultaneous use of methods (1) and (2), where at $r = 3/4$, and with $u_1 = 1$ and $u_2 = 99$, the price of good 1 is $p_1^k = 0.0219072\ldots$ and the wage is $w^k = 0.01385309\ldots$

System (h) is defined by the simultaneous use of methods (1) and $(2')$, where the price of good 1 is $p_1^h = 0.025669\ldots$ and the wage is $w^h = 0.0139280\ldots$ Thus $w^h > w^k$.

But it is system (k) which is cost minimising: we can show that at the prices of (k), the method of production likely to be used presents a negative surplus. Indeed, according to the table above, the cost of production is $(1 + r)0.5p_2^k + w^k = (1 + r)0.5((1 - p_1^k)/99) + w^k = 0.022497$ while the production of one unit of good 1 bears the value p_1^k, that is, 0.0219072.

Thus, using method $(2')$ does not decrease production costs; system (k) is the cost minimising system while $w_h > w_k$, at the considered rate of profit. *Consequently, at a given r, the minimisation of production costs does not imply the maximisation of wages any more.* And comparing the wage–profit curves cannot be considered as relevant.

Note on the importance of the choice of the numeraire: if we choose $u_1 = u_2 = 1$ as the numeraire for prices, (k) is still the production cost minimising system, but this time $w_k > w_h$. The paradox, or rather the lack of equivalence emphasised above, vanishes. This shows that the domination of one wage–profit curve over another is not necessarily independent of the numeraire; similarly, with a specific numeraire, switching points, which would not exist with a different numeraire, may appear between two curves (we have seen that in a system with single-product industries and circulating capital, the order of the $w(r)$ curves was independent of the numeraire).

We have shown in chapter 3 that for a given technique or method of production, we could obtain the properties of simple production systems in the interval $[R_0 \ R[$. Now, if we consider two techniques (k) and (h)

respectively characterized by intervals $[R_0^k \ R^k[$ and $[R_0^h \ R^h[$, it is only for $r \in [R_0^k \ R^k[\cap [R_0^h \ R^h[$ that the production costs minimising system is also w maximising, with r given and whatever d. There is no guarantee when r does not belong to that interval.

But the chosen value of the rate of profit, namely $r = 3/4$, does not belong to the interval $[1(\sqrt{17} - 1)/2]$ where the c.m.s exists and coincides with the w-maximising system, given r and whatever d.

The condition is more restrictive than the one indicated by Sraffa (P.S. 96) in *Production of Commodities by Means of Commodities*; he has pointed out (P.S. 72) that the curve (w, r) could be increasing in joint production, but he believed[12] that the decreasing character of the compared techniques' (w, r) curves was sufficient to ensure the equivalence of the minimisation of production cost and the maximisation of w given r (or of r given w). However, the decreasing condition is no doubt necessary but not sufficient. It is only in the interval indicated above that the equivalence is ensured; for curves (w, r) may be decreasing beyond that interval.

7.3.3 Stability condition of the choice of technique

Let $[A_k, B_k, L_k]$ and $[A_h, B_h, L_h]$ be square systems composed of an equal number of goods and methods of production. Both systems differ only by one activity.

Prices in both systems are defined, at a given r, by

$$[B_k - (1+r)A_k]p_k = w_k L_k \quad \text{and} \quad [B_h - (1+r)A_h]p_h = w_h L_h \qquad (1)$$

Definition
 A c.m.s is said to be stable when the choice of technique retained is the same whatever the price system.

In other words, the c.m.s is stable when we cannot have

$$[B_h - (1+r)A_h]p_k \le w_k L_h \text{ if } [B_k - (1+r)A_k]p_h \le w_h L_k$$

Theorem
 There is a stable c.m.s when different production systems satisfy the same needs in a golden rule situation $(r = g)$.

This assumption means that the same needs d can be satisfied by both techniques h and k in a golden rule situation, that is to say

$$y_h[B_h - (1+r)A_h] = d = y_k[B_k - (1+r)A_k] \qquad (2)$$

Assume that system (h) is the c.m.s, then we obtain

$$[B_k - (1+r)A_k]p_h \le w_h L_k$$

By pre-multiplying both terms of that inequality by $y_k > 0$, we obtain

$$y_k[B_k - (1+r)A_k]p_h < w_h y_k L_k$$

or, by (2)

$$dp_h < w_h d[B_k - (1+r)A_k]^{-1}L_k \tag{3}$$

According to (1), $[B_k - (1+r)A_k]^{-1}L_k = \dfrac{1}{w_k}p_k$ and (3) writes

$$dp_h < w_h \cdot \frac{1}{w_k} dp_k \tag{4}$$

By normalising prices in both systems by $dp_h = dp_k = 1$, we deduce from (4) that

$$w_k < w_h \tag{5}$$

Thus $[B_h - (1+r)A_h]p_k \leq w_k L_h$ is impossible. Otherwise, by pre-multiplying $y_h[B_h - (1+r)A_h]p_k < w_k y_h L_h$ by $y_h > 0$, that is according to (2)

$$dp_k < w_k d[B_h - (1+r)A_h]^{-1}L_h$$

and according to (1)

$$dp_k < w_k \cdot \frac{dp_h}{w_h}$$

Since $dp_k = dp_h = 1$, we would have $w_h < w_k$, which is at variance with (5).

We can note that the condition of the existence of the c.m.s is not established in the example developed in section 7.3.1., with $r=0$ (original hypothesis); it is clear that in a golden rule situation ($r=g=0$) both production systems cannot satisfy the same wants (see figure 7.4).

Another interesting example was developed by Salvadori (1981) who shows that in joint production the introduction of an innovation though profitable for the innovative capitalist may entail a decrease in the general rate of profit. We can quite easily show that the golden rule has not been respected.

Consider the following production system (see table 7.3).

The wage is now 'advanced' and consists in one unit of good (2) for each worker. If we simultaneously use methods (1) and (2') the prices of both goods are determined at the same time as the rate of profit r by the following equation system

$$\begin{cases} (0.5p_1 + 0.5p_2 + p_2)(1+r) = p_1 + 2p_2 \\ (0.5p_2 + p_2)(1+r) = p_1 \end{cases}$$

Table 7.3.

	input			output	
	good 1	good 2	labour	good 1	good 2
method 1	0.5	0.5	1	1	2
method 2	0	3	1	3	0
method 2'	0	0.5	1	1	0

With $p_1 + p_2 = 1$ as the normalisation condition, we obtain the following solution to system (h) above

$$p_1^h = \frac{6 - \sqrt{6}}{5} \qquad p_2^h = \frac{\sqrt{6} - 1}{5} \qquad r^h = \frac{2\sqrt{6} - 3}{3} = 0.63299\ldots$$

But, system (h) is not cost minimising; we can indeed notice that for the values of prices and rate of profit indicated above, using method (2) entails an excess profit. Since that method uses three units of commodity (2) and one unit of labour to produce three units of commodity (1), the production cost can easily be calculated by taking into account the fact that the 'advanced' wage is composed of one unit of commodity (2) and that the rate of profit is r^h

$$(3p_2^h + p_2^h)(1 + r^h) = \frac{4(\sqrt{6} - 1)}{5} \left(\frac{2\sqrt{6} - 3}{3} + 1 \right) = \frac{8}{3} \frac{(6 - \sqrt{6})}{5}$$

which is less than the value of output, namely $3p_1^h = 3 (6 - \sqrt{6})/5$.

Thus the use of method (2) entails an excess profit at the going prices p^h and the rate of profit r^h; as a consequence, capitalists will be encouraged to replace (2') by (2), hence the new system (k) which simultaneously determines the prices of both goods and the new rate of profit

$$\begin{cases} (0.5p_1 + 0.5p_2 + p_2)(1 + r) = p_1 + 2p_2 \\ (3p_2 + p_2)(1 + r) = 3p_1 \end{cases}$$

Owing to the normalisation condition $p_1 + p_2 = 1$, we obtain the following solution to system (k)

$$p_1^k = \frac{33 - \sqrt{193}}{28} \qquad p_2^k = \frac{\sqrt{193} - 5}{28}$$

$$r^k = \frac{\sqrt{193} - 9}{8} = 0.6115 < r^h = 0.63299$$

Table 7.4.

	input			output	
	good 1	good 2	labour	good 1	good 2
method 1	2	0	1	5	1
method 2	0	1	1	1	3
method 2'	1	0	1	1	3

Therefore, owing to the existence of a positive excess profit at the price system initially applied (i.e., h), the replacement of method (2') by method (2) leads to a decrease in the average or general rate of profit. *Thus it seems that in joint production, the introduction of a technical innovation, though profitable for the innovative capitalists, may entail a decrease in the general rate of profit.*

We can easily check that the rhythm of accumulation cannot be greater than 33%, a rate at which the system does not present any surplus of good 2; the paradox emphasised by Salvadori springs from the non-respect of the golden rule. We may add that at $r = g = 33\%$, only the first activity is used: good (1) then becomes a free good and only good 2 is an economic good. This is a truncation of the system, a problem we shall revert to later on.

7.3.4 Identifying the method to be superceded

Consider an economy with two goods and three methods of production characterised in table 7.4 (see Salvadori 1984, p. 183).

We assume that $r = 3/2$ and $p_1 + p_2 = 1$.

System (k) is defined by the simultaneous use of methods (1) and (2), and we obtain

$$w^k = \tfrac{2}{3} \qquad p_1^k = \tfrac{1}{3} \qquad p_2^k = \tfrac{2}{3}$$

System (h) is defined by the simultaneous use of methods (1) and (2') and we obtain

$$w^h = \tfrac{3}{7} \qquad p_1^h = \tfrac{4}{7} \qquad p_2^h = \tfrac{3}{7}$$

Thus, we do have *two possible systems of production* (in the sense that prices and distributive variables are simultaneously positive), *but none of them is cost minimising*. Indeed:

System (k) is not the c.m.s.: at the prices prevailing in (k), method (2') shows a positive surplus, which can be easily checked; the production

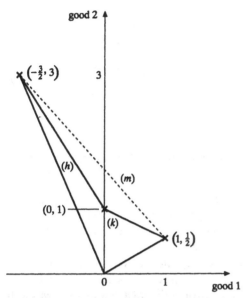

good 2

$\left(-\frac{3}{2}, 3\right)$

3

(h)

(m)

(0, 1)

(k)

$\left(1, \frac{1}{2}\right)$

0

1

good 1

Figure 7.5

cost $(1+r)p_1^k + w^k = 5/2.1/3 + 2/3 = 9/6$ is less than the value of this activity's output, $p_1^k + 3p_2^k = 1/3 + 3.2/3 = 7/3 = 14/6$.

System (h) is not the c.m.s. either: at the prices prevailing in (h), method (2) shows a positive surplus; the production cost $(1+r)p_2^h + w^h = 5/2.3/7 + 3/7 = 3/2$ is here again less than the value of output, $p_1^h + 3p_2^h = 4/7 + 3.3/7 = 13/7$.

In such a situation there is no cost minimising system: at the prices prevailing in (k), capitalists consider that method $(2')$ is more profitable; when it is adopted and replaces (2), a new price system (h) appears for which method (2) becomes more profitable! We are then confronted with a *permanent oscillation between two production price systems*; neither of them can be stable.

Let us now re-examine that example. Matrix $B - (1+r)A$, characterising the three methods of production writes, with $r = g = 3/2$:

$$[B - (1+r)A] = \begin{bmatrix} 0 & 1 \\ 1 & \frac{1}{2} \\ \frac{-3}{2} & 3 \end{bmatrix}$$

Hence see figure 7.5 plotting the net g-products.

Recall that we have compared two systems, (k) composed of methods (1) and (2) and system (h) composed of methods (1) and $(2')$. But it appears clearly (see figure) that any demand perfectly satisfied by (k) can also be

Table 7.5.

| | input | | | output | |
	good 1	good 2	labour	good 1	good 2
method 1	0	1	1	1	1
method 2	5	0	1	5	5
method 2'	2	0	1	4	4

perfectly satisfied by (m) which is composed of methods (2) and (2'); the efficiency frontier (broken line on diagram) has been defined on the basis of (m) which can be easily established as the c.m.s. Thus, the problem of switch in methods of production has been ill-defined: we have compared only two systems (k) and (h), which differed by only one method (2) and (2') while it was method (1) which had to be replaced, the c.m.s. being composed of (2) and (2'). Though the problem of the introduction of a new method was well defined, that of the elimination of a method was not.

In this connection, Sraffa warned:

With single-product industries, each process or method of production is identified by the commodity which it produces, so that when an additional, $(k+1)^{th}$, method is introduced there is no doubt as to which of the pre-existing methods it is an alternative to.

When, however, each process or method produces several commodities, and each commodity is produced by several methods, this criterion fails. And the problem arises of how to identify among the pre-existing methods the one to which the new method is an alternative. (P.S., section 96)

Thus it is in the whole set of possible production systems that the problem of switch in methods of production has to be contemplated; it entails the adoption of a new method of production and also the elimination of a pre-existing one, the cost minimising criterion under the constraint of satisfying demand, ensuring in a golden rule situation, the existence and stability of the c.m.s.

However, there is no guarantee that when it exists, the c.m.s. includes non-negative elements. Let us now address that issue.

7.3.5 Ruling out negative prices through system truncation

Consider an economy with two goods and three methods of production with the characteristics shown in table 7.5.

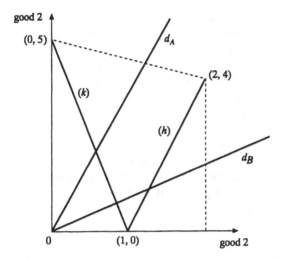

Figure 7.6

System (k) is defined by the simultaneous use of methods (1) and (2) where $w^k = p_1^k = 5/6$ and $p_2^k = 1/6$ for $r = 0$ and $p_1 + p_2 = 1$. This system is not cost-minimising since at the prices of (k) and owing to the wage and rate of profit values, method $(2')$ shows a positive surplus: the production cost (at $r = 0$) is indeed $2\,p_1^k + w^k = 3w^k = 3.5/6 = 5/2$ less than the value of output $4p_1^k + 4p_2^k = 4\,(p_1^k + p_2^k) = 4$.

Capitalists are thus led to replacing method (2) by method $(2')$ which is less costly; but the simultaneous use of method (1) and $(2')$ defines system (h) where $w^h = p_1^h = 4/3$ and $p_2^h = -1/3 < 0!$

Such a phenomenon can be easily explained. At $r = 0$, matrix $B - (1 + r)A$ writes

$$[B - A] = \begin{bmatrix} 1 & 0 \\ 0 & 5 \\ 2 & 4 \end{bmatrix}$$

Hence the net g-product diagram depicted in figure 7.6 (with $r = g = 0$).

It appears clearly that the simultaneous use of methods (1) and $(2')$ which define system (h) shows a curve of consumption possibilities with a positive slope or, which is equivalent, negative (production) prices. We have already indicated (chapter 1) that this is the sign of an inefficient system; it is indeed quite clear that method (1) is dominated by method $(2')$ (with $r = g = 0$) and that the simultaneous use is inefficient; such an inefficiency is revealed by non-positive elements in the price system.

Thus system (h) can never be used and method (1) has to be superceded if method (2') is available. If so, two situations have to be contemplated:

either the structure of demand is included within the cone of net products, determined by the simultaneous use of methods (2) and (2'), i.e., $d_2/d_1 > 4/2 = 2$: demand can then be perfectly satisfied by system (m) composed of (2) and (2'), and production prices are strictly positive for both goods (see position d_A).

or demand is outside the cone previously defined, i.e., $d_2/d_1 < 2$.

In such conditions (see d_B on figure 7.6) method (1) cannot be used since it is dominated by method (2') which will be the only one used. As a result good (2) is supplied in excess and thus, provided we assume the free disposal of the good produced in excess, the free good is available at zero price and good (1) which is the sole economic good has a positive price.

Thus, the appearance of negative elements in the c.m.s shows that one method of production is inefficient. Eliminating it would lead, with some structures of demand, to the impossibility of perfectly satisfying demand, and thus supply exceeds demand. Assuming the free disposal of free goods means that they are available at zero price and the costs of production are positive only for economic goods, the supply of which strictly equals demand.

It is worth noting that the conditions related to the positivity of the c.m.s. hold for $r = g = 0$ and when Koopmans' concept of the efficiency frontier can be used. In the general case when $r = g \neq 0$ the concept of g-efficiency frontier has to be used.

Therefore, the appearance of negative prices reveals an inefficiency of the system springing from the simultaneous use of two methods of production with one dominating the other. Ruling out the dominated method of production leads to the impossibility of perfectly satisfying wants and thus an excess supply of goods. By the von Neumann rule these products are available at zero price provided we assume their free disposal. Then, only the goods which perfectly satisfy wants have positive production prices. Thus the efficiency condition implies the positivity of the c.m.s.

As a conclusion, the difficulties related to the existence, non-unicity and non-positivity of the c.m.s. can be relaxed if we take into account the necessity to satisfy demand in a golden rule situation, by eliminating inefficiencies; *in other words, minimising costs under the constraint of satisfying demand in a context of g-efficiency.*

If the retained structure of wants corresponds to the workers' consumption basket, the system is a c.m.s. which, given $r = g$, ensures the maximisation of wages. Hence the following proposition:

If the compared systems of production produce the basket of goods consumed by workers under g-efficiency, the c.m.s. coincides with the system which at the considered rate of profit, maximises the real wage.

7.4 Depreciation of machines

By 'machines' or 'fixed capital' we mean any means of production whose period of use is greater than the reference period of time, generally a year. Consequently we know that the distinction between fixed capital and circulating capital is quite arbitrary.

In 'references to the literature' (Appendix D) Sraffa notes that 'the plan of treating what is left of fixed capital at the end of the year as a kind of joint-product may seem artificial if viewed against the background of the continuous flow of industrial production, but it fits easily into the classical picture of an agricultural system ...'. This method, introduced by Torrens, adopted by Ricardo in the third edition of the *Principles*, then by Malthus in the *Measure of Value* and later by Marx, seems to have fallen into oblivion afterwards.

The depreciation of the machine (we speak here of 'truncation') means that it has to be decided how long the machine is going to be used. This is closely connected to the analysis of switch in methods of production previously carried out; indeed, the decision to depreciate a machine, or stop using it, is made to satisfy the same needs as those satisfied when a method of production is abandoned, considering the worn-out machine as a free good. Of course, the life span of a machine may be fixed, independently of economic considerations. But such an hypothesis that we shall first address, is neither the most frequent nor the most interesting one.

7.4.1 Fixed life span hypothesis

This point of view implies that the same machine, at different ages, should be treated as so many different products, each with its own price. In order to determine these prices, an equal number of additional equations (and therefore of processes) is required.

Accordingly, an industry which employs a durable instrument must be regarded as being subdivided into as many separate processes as are the years of the total life of the instrument in question. Each of these processes is distinguished by the fact that it uses an instrument of a different age; and each of them 'produces', jointly with a quantity of a marketable commodity, an instrument a year older than the one which it uses – with the exception of the process using the expiring instrument in its last year, which produces singly the marketable commodity (or, at most, in addition, the residual scrap if it has any value). (P.S. 74).

Table 7.6.

	Inputs						Outputs				
		machines						machines			
wheat	M_0	M_1	M_2	M_3	labour	wheat	M_0	M_1	M_2	M_3
a_0					l_0		1			
a_1	1				l_1	b_1		1		
a_2		1			l_2	b_2			1	
a_3			1		l_3	b_3				1
a_4				1	l_4	b_4				

Let us now consider a single machine produced with wheat and labour and used over four periods of time and then becomes scrap without any value. Each period of time can be characterised as a process, a particular method of production: the first process uses wheat, the new machine denoted by M_0, and labour and produces a certain quantity of wheat written b_1 as well as the worn machine M_1; the second uses wheat the worn machine M_1, and labour and produces a quantity of wheat denoted by b_2 as well as the worn machine M_2; the third uses wheat the worn machine M_2 and labour and produces a quantity of wheat denoted by b_3 as well as the worn machine M_3; the latter is finally used by the fourth process, which again produces wheat and a worn-out machine, since it has reached its last year of usefulness. Therefore, we have one activity producing the new machine and four activities producing wheat using machines at different ages appearing as many distinct machines each with its own price (see table 7.6).

Consequently, there are five equations and seven unknowns: the price of wheat, the price of the new machine, the three prices of the worn machines, the wage w and the rate of profit r. Owing to the normalisation equation, we have here again one degree of freedom.

Now consider the more general case of a system producing k goods (the new machine included) with circulating capital and labour, and each method produces one and only one good (for simplicity's sake we have ruled out the hypothesis of joint production). Wheat is produced by means of the new machine used over T periods of time: hence T production equations of wheat, with each method using an input vector a_h, a quantity of labour l_h, a worn machine M_{h-1} and producing a quantity b_h of wheat and a worn machine M_h (except for the last process which only produces wheat).

By writing p the price vector (with k components) in circulating capital inputs, p_h^m (with $h = 0,1,2,\ldots,T-1$) the prices of the different machines, p_h

the price of wheat, A the intermediate consumption matrix of sectors different from wheat and L the vector of needs in direct labour of these sectors, we have

$$
\left\{
\begin{array}{ll}
(1+r)Ap + wL & = p \\
(1+r)[a_1 p + M_0 p_0^m] + w l_1 & = b_1 p_b + M_1 p_1^m \\
(1+r)[a_2 p + M_1 p_1^m] + w l_2 & = b_2 p_b + M_2 p_2^m \\
\cdots\cdots\cdots\cdots\cdots\cdots\cdots\cdots\cdots\cdots\cdots\cdots\cdots\cdots\cdots\cdots \\
(1+r)[a_{T-1} p + M_{T-2} p_{T-2}^m] + w l_{T-1} & = b_{T-1} p_b + M_{T-1} p_{T-1}^m \\
(1+r)[a_T p + M_{T-1} p_{T-1}^m] + w l_T & = b_T p_b \\
\text{with } up = 1
\end{array}
\right.
$$

Thus we have $k + T + 1$ equations and $k + T + 2$ unknowns: the k prices of goods produced by means of circulating capital (the new machine included), the price of wheat, the $(T-1)$ prices of the worn-out machines and the two distributive variables, hence $k + 1 + (T-1) + 2 = k + T + 2$.

7.4.2 The integrated equation and 'the suppression of joint production'

Joint production appears in the $(T-1)$ processes using the first $(T-1)$ machines and producing wheat as well as a worn-out machine, which is an intermediate product.

The method to suppress intermediate products proposed by Sraffa (P.S. 76) can be generalised;[13] the purpose is to combine in a single expression all the elements of the machine system by multiplying them by $(1+r)^{T-t}$. Indeed, if we multiply the T equations respectively by $(1+r)^{T-1}$, $(1+r)^{T-2},\ldots,(1+r)$, 1 and add them, the machines of intermediate ages (above zero and under T years) which appear on both sides cancel out and we obtain the integrated equation

$$
(1+r)\sum_{t=1}^{T}(1+r)^{T-t}a_t p + (1+r)^T M_0 p_0^m + w\sum_{t=1}^{T}(1+r)^{T-t}l_t
$$
$$
= \sum_{t=1}^{T}(1+r)^{T-t}b_t p_b
$$

or also

$$
(1+r)\hat{a}p + (1+r)^T M_0 p_0^m + w\hat{l} = \hat{b} p_b
$$

with

$$
\hat{a} = \sum_{t=1}^{T}(1+r)^{T-t}a_t
$$

$$\hat{l}= \sum_{t=1}^{T}(1+r)^{T-t}l_t$$

$$\hat{b}= \sum_{t=1}^{T}(1+r)^{T-t}b_t$$

The production equations of wheat (with a simultaneous production of worn machines) are thus replaced by the 'integrated' equation above which provides the necessary information and where wheat (and only wheat) is produced using an input vector, labour and the new machine. In a way, such an integrated equation is a 'simple'-production equation since only wheat appears as produced by the system. It is not, however, a usual production equation: the $\hat{a}$, $\hat{l}$ and $\hat{b}$ are indeed functions of r. Therefore, it is not really a simple production system, but simple production taking into account discounts, in short fixed capital.

The treatment of machines, or the taking into account of fixed capital was explained in the first formulation; the integrated equation ignores the latter without eliminating it.

By combining the integrated equation and the k production equations different from wheat, namely $p=(1+r)Ap+wL$, we obtain the set of activities producing finished goods (among them wheat and the new machine). We can show without any difficulty[14] that under the usual productivity conditions there exists a maximum rate of profit $R>0$ and the prices of finished goods are positive for any $r\in[0\ R]$. We can also demonstrate that the system has a strictly positive[15] standard commodity and that the wage–profit relation is linear and decreasing provided prices and wages are expressed in terms of that standard commodity.

It is amazing that the previous characteristics are independent of all hypotheses on the prices of intermediate goods, that is to say, worn machines. However, analysing them is necessary to study depreciations and their consequences.

7.4.3 Efficiency and prices of machines

Let us revert to the price equation characterising the T periods of the machine's usefulness. We have

$$(1+r)(a_hp + M_{h-1}p^m_{h-1}) + wl_h = b_hp_b + M_hp^m_h$$

After rearranging the equation and owing to $M_h = M_{h-1} = 1$ (it is indeed the same machine or rather the same quantity of machines which is used as inputs and outputs)

$$(1+r)p^m_{h-1} - p^m_h = b_hp_b - (1+r)a_hp - wl_h = F_h(r)$$

$F_h(r)$ can be interpreted as the net return of the hth process: it is indeed the difference between the value of the output of wheat and that of used inputs, taking into account the rate of profit r and the wage w.

Using the integrated equation allows to consider here w, r, p_b and p as fixed and exogenous. Hence the recurrent form of the machines' price equation

$$p_{h-1}^m = \frac{F_h(r) + p_h^m}{1+r} \qquad \text{with } h = 1, \ldots, T-2$$

$$p_{T-1}^m = \frac{F_T(r)}{1+r}$$

Thus, we can calculate without any difficulty the price of a worn machine of age h by first multiplying the different values of $p_h^m, p_{h+1}^m, p_{h+2}^m, \ldots, p^m{}_{T-1}$ successively by $1/1, 1/(1+r), 1/(1+r)^2, \ldots, 1/(1+r)^{T-h-1}$.

$$p_h^m = \frac{F_{h+1}}{1+r} + \frac{p_{h+1}^m}{1+r}$$

$$\frac{p_{h+1}^m}{1+r} = \frac{F_{h+2}}{(1+r)^2} + \frac{p_{h+1}^m}{(1+r)^2}$$

$$\cdots\cdots\cdots\cdots\cdots\cdots\cdots$$

$$\frac{p_{T-1}^m}{(1+r)^{T-h-1}} = \frac{F_T}{(1+r)^{T-h}}$$

Summing up, we obtain

$$p_h^m = \sum_{t=1}^{T-h} \frac{F_{h+t}}{(1+r)^t}$$

Thus, the price of a worn machine of age h appears as the sum of the expected net returns F_t at each period, discounted by the rate of interest r.

If the machine is new, its production price is equal to the sum of discounted expected net returns over the period of use

$$p_0^m = \sum_{t=1}^{T} \frac{F_t}{(1+r)^t}$$

Thus, the price of the new machine can be determined either by production (and distribution) conditions, or by the conditions of use (and discount). Both methods of valuing are equivalent. The new machine, a new capital good, is therefore at a point where intertemporal and input–output analyses meet.

The price of the worn machine, the intermediate good (at a given r), will vary with age. More precisely, the variations in the flow of net incomes F_h during the period of use will play a determining role. In this respect, it will be convenient to speak of evolution in the machine's *efficiency*; this term may be misleading though: recall that it is economic efficiency which is in question and it depends on prices and more generally on the rate of profit.

From the previous formula determining p_h^m, let us consider the case of a machine the net returns of which would remain positive whatever its age: it is quite obvious that the price of the worn machine would also be positive

$$F_h > 0 \quad \forall h \Rightarrow p_h^m > 0$$

This holds only if, at a given r, the efficiency is constant or possibly increasing. In a number of cases, however, the F_hs become negative when the machine is in its last years of usefulness, which results in negative book-values for old machines.

The issue of net flows of negative returns has to be elaborated: a negative net flow does not necessarily mean that the price of the worn machine for that specific period is negative: $F_h < 0$ does not imply $p_h < 0$. A machine with h years may have a positive price even if net returns are negative during period h and even in the next periods. For example, consider the case of a machine with negative net returns between 0 and θ and positive prices in each of the periods in question; the positive net returns of the periods following θ compensate for the negative net returns of the first periods of use: this is the case for dams, machines which are being built, works in progress.

However, if the machine has negative net returns from $t = \theta$ until the end of its last year of usefulness, its price will become negative at $t = \theta$ at the latest. Suffice to use the recurrence formula

$$p_{T-1}^m = F_T(r)/(1+r)$$

Theorem
The wage prices $\hat{p}$ of the k final goods are increasing functions of r in interval $[0 \ R]$ if all the prices of the intermediary goods (worn machines) are positive in that interval.[16]

Indeed, by differentiating both sides of

$$B\hat{p}(r) = (1+r)A\hat{p}(r) + L$$

we obtain

$$B\frac{d}{dr}\hat{p}(r) = (1+r)A\frac{d}{dr}\hat{p}(r) + A\hat{p}(r)$$

that is

$$[B - (1+r)A] \frac{d}{dr} \hat{p}(r) = A\hat{p}(r)$$

By multiplying both members of the last equality on the T processes using the machine by $(1+r)^{T-t}$ and by adding corresponding terms using the same notations as in section 7.4.2, we obtain

$$[\hat{B}(r) - (1+r)\hat{A}(r)] \frac{d}{dr} \hat{p}(r) = \hat{A}(r)\hat{p}(r) + \sum_{t=1}^{T} M(t-1)\hat{p}_m(t-1)$$

that is

$$\frac{d}{dr} \hat{p}(r) = [\hat{B}(r) - (1+r)\hat{A}(r)]^{-1} = \left\{ \hat{A}(r)\hat{p}(r) + \sum_{t=1}^{T} M(t-1)\hat{p}_m(t-1) \right\}$$

where $[\hat{B}(r) - (1+r)\hat{A}(r)]^{-1} > 0$ since in model $[\hat{A}(r), \hat{B}(r)]$ there are no machines any more and we revert to the simple production model.

The obvious consequence of this is that relation (w, r) can be increasing only if the prices of some intermediate goods become negative in interval $[0 \ R]$. Therefore, any 'anomaly' in curve (w, r) means that the prices of some intermediate goods become negative; the converse is not true: some prices may be negative without any anomaly, or increase appearing in curve (w, r), (we have seen earlier that relation (w, r) is linear and *decreasing* only if Sraffa's standard commodity is used as a numeraire). Let us now explain the appearance of negative prices for intermediate goods.

7.4.4 The capital life span

Why would some worn machines have negative prices? Because they have been used too long; owing to the going rate of profit r, they should have been 'depreciated', superceded.

To show this, let us first assume that it is the oldest machine which has a negative price. By the previous definition

$$p_{T-1}^m = \frac{F_T(r)}{1+r} \qquad \text{with } F_T(r) = b_T p_b - (1+r)a_T p - wl_T$$

given r, $p_{T-1}^m < 0 \Leftrightarrow F_T(r) < 0$. If the price of the oldest machine is negative then the process using that machine does not derive the average profit from the capital invested

$$F_T(r) < 0 \Leftrightarrow b_T p_b < (1+r)a_T p + wl_T$$

Thus, there is no reason for this process to be used: wheat can indeed be produced by another method and needs to be satisfied at a lower cost. Under the assumption of free disposal of that machine – a problem we shall revert to – let us consider the machine as a free good and simultaneously abandon the activity in question.The depreciation procedure may also be continued until positive prices are obtained for all the machines used.

Remember though that this analysis has been carried out for a given value of r and depreciation may be different at another value of r. No relationship can be established between the economic life of capital goods and the value of the rate of profit; contrary to what neo-Austrian authors believed in a less formal context (see Hayek, 1931) that a decrease in the rate of interest (profit) does not necessarily lead to a longer production process. Further, the possibility of returns to depreciation cannot be ruled out; in other words it may happen that the life span of a machine that is optimal in a given interval of variation in the rate of profit, stops being so and then becomes optimal anew when the rate of profit increases (or decreases). Examples of that kind have been given by Hageman and Kurtz (1976) and Schefold (1978).

If depreciation is the consequence of negative prices, conversely, we may conceive the possibility of a longer period of use of some capital goods. The initial hypothesis of a machine's fixed life span is of course excessive in a number of cases; conversely, we may put forward that it is always profitable to lengthen the life of a machine as long as the method of use (and of servicing) allows a positive book-price. This explains the 'venerable' age of some equipment.[17]

It is worth adding that the free disposal hypothesis is rather questionable. In many cases the removal (and dismantling) costs of the equipment are significant. An alternative hypothesis would be that of fixed costs independent of the age of the machine, that would be taken into account every time an activity is to be stopped. But this often leads to a non-optimal use of the means of production; depreciation may thus be accelerated.

7.5 Optimisation and production prices

Is it possible to link the traditional analyses of choices of techniques and the presentations in terms of optimisation? Obviously both approaches are conflicting: if we take the rate of profit as the exogenous variable, the objective function of the canonical linear programming indicates a minimisation of wages; while in Sraffa's case of switch in techniques, the aim is to reach the highest wage at the considered rate of profit.

A simple case, that can easily be stated in general terms, allows us to show that the contradiction is only apparent, provided simple production prevails. In that case the solution wage is indeed the lowest wage satisfying the linear programming constraints and simultaneously the highest wage springing from the choice of technique. Let us add that in both cases the aim is to minimise production costs at the considered rate of profit. But in joint production, the wage maximisation criterion has no general value any more (given r). It is the cost minimisation criterion, von Neumann's rule of profitability, which has to be considered.

The problem is the same when it is the wage, and not the rate of profit any more, which is taken to be exogenous. But then, the optimisation programming is not linear any more and von Neumann's model becomes more relevant.

Also, it appears that if the choice of the exogenous distributive variable is unimportant mathematically speaking, it is quite important as far as its economic meaning is concerned. When r is exogenous, w is positive only in a context of full employment.

While when w is exogenous it has a positive value even in a situation of underemployment, the value of the rate of profit being obtained by solving the model.

The analyses that follow have been carried out within the usual context for this kind of exercice (steady-state regime, golden rule and constant returns to scale unless otherwise stated). Thus, we shall distinguish two cases.

7.5.1 When the rate of profit is exogenous

Using the usual notations, let us consider an economy with n activities producing k goods (with $n > k$). The unit level of operation for each activity is determined by the condition $l_i = 1$. We adopt the general case with some activities producing several goods (pure joint production or worn-out machines); final consumption is defined by vector d, with its level being a scalar c; y is the activity level vector, yA and yB are the intermediate consumption vector and the production vector respectively. The inequation system determining the equilibrium conditions for the whole set of goods is

$$yB \geqq (1 + g)yA + cd$$

or

$$y[B - (1 + g)A] \geqq cd$$

The available output of each good must be at least equal to the intermediate consumption (yA), accumulation (gyA) and final consumption cd.

The only primary factor of production considered here is labour which is taken to be homogeneous. The labour force coefficients for each activity are set equal to unity ($l_i = 1$) to allow a convenient normalisation of activity levels. The quantity of labour used in the whole economy is yL. If we assume that the quantity of available labour during the period in question equals N, then we have: $yL \leq N$. Recall, that it may be convenient to choose such units of measure to express the quantity of labour so that $N = 1$; this does not have any consequences on the general operation of the model, nor does it entail any new implicit hypothesis on the equilibrium conditions of the labour market; thus we have $yL \leq 1$.

If we take c as the social utility function of households' final consumption, the structure of which is taken to be fixed, we obtain the following primal programming and the corresponding dual relations that we shall explain

PRIMAL	DUAL
Max c	Min w
$y[B - (1+g)A] \geqq cd$	$p \geq 0$
$yL \leq N$	$w \geq 0$
$y \geq 0$	$[B - (1+g)A]p \leq wL$
$c \geq 0$	$D \leq dp$

The column-vector p is composed of the different goods' dual prices and number w is the dual price corresponding to labour. Let a^i and b^i, be the ith columns of matrices A and B respectively; d_i is the ith element of the final consumption vector. By the complementarity relations, if the supply of a good exceeds demand, its dual price is zero; it is positive in the opposite case

$$y[b^i - (1+g)a^i] > cd_i \Rightarrow p_i = 0$$
$$y[b^i - (1+g)a^i] = cd_i \Leftarrow p_i > 0$$

It is worth adding that the complementarity relations also hold for the dual price of labour: the wage can be positive only if the quantity of available labour is totally used (we shall revert to this issue later)

$$yL < N \Rightarrow w = 0$$
$$yL = N \Leftarrow w > 0$$

To every variable y_j corresponds a dual relation $[b_j - (1+g)a_j]p \leq wl_j$ where b_j and a_j represent the jth rows of matrices A and B. Owing to the complementarity relations we can write

$$[b_j - (1+g)a_j]p < wl_j \Rightarrow y_j = 0$$
$$[b_j - (1+g)a_j]p = wl_j \Leftarrow y_j > 0$$

Consequently, only the activities allowing us to reach the rate of profit are used at the optimum (the rate of profit is equal to the rate of growth owing to the golden rule hypothesis and the solution of the previous programming). We recognise here the determination process of production prices, with $r = g$.

Finally, the last relation of the primal can be interpreted by using the complementarity relations

$$c > 0 \Rightarrow D = dp$$
$$c = 0 \Leftarrow D < dp.$$

If the supply price, the value of economic goods (dp) is too high, higher than an exogenous value D which can be interpreted as the available purchasing power for final consumption, we should have $c = 0$, owing to the complementarity relation $c(dp - D) = 0$. Such a case is ruled out here since we assume that $c > 0$, and as a result $dp = D$; which comes down to the usual normalisation condition.

The economic constraints are: $y \geq 0$, $p \geq 0$, $w > 0$ and $c > 0$ so that by making $M = B - (1 + g)A$, the programming can write

PRIMAL	DUAL
Max $0.y + 1.c = c$	Min $0.p + 1.w = w$
$-yM + cd \leq 0$	$p \geq 0$
$yL + c.0 = N$	$w > 0$
$y \geq 0$	$-Mp + wL \geq 0$
$c > 0$	$dp + w.0 = D$

Maximizing c comes down to maximizing $D.c$ or $0.y + D.c$ with D given and minimising w comes down to minimising $N.w$ or $0.p + N.w$, given N.

By writing

$$\underset{(1,k+1)}{a} = (0,0,\dots,0,N), \quad \underset{(1,n+1)}{x} = (y_1, y_2, \dots, y_n, c)$$

$$\underset{(k+1,1)}{u} = \begin{pmatrix} p_1 \\ p_2 \\ \vdots \\ p_k \\ w \end{pmatrix}. \quad \underset{(n+1,1)}{f} = \begin{pmatrix} 0 \\ \vdots \\ \vdots \\ 0 \\ D \end{pmatrix}.$$

and $$\underset{(n+1,k+1)}{H} = \begin{pmatrix} -M & L \\ d & 0 \end{pmatrix}$$

This programming then writes in the traditional form

PRIMAL	DUAL

Max $xf = c$	Min $a.u = w$

$xH \leq a$	$u \geq 0$

$x \geq 0$	$Hu \geq f$

Let us now revert to the objective function of the dual programming; it may be curious that the aim is to minimise the wage while the analysis of switch in methods of production puts the emphasis on the maximisation of the wage – though wrongly since the aim is always to minimise the costs of production. In simple production, the cost minimising criterion and the wage maximising criterion are indeed equivalent (with r given). But such an equivalence does not hold in joint production and only the cost minimising criterion (or von Neumann's rule of profitability) is relevant.

We shall address the problem first in a context of simple production with each activity being specialised in the production of a single good, then in a context of joint production, keeping the system of production with two goods. Note that in both cases the dual programming has to be considered as a whole. Indeed, given $r = g$ and given the structure of demand, the objective is to find the lowest wage such that no activity makes excess profits. Let us first contemplate the case of simple production with the following example. Let

$$A = \begin{bmatrix} 5 & 2 \\ \frac{1}{3} & \frac{4}{3} \\ 4 & 3 \end{bmatrix} \qquad L = \begin{bmatrix} 1 \\ 1 \\ 1 \end{bmatrix} \qquad B = \begin{bmatrix} 10 & 0 \\ 0 & \frac{10}{3} \\ 0 & 10 \end{bmatrix}$$

be a simple production system with two goods and three activities. The production price equations are written for $r = g = 0$ and completed by the normalisation condition $dp = 1$ with $d = (1 \ 1)$. We assume $c > 0$ and $D = 1$.

$$\begin{cases} 5p_1 + 2p_2 + w = 10p_1 \\ \frac{1}{3}p_1 + \frac{4}{3}p_2 + w = \frac{10}{3}p_2 \\ 4p_1 + 3p_2 + w = 10p_2 \\ p_1 + p_2 = 1 \end{cases}$$

Hence by substitution, the three relations $w(p_1)$ defined at $r = 0$

$$\begin{cases} w = 7p_1 - 2 & (1) \\ w = 2 - \frac{7}{3}p_1 & (2) \\ w = 7 - 11p_1 & (3) \end{cases}$$

These three relations are shown in figure 7.7 as well as the normalisation

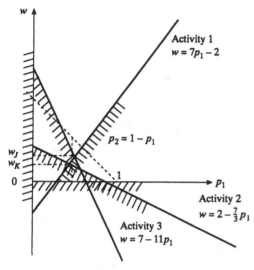

Figure 7.7

condition $dp = 1$ that is, $p_2 = 1 - p_1$. Owing to the constraints, the optimisation programming leads us to seek the lowest w such that

$$w \geq 7p_1 - 2$$
$$w \geq 2 - \tfrac{7}{3}p_1$$
$$w \geq 7 - 11p_1$$

with w, p_1, and p_2 positive.

Thus the solution is given by the ordinate of the intersection point J defined by the $w(p_1)$ lines of activities (1) and (3), that is to say w_j; thus, activities (1) and (3) are retained, while the second is not: indeed, for $w_k < w_j$, the third activity would make profits greater than the average profit (here $r = 0$) and the inequalities of the dual programming would not be satisfied (see figure 7.7).

It is actually the lowest wage satisfying the constraints (any $w > w_j$ would satisfy them equally, but w_j is the minimum wage) and simultaneously the highest wage allowing positive prices for all the goods: $w_j > w_k$. Note also that the same programming serves to define the system allowing us to ensure the minimisation of production costs at the considered rate of profit ($r = g = 0$). Indeed, for $w = w_j$, the inequalities $[B - (1 + g)A]p \leq wL$ turn into equalities for the activities retained as the optimal solution to the programming in order to form the cost minimising system at the considered rate of profit. Activities that are not retained have too low a profitability and their production costs are too tight.

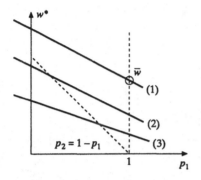

Figure 7.8a

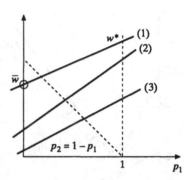

Figure 7.8b

In joint production, each method can simultaneously produce both goods and the configurations cannot be ruled out.

As in the previous case, lines (1), (2) and (3) represent the $w(p_1)$ relations at a given r. The broken line represents $p_2 = 1 - p_1$ since by assumption we have $d = (1 \; 1)$. In both cases, activity (1) dominates activities (2) and (3); thus, in both cases, it will be the only one to be used. But in the first case $p_1 = 1$ and $p_2 = 0$ while in the second $p_1 = 0$ and $p_2 = 1$. Only one activity is used and it produces both goods, with only one of them being an economic good the other being a free good. The solution $\bar{w}$ is shown on figure 7.8; it is the result of the price non-negativity constraint.

Note that in this case the solution $\bar{w}$ does not correspond to the maximum wage w^* which could appear in one or the other considered cases but which would not ensure the minimisation of production costs (the corner solutions which may appear in joint production are impossible in simple production where, contrary to joint production, two activities are needed to produce two goods).

Of course, in joint production, the choice of techniques depends on the structure of demand d while it is independent of it in simple production (non-substitution theorem). We can see that in case of joint products, with another structure of demand $d = (d_1 \; d_2)$ we have, $p_2 = \dfrac{1}{d_2} - \dfrac{d_1}{d_2} p_1$ and a change in the respective slopes and positions of lines (1), (2) and (3) consequently modifies both the number of economic goods produced and the number of activities retained.

A final issue deserves our attention: that of the reasoning behind the determination of wages. It is assumed here that the rate of profit is exogenously determined: in such conditions, the wage appears as the dual price of labour and is positive only if the available quantity of labour is totally used; which is far from being the case in real economies. Hence the questioning of the hypotheses retained and possibly of the framework of analysis itself. Lacaze has analysed the problem quite well, he states that 'the solution simply consists in admitting – a confession of helplessness – that beside the official economy exists a sub-economy that we cannot take into account'. And thus a part of the active population will be 'out of the model' (see Lacaze, 1976a, pp. 1–72). We find it preferable to revert to the initial hypothesis according to which the rate of profit is exogenously determined and to contemplate the other side of the alternative.

7.5.2 When the wage is considered as exogenous

We know that in *Production of Commodities by Means of Commodities* Sraffa sometimes chooses the wage and at other times profit as the exogenous variable. In the classical theory, the wage is determined by the historical and social wants of the workforce to reproduce itself, and the rate of profit then appears as an endogenous variable. This is the hypothesis that we shall use here.

If the wage is exogenously determined and fixed at the real level $d = (d_1, \ldots, d_k)$, the aim of the primal cannot be the maximisation of c but of g for a given real wage. Hence the following programming, assuming that the wage is 'advanced'

PRIMAL	DUAL
Max g	Min r
$y[B - (1+g)A] - (1+g)yLd \geqq 0$	$p \geqq 0$
$y \geqq 0$	$[B - (1+g)A]p - (1+r)Ldp \leqq 0$
$g \geq 0$	$r \geq 0$

By writing A^* the socio-technological matrix $A + Ld$, the (non-linear) programming writes

PRIMAL	DUAL
Max g	Min r
$y[B - (1+g)A^*] \geqq 0$	$p \geqq 0$
$y \geqq 0$	$[B - (1+g)A^*]p \leqq 0$
$g \geq 0$	$r \geq 0$

We find here von Neumann's model; workers' wages are non-zeros and integrated to the socio-technological matrix A^*.

From the price equations related to the methods actually used, we obtain the price system translating Marx's hypotheses, that is to say, R^* being the solution r

$$[B - (1 + R^*)A^*]p = 0 \qquad Bp = (1 + R^*)A^*p.$$

Note that there is unemployment and consequently the dual price of labour is zero. Further, suffice to apply the same reasoning as the one used in the case when the rate of profit is considered as exogenous to re-interpret the dual programming: indeed, the objective is to find *the lowest rate of profit r such that no activity makes any excess profit.*

Any activity i shows a valuing of inputs and outputs such that

$$(1+r)(a_{i1}^* p_1 + a_{i2}^* p_2) = b_{i1} p1 + b_{i2} p_2$$

We choose to normalise prices by the condition $d_1 p_1 + d_2 p_2 = 1$. By substitution, we obtain the following relation

$$r = \frac{p_1(d_2 b_{i1} - d_1 b_{i2}) + b_{i2}}{p_1(d_2 a_{i1}^* - d_1 a_{i2}^*) + a_{i2}^*} - 1$$

and

$$\frac{dr}{dp_1} = \frac{d_2(b_{i1} a_{i2}^* - b_{i2} a_{i1}^*)}{[p_1(d_2 a_{i1}^* - d_1 a_{i2}^*) + a_{i2}^*]^2}$$

Note that if activity i is specialised in the production of good 1 ($b_{i2} = 0$) relation $r(p_1)$ is increasing since $\frac{dr}{dp_1} > 0$; relation $r(p_1)$ is decreasing if activity i is specialised in the production of good 2 ($b_{i1} = 0$).

If two goods are jointly produced by activity i, relation $r(p_1)$ is increasing or decreasing depending on whether $b_{i1} a_{i2}^* - b_{i2} a_{i1}^*$ is positive or negative.

Owing to the expression of the model

$$(1+r)A^* p \geq Bp$$

the whole part located under $r(p_1)$ must be excluded (see shaded areas on the figures). Further, we have also excluded $p_1 < 0$ and $p_1 > \frac{1}{d_1}$ (which would lead to $p_2 < 0$).

On figure 7.9a activities (α) and (β) are simultaneously used. The rate of profit R and the price p_1 of good 1, solution to the system, appear on the figure.

Price p_2 is then equal to $\bar{p}_2 = \frac{1}{d_2}(1 - d_1 \bar{p}_1)$. Activity ($\gamma$) which is dominated by (α) is not used.

On figure 7.9b the three activities can be simultaneously used. The solution to the problem is given by $(R, \bar{p}_1)$ and price $\bar{p}_2$ is immediately deduced.

The case shown on figure 7.9c can appear in joint production only. Method (γ) dominates the others. The lowest solution rate of profit is R at which

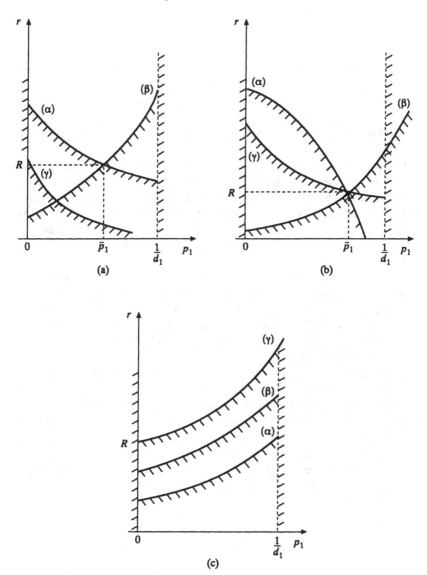

Figure 7.9

$$\bar{p}_1 = 0 \text{ and } \bar{p}_2 = \frac{1}{d_2}$$

We could obtain without any difficulty the case when the three curves are decreasing; good 1 is then the sole economic good.[18]

At the micro-economic level, the choice of techniques lies in von Neumann's rule of profitability; the methods that are not retained are 'non profitable' (von Neumann 1945–6, p. 1), they do not allow the minimisation of production costs.

It appears clearly that in the case of switch in techniques, it is not a misuse of language to speak of maximisation of wage (given r) or of maximisation of profit (at a given real wage). If in simple production such a treatment may be appropriate, it becomes irrelevant in the more general case, that is to say when there is joint production. The most general criterion and always the most relevant is that of the minimisation of costs, with production satisfying demand.

In a way, the idea of a maximum rate of profit in a square system may cause some problems; it is true that at the considered level of wage, the solution to the rate of profit is the highest of those that can be obtained with the available methods of production. And for the methods actually used, it is also the lowest acceptable rate of profit, that which ensures the minimisation of production costs.

It appears also clearly that the choice of the exogenous distributive variable is not without consequences. Assuming that a given rate of profit is exogenous implies that the wage appears as the dual price of labour, which is positive only when the constraint is saturated, when there is full-employment. It may be more interesting to consider the real wage (or the real wages of the different categories of workers) as data. Thus, the corresponding mathematical model is a non-linear programming model, von Neumann's model, while the first case corresponds to a linear programming model.

8   The dynamic evolution

Up to now our analyses have been carried out within a timeless context; we have enhanced the structures of prices, at given r or g, and the corresponding wage rates, on the one hand, and the activity structures and the resulting consumption levels, on the other hand; thus we have dealt with structures and not with change.

We shall first address the dynamic evolution of prices and quantities by assuming constant returns to scale. Then we shall analyse the accumulation process in a more general context with some activities using natural resources, land whose availability is limited thus creating a scarcity constraint. The regulating price of wheat, and more generally of the good produced in increasingly costly conditions, will be fixed by the most costly method of cultivation. The land using that method being first considered as over abundant shall have a zero price and its owner will divert no profit from it. As far as the other lands are concerned, we shall show that their owners divert from them differential rents which are residual: lands and methods of cultivation are closely related and are at the heart of our analysis. Within the same framework, we shall analyse the consequences of the introduction of new techniques or changes in the methods of production.

When the 'land' using the most costly method of cultivation is fully used, the rent phenomenon becomes general; intensive cultivation entails the appearance of positive rents for all natural resources; then the prices of 'wheat' and 'land' (and thus the intensive rent) are determined simultaneously. Therefore, the determination of prices is deeply altered by scarcity.

8.1 Accumulation and distribution with constant returns

Let us recall that in such a situation, production and labour steadily grow at a (yearly) rate g while the prices of dated goods steadily decrease at a (yearly) rate r. The dynamic point of view allows us to better understand the opposition between the hypothesis of 'advanced' wages and that of wages paid *ex post*, that is to say, paid on surplus. Then the normalisation equation of prices can be reinterpreted: the numeraire is not the currency, but the normalisation equation can be interpreted as a money expression of prices. We shall specify how in such a situation inflation may spring from the conjunction of firms' behaviour and the rigidity to a decrease in prices and wages. Finally, we shall ponder on the consequences of the possibility to choose given to consumers, or in other words the consequences of moving from the hypothesis of complementarity of goods to the hypothesis of substitution; we will show that the production price system limits market prices if it does not totally determine them.

Our purpose is thus to specify the dynamic evolution of quantities and prices assuming constant returns to scale until the end of time. The environment remains unchanged: there are no technical improvements the consequences of which will be developed later. But we shall examine the influence of agents' behaviour (firms or workers) on the evolution of prices.

We know that in the case of single product industries with circulating capital,[1] systems of activity levels and prices in a golden rule situation, that is to say with $r = g$, are

$$y = (1 + g)yA + cd \text{ with } yL = 1$$
$$p = (1 + r)Ap + wL \text{ with } dp = 1$$

These are two timeless models, two pictures of economic systems. In both cases, at $r = g$ which is exogenously fixed, structures are defined: the structure of activity levels and a number (c) of baskets of consumption goods (d) resulting from the use of a given quantity of labour (one unit) by the economic system; the structure of prices and wages per worker, when the values of some baskets of commodities are set equal to 'one'.

8.1.1 Growth of quantities

Let us first address the temporal analysis of the activity level system: the quantities produced are $y_t I$ or $y_t B$ depending on whether we are in a context of 'simple' or 'joint' production, y_t being the vector of activities in period t. We assume for the time being that the environment remains unchanged (there are no technical improvements or new methods of production available) and the output is produced in a context of constant returns to scale with an unlimited supply of labour at the offered wage level. There is no scarcity constraint related to natural resources (a problem we shall revert to) and the reserves of labour power are over abundant (we assume that the rhythm of accumulation is less than the natural growth rate of the labour power). This is a case of proportional growth in a situation of underemployment, with all the resources growing by assumption at the same rate g.[2] At each period, growth is limited by the amount or the stock of means of production used; such a stock grows from one period to another at a rate g; thus, the constraint is steadily relaxed at a rate g and the dynamic system writes $y_t I = (1+g)y_{t-1}A + c_t d$ with $y_0 L = 1$. Production ($y_t I$ or $y_t B$) and employment steadily grow at a rate g and thus we have

$$y_t I = (1+g)y_{t-1} I$$
$$y_t L = (1+g)y_{t-1} L$$

Therefore, we have

$$c_t = (1+g)c_{t-1} \text{ and } \frac{c_t}{y_t L} = \frac{c_{t-1}}{y_{t-1}L} = \ldots = \frac{c_0}{y_0 L} = c_0$$

Thus, the relative structure of activity levels remains fixed while production and employment grow steadily owing to the constant rhythm of accumulation g, taken to be given; c_t appears as an indicator of consumer goods production (at time t) which develops steadily at a given g, while the production of consumer goods per unit of labour $c_t/y_t L$ remains at the constant level c_0, in the absence of technical improvements.

8.1.2 The evolution of the price system

As far as the temporal evolution of the price system p_t is concerned, we can write

$$p_t = (1+r)Ap_{t-1} + w_{t-1}L \text{ with } dp_0 = 1$$

or

$$p_t = (1+r)Ap_{t-1} + w_t L \text{ with } dp_0 = 1$$

The first formulation corresponds to the hypothesis of 'advanced' wages made by Marx and the Classical school, while the second refers to Sraffa's hypothesis according to which the wage is paid *post factum*, on surplus.

In both cases we face a problem of intertemporal equilibrium, making it necessary to distinguish goods of the same nature on the basis of the date or moment of their production or consumption. We know that from the relative prices $p_{i,t}$ of the same product available at different dates[3] we can define *an interest rate $r_{i,t}$ which is specific to that product*: the rate $r_{i,t}$ is thus 'the interest rate provided for in a contract concerning the lending of one unit of product i between dates t and $t+1$. With such a definition of the specific interest rate, we have $p_{i,t+1} = \dfrac{1}{1+r_{i,t}} p_{i,t}$

'Generally', adds Malinvaud (1982), 'the interest rates specific to one period and several goods do not coincide. In order to make them coincide, discounted prices should be such that the ratios $p_{i,t+1}/p_{i,t}$ have the same value for all the products. But there is no reason for such a situation to happen.'

Later, the author shows 'in what sense relative prices p_i and the interest rate r are defined in a unique way with respect to all programming corresponding to a stationary regime'.[4] Such a proposition can easily be applied to the case of proportional growth.

Thus, with proportional growth (that is, when the growth rate g is the same for all the products) we have $r_{i,t} = r = g$ $\forall i$ $\forall t$ and

$$p_{i,t+1} = \frac{1}{1+r} p_{i,t} \forall t$$

Thus, the dated prices of the different goods steadily *decrease* as time goes by at a yearly rhythm that is identical to the rate of profit or the rate of growth.

The excess profit made in period t by the ith activity must be zero, and with the goods produced appearing one period after those used, this writes

$$p_{i,t+1} - a_i.p_t - l_i w_t = 0$$
$$\frac{1}{1+r} p_{i,t} - a_i.p_t - l_i w_t = 0$$

Hence the usual notation of production prices under the hypothesis of 'advanced' wages

$$p_{i,t} = (1+r)(a_i p_t + l_i w_t)$$

If the wage is paid '*post factum*', we have

$$p_{i,t+1} - a_i p_t - l_i w_{t+1} = 0$$
$$\frac{1}{1+r} p_{i,t} - a_i.p_t - l_i \frac{w_t}{1+r} = 0$$

that is $p_{i,t} = (1+r)a_i.p_t + l_i w_t$

8.1.3 The numeraire and the money expression of prices

Regarding the dynamic evolution of prices, we may notice that the normalisation condition $dp_0 = 1$ is given once and for all and it is on the basis of that normalisation condition that the steady decrease in each dated price is assessed. If we had $dp_0 = dp_1 = dp_2 = ... = dp_t = $ cst, in a steady regime the structure of prices would have been constant, with absolute prices remaining constant.

But the condition is $dp_0 = 1$ with $dp_t \neq 1$ and $t \neq 0$. Hence the (downward) evolution of absolute prices, while relative prices, the structure of prices, remain constant. In fact the important condition is $up_0 = \text{cst} = D$, whatever $u \geq 0$; it is only for convenience's sake that we have set $u = d$ and the constant equal to unity.

Thus the numeraire is not the currency and the condition $up_0 = D$ is nothing but the money expression of prices at $t = 0$. Here the currency is not a commodity; the conditions of money creation are not contemplated in the model which however is not a real model. Prices are expressed in terms of the currency by the previous condition (and we may change from the monetary economy to the real economy, from absolute prices to relative prices by normalising prices differently). As for the creation of money, which is not analysed here, we assume it is endogenous.

8.1.4 Mark-up, rigidity to decrease and inflation

The previous developments lie on a very strong and peculiar hypothesis, that of 'endless tranquillity', of the permanent regime. The considered price system has always been existing and always will be, the rate of profit adopted is the equilibrium rate of profit and the whole set replaces itself over periods. However, the actual evolution of prices seems to be quite different from what was described in theory: firms may not know the equilibrium rate of profit, prices do not decrease at each period.

In what follows we will show that some inflationary evolutions may be explained while keeping the framework of constant returns (or even by totally ignoring the evolution of quantities); a fortiori, the appearance of diminishing returns, the limited endowments in natural resources, the evolution of the quantities produced reinforce the trends that we shall emphasise, notably using Nikaido and Koyabashi's (1978) work, as well as those due to F. Catz and J. Laganier (1982 and 1984) and Y. Fujimori (1982).

In order to do so, let us first specify the formalisation that we shall use in the present chapter. Time is discretely divided into periods $t = 0, 1, \ldots$; prices and wages at each period are denoted by p_t and w_t and are exogenously initialised by the data of p_0 and w_0. Prices are determined by the capitalists on the basis of mark-up first and then under the hypothesis of price rigidity.

Capitalists' mark-up can be formalised as follows

$$p_{t+1} = (1 + \bar{r})Ap_t + LW_t$$

$\bar{r}$ is the rate of profit demanded by firms. This equation shows that capitalists set the price of period $t+1$ on the basis of the costs recorded in period t and the demanded rate of profit $\bar{r}$.[5] Further, we assume that there are m categories of workers (W_t is thus a vector $(m \times 1)$ and L is a matrix $(k \times m)$) and that they demand a wage which maintains their purchasing power. With D standing for the matrix of socially recognised consumption wants, we have $W_{t+1} = Dp_t$. It is worth noting that such a formulation does not necessarily imply that wages are totally consumed: workers put forward claims to maintain their purchasing power but not to consume.

The rigidity of prices and wages is formalised in system I; firms and workers are respectively opposed to any decrease in prices and wages

$$\text{(I)} \quad \begin{cases} p_{t+1} = \text{Max} \left[(1+\bar{r})Ap_t + LW_t, p_t \right] \\ W_{t+1} = \text{Max} \left[Dp_t, W_t \right] \end{cases}$$

We may also consider systems II or III, respectively, taking into account the rigidity of prices and wages only.

$$\text{(II)} \quad \begin{cases} p_{t+1} = \text{Max} \left[(1+\bar{r})Ap_t + LW_t, p_t \right] \\ W_{t+1} = Dp_t \end{cases}$$

$$\text{(III)} \quad \begin{cases} p_{t+1} = (1+\bar{r})Ap_t + LW_t \\ W_{t+1} = \text{Max} \left[Dp_t, W_t \right] \end{cases}$$

We may also contemplate the existence of partial rigidity for some prices and some wages. In fact, the general logic of the model can be described using system I which is the simplest[6] and the one we shall limit ourselves to (changing to the hypothesis of advanced wage is quite easy to do). Let r be the rate of profit, which is the solution to the intertemporal model.

$$\begin{cases} p = (1+r)Ap + Lw \\ W = Dp \\ up = 1 \end{cases}$$

Let us now consider three cases in which the equilibrium rate of profit r and the demanded rate of profit $\bar{r}$ are compared:

1st case
$\bar{r} = r$: the demanded rate of profit equals the equilibrium rate of profit.

Then, we can show that system (p_t, W_t) converges towards the limit system (p^*, W^*) which has the following characteristics:
(a) prices and wages adjust in relative values towards production prices and the wages of the reference timeless model;[7]

(b) absolute prices stabilise at a level determined by the initial conditions (p_0, W_0). System I which includes rigidities does not allow any decrease in prices or wages, with initialisation (p_0, W_0) playing in a way the role of a ratchet. Indeed, (p_0, W_0) may be interpreted as a system of prices and wages springing from a shock on a vector (p_{-1}, W_{-1}) which was an equilibrium price system. Inflation so to speak adjusts to the greatest initial shock (see Catz and Laganier 1984) and restores the equilibrium of the rate of profit as in the timeless system; of course this implies that the reasons for the shock are temporary and will not happen again. If they do happen again, there will be another propagation.

2nd case
$\bar{r} < r$: the demanded rate of profit is less than the equilibrium rate of profit.

System (p_t, W_t) converges towards system (p^*, W^*) which does not ensure the adjustment of the rate of profit and therefore is not a production price system. All the industries and categories of workers are provided with the necessary minimum ($\bar{r}$ for every industry or activity, dp^* for every category of workers), with some industries or some categories of workers still enjoying the additional remuneration steming from the initial shock.

There is no conflict in the aggregate distribution; inflation is neither general nor permanent; it allows a partial redistribution of the profits or wages springing from the initial shock.

3rd case
$\bar{r} > r$: the demanded rate of profit is greater than the equilibrium rate of profit. There is a conflict in the aggregate distribution between capitalists and workers. We can show then that within the framework retained for system I, all prices increase: whatever the initial structure (p_0, W_0) there is a period of time from which all the prices and wages tend towards infinity; inflation is general with a general increase in prices and wages.

Consequently, the price and wage setting process from one period to another is simplified; since all prices and wages at a given period are greater than the previous period's, system I writes

$$(\mathrm{I}') \quad \begin{cases} p_{t+1} = (1+\bar{r})Ap_t + LW_t \\ \overline{W_{t+1} = Dp_t} \end{cases}$$

From which we obtain, by setting

$$\bar{A} = \begin{bmatrix} (1+\bar{r})A & L \\ D & D \end{bmatrix} \quad \text{and } \bar{p}_t = \begin{bmatrix} p_t \\ W_t \end{bmatrix}$$

(I") $\bar{p}_{t+1} = \bar{A}\ \bar{p}_t$

Relation $\bar{p}_{t+1} = \bar{A}\ \bar{p}_t$ has two consequences:

the structure of prices $\bar{p}_t$ converges towards the structure of eigenvector $\bar{p}$ on the right of $\bar{A}$, corresponding to the dominant eigenvalue $\bar{a}$ defined by

$$\bar{A}\ \bar{p} = \bar{a}\ \bar{p}$$

where $\bar{a} > 1$ since $\bar{r} \geq r$

the levels of prices and wages all tend towards $+\infty$ for, by iteration, we obtain

$$\bar{p}_t = \bar{A}^t\ \bar{p}_0$$

where matrix $\bar{A}$ has a dominant eigenvalue $\bar{a} > 1$.

This is thus an inflationary situation without distortions in relative prices. The levels of prices and wages increase at each stage at a rate $i = \bar{a} - 1$. The demanded rate of profit $\bar{r}$ is thus decreased by the value of the inflation rate i and everything goes as if the rate of profit r' was included between r and $\bar{r}$.

The result according to which there is a structure convergence of relative prices in spite of the increase in their absolute levels is of course questioned if economic agents' behaviour becomes unstable. If for instance, during the inflationary process, some industries or activities increased their desired margin or profit rate.

Remark

The previous results hold in system (II) where only prices are rigid. On the other hand, in system (III), where rigidity only applies to a decrease in wages, a difference appears when $\bar{r} > r$ (see Catz and Laganier, 1984): the structure convergence is not necessarily insured any more.

8.1.5 Intertemporal general equilibrium and production prices

A number of recent works have tried to link the intertemporal general equilibrium theory and the production price theory. According to F. Hahn (1982), production prices are only a peculiar aspect of prices in an intertemporal general equilibrium when the parameters of the model are chosen in a specific way. Contrary to Hahn, who chose for his analysis a general equilibrium model with finite horizon, Dumenil and Levy (1983) believe that an infinite horizon is more appropriate: when time tends towards infinity, there exists an equilibrium price system which converges towards a vector of production prices, independently of the economic parameters' values: utility function, initial stock. Such propositions have been demonstrated within a very simplified economy by Dana and Levy (1984) then within a more general framework by Dana, Florenzano, Le Van and Levy (1984). The authors consider an economy with any (finite) number of consumers. Producers have at their disposal a set of simple methods of production with a possible substitution of inputs and constant returns to scale. It is also assumed that the socio-technological conditions remain unchanged as time goes by. They notably show that:

'We can obtain two main results: Under standard assumptions [the] intertemporal general equilibrium model has an equilibrium whose prices allow at each period a uniform maximum profit rate for every producer.
    Recall that production prices are stationary prices which allow a maximum profit rate uniform for every producer; when such a price system exists, the sequence of the undiscounted prices of the general equilibrium converges towards the production prices system. Then the maximum profit rate calculated at each period with undiscounted prices is uniform and converges towards the stationary maximum profit rate associated with the production prices. (Dana and Levy 1984, p. 1)

8.1.6 Production prices and consumers' choices

The analyses dealing with production prices usually assume, at least when the problem is addressed, that the structure of final demand is fixed. Schefold (1985b, pp. 15 and 46) explains and supports such an hypothesis by using different arguments, the most important being the existence of a hierarchy of wants, different consumption structures due to the existence of different social classes or groups, habits and social conventions. We may add that if we are to study permanent regimes, the assumption is quite normal or tempting. In a nutshell, we are dealing with wants and not preferences.

Then what kind of problems can the introduction of a preference function with a possible substitution of goods cause?[8]

We shall limit our analysis to a simple model with two goods, and the utility function having the usual properties. The consequences of the new assumption may be different depending on what type of model is retained.

Under simple production, case A (figure 8.1), and more generally when economic goods are g-separately reproducible, the possibility of choosing the consumption structure as a function of the prices of goods does not change anything in the way the problem is solved. By assuming that the efficient system is determined (at a given $r = g$) by activities (i) and (j), the representative consumer maximises his utility at the tangency point of one of the indifference curves and the curve of transformation between goods, which is nothing but the curve of consumption possibilities $M_i(g) - M_j(g)$. At this point, the ratio of both goods' marginal utilities equals the inverse of

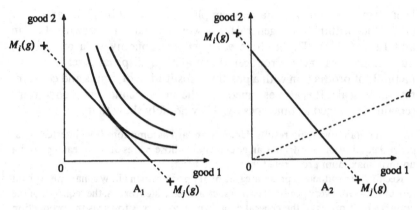

Figure 8.1a   Figure 8.1b

their price ratio; the latter, whether it is possible to choose the consumption structure as a function of prices or not, is determined by the absolute value of the consumption possibilities' slope (in A_1 and A_2). It is therefore on the basis of the so-called production price system that consumers make their choice. Thus, the production system is always square (subject to exceptions), and prices are identical whatever the assumption made about the utility function: it does not matter for the consumer whether goods are complements or substitutes. Obviously, in both cases there is no reason for the consumer's choice to be the same and the activity and production structures will be different. But the possibility consumers have to alter the consumption structure has no consequences whatsoever on the equilibrium price or the choice of techniques; this is due to the non-substitution theorem.

If the two goods are not g-separately reproducible, then distinctions are to be made. If the utility function is such that one of the indifference curves is tangent to one of the facets of the efficiency frontier (see figure 8.2) we come to the same conclusion as previously: the production system is (normally) square, and equilibrium prices are the traditional production prices. Whether the utility function lies on the assumption of complementarity or substitution of goods has no importance either.

However, other possibilities have to be contemplated. In case C_1 (figure 8.3), the indifference curve does not meet a facet but a peak of the efficiency frontier. Then, equilibrium prices are not determined by the structure of production prices any more, but fixed by the market (and equal to the slope of the indifference curve at the point where it meets the peak of the frontier). It is worth noting that market prices denoted by p_1 and p_2 are then limited by the reproduction conditions of the two goods in both alternative systems

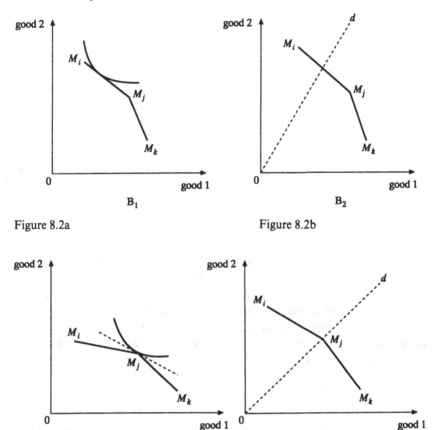

Figure 8.2a   Figure 8.2b

Figure 8.3a   Figure 8.3b

using a common method M_j. Indeed, to the right and left of M_j, we have two production price systems the structures of which are respectively given by the slopes of lines $M_j M_i$ and $M_k M_j$, (in absolute values).

Clearly, we have

$$\left(\frac{p_1}{p_2}\right)_{\text{left}} < \frac{u_2'}{u_1'} = \frac{p_1}{p_2} < \left(\frac{p_1}{p_2}\right)_{\text{right}}$$

Such indetermination also shows in C_2 where the line representing the structure of consumption (taken to be fixed here) coincides with one edge of the cone (here, with OM_j). In both cases the production system is not square any more; indetermination which is obvious in the case of fixed consumption structure (C_2) is relaxed by consumers' preferences (C_1). Note

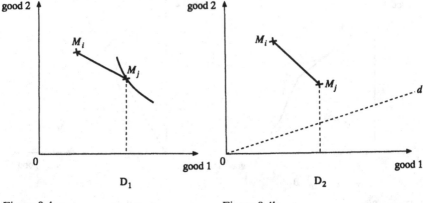

Figure 8.4a   Figure 8.4b

that while this case is quite exceptional in the case of complementarity of goods, it is quite common in the case of substitution.

Finally, case D (figure 8.4) can be considered as a variant of the previous case. In the complementarity hypothesis (D_2) good 2 is produced in excess and has a zero price; the production price system only applies to the economic good. In the 'neo-classical' case (D_1) both goods are economic goods and market prices p_1 and p_2 are then constrained by

$$\left(\frac{p_1}{p_2}\right)_{\text{left}} < \frac{u_2'}{u_1'} = \frac{p_1}{p_2} < \frac{p_1}{p_2} = +\infty \text{ since } p_2 = 0$$

Thus, the possibility of modifying the structure of consumption considerably reduces the importance of free goods since low prices often lead to a higher demand for the good in question. Equilibrium prices are then market prices the structure of which is twice limited; first by the limit hypothesis holding that one of the goods is available at zero price; second, by the structure of production prices stemming from the simultaneous use of the two methods to produce the two goods; a decrease in prices below that limit would imply that method M_j will be abandoned and method M_i will be the only one used owing to a significant change in consumers' preferences and thus in the shape of the indifference curve. The existence of 'square' systems is here quite exceptional.

In the more common case where both goods are commodities, whatever the assumption made on the utility function, we have previously seen (case C) that the production systems were not always square; equilibrium prices are then market prices which are limited, so to speak, by the structures of production prices. Therefore, generally, production price systems limit market prices if they do not determine them totally; such a strict determination is more particularly ensured when the goods in question are g-separately reproducible (see case A).

Note

Consider a decomposable model where a non-basic good enters its own production in great proportions (Sraffa's beans example). Such a non-basic good is a blocking good whose price tends towards infinity when the rate of profit r prevailing in the economy tends towards the maximum rate of profit R of the model. Therefore, the fixed-demand-structure hypothesis does not hold when one of the goods is a blocking good and when the rate of profit r approaches R.

8.2 Accumulation and increasing difficulties to produce

In the accumulation regime that we have just described, the economic system develops steadily (hence the use of the term 'permanent regime'), the means of production used as capital steadily increase at a rate g as well as the labour-power used. The system is not constrained, and it produces with constant returns all the means of production that it may need and freely uses the unlimited labour supply at the current rate.

Let us now assume that some activities use natural resources, 'lands', whose quantity or available surface is limited. As a consequence, the permanent regime of accumulation will face scarcity constraints at certain dates; then production will have diminishing returns.

The regulating price of wheat, and more generally of the good produced in increasingly costly conditions, will be fixed on the basis of the less profitable cultivation method, the one used on the land cultivated to produce additional quantities of wheat and satisfy demand. By assumption, that land is not fully used;[9] it is over abundant and available at zero price; thus land owners do not retrieve any rent from it. As far as the other land is concerned, we shall show that the differential rents provided by such land are residual: they are indeed determined once the wage and the production prices of all the commodities are known (at a given r).

It is worth noting in the following developments, that land and the cultivation method are closely related. Land has no qualities per se: the nature of one piece is not better than another; to produce, land must be cultivated. The production process or the cultivation method, does not limit itself to producing wheat; it gives value to land and, as we shall see, allows its reproduction. Reasoning in terms of joint production will allow us to emphasise that essential element, namely the joint production of wheat and land by means of inputs, intermediate consumptions (fertiliser, seed).

Thus, at least in a way, land has no natural qualities; or more precisely it is dependent on the method of cultivation used. Of course, we may assume that identical methods of cultivation are applied on different land: this is a specific case that we shall examine later on. In what follows, it is generally assumed that there is no reason for the methods used on any land to be identical.

8.2.1 Land and joint production

By 'land' we mean all natural resources and means of production employed in production but not themselves produced, allowing in some conditions to provide the owner with a specific income that we shall call 'rent'.[10]

Let us assume for the time being that land is all of the same quality and it is not altered by use; notations are then highly simplified. Consider the ith process: it uses produced and reproducible means of production (represented by the row-vector a_i), a certain quantity of direct labour l_i, and a given quantity of t_i (surface area) of natural resources, land. Then we obtain a quantity b_{ij} of the jth good (the wheat crop) and we retrieve the land used without it disappearing in the process.

This is a very specific case of joint production: we assume that (a) only one type of crop is obtained on that land (wheat *or* carrots but *not* wheat *and* carrots, which rules out the traditional meaning of joint production); (b) land is not altered by the production process: it is the same product whose price per unit (acre for instance) is denoted by p_T.

In such conditions, and assuming that the wage w is paid on surplus[11] and that the rate of profit applies to the money spent by the entrepreneur to buy produced or non-produced means of production, the equation characteristic of the ith process writes

$$(1+r)(a_ip + t_ip_T) + wl_i = b_{ij}p_j + t_ip_T \tag{1}$$

After rearranging the equation and by applying the same procedure as the one used in chapter 7 about machines, we obtain

$$(1+r)t_ip_T - t_ip_T = b_{ij}p_j - (1+r)a_ip - wl_i = F_i(r)$$

By writing $F_i(r)$ the net return in final good of the ith process, we have

$$rt_ip_T = F_i(r) \Rightarrow p_T = \frac{F_i(r)}{rt_i} \tag{2}$$

If we assume that, owing to the method of cultivation used, the 'natural' properties of land do not change as time goes by, the net return of the process in question is constant (at a given r); by writing $\rho = \rho(r)$, the return or rent per acre, we have

$$p_T = \frac{\rho}{r} \qquad\qquad (3)$$

Therefore, land appears as a means of production which is not produced and its price can be considered as determined by the capitalisation of the rent at the going rate. Under the previous assumptions, every acre yields ρ a year; the value of one acre is then the sum of the values of discounted net returns over an infinity of periods

$$p_T = \frac{\rho}{1+r} + \frac{\rho}{(1+r)^2} + \cdots \frac{\rho}{(1+r)^n} \rightarrow \frac{\rho}{r} \text{ when } n \rightarrow +\infty$$

Equation (1), showing the price of land, can transform into equation (4) which is equivalent and shows the rent; indeed, from (1) we obtain

$$(1+r)a_ip + t_ip_T + rt_ip_T + wl_i = b_{ij}p_j + t_ip_T$$

And by using (3) and simplifying, we obtain

$$(1+r)a_ip + \rho t_i + wl_i = b_{ij}p_j \qquad\qquad (4)$$

Thus formulations (1) and (4) are equivalent: the first emphasises the production aspect, the second emphasises the distribution aspect. Underlying the equivalence is necessary to make the comparison between economists' and agronomists' approaches easier. For most of the English classics of the nineteenth century, land was an indestructible and reproducible factor of production: Ricardo speaks of 'the original and indestructible powers of the soil' (*Principles* 1984, chapter II, p. 33). While for agronomists, fertility is produced; in 1855, an agronomist noted that 'from one improvement to another, arable land is constructed just as a furnace would be'.[12] For agronomists, it is quite clear that there is 'production, destruction, and reproduction of land's productive capacity' (Barthélemy 1982, p. 63)

As a matter of fact some economists supported that position. Among them Anderson, who certainly was before Ricardo and West, the genuine founder of the theory of rent,[13] wrote in 1777 that soils of the least fertile class could be sufficiently improved through cultivation to move to the superior class. Marx presents Anderson's theses as follows:

Anderson . . . explained the difference between land which pays rent and that which does not, or between lands which pay varying rents, by the *relatively* low fertility of the land which bears *no* rent or a *smaller* rent compared with that which bears a rent or a greater rent. But he stated expressly that these degrees of relative productivity of *different* types of land, i.e., also the relative low productivity of the worse types of land compared with the better, had absolutely nothing to do with the *absolute* productivity of agriculture. *On the contrary*, he stressed not only that the absolute productivity of *all* types of land could be constantly improved and must be improved with the progress in population, but he went further and asserted that the *differences* in *productivity* of various types of land can be progressively *reduced*. (*Theories of Surplus Value, Collected Works*, vol. 32, p. 346)

But equation (4) clearly emphasises that fertiliser, labour and the whole set of inputs used produce not only wheat but also land. It has also been underlined that by a simplified assumption, land is not altered by the production process. This does mean that the cultivation method used is such that it reproduces land as it was before. (We shall see later on how the treatment can be generalised and contemplate methods of production with a change in the quality of land.) Thus, obviously land appears as a good that is not produced (this is its main characteristic) but also as a good that can be damaged and consequently partly reproducible.

As for any other good, the rule of free goods also applies to land: only goods whose supply does not exceed wants can have a positive price. If the whole surface area of land is not fully used, its price will be zero as well as the rent perceived by its owner(s). Only fully used land may have a positive price and thus provide their owners with a positive rent. Let us now specify the determination of that rent (and thus the price of land).

8.2.2 *Fertility order and differential rent*

If up to now we have assumed that only one plot of land produced wheat, we shall now assume that there are h plots available for that purpose and that land is not used in the rest of the production system. Moreover, to simplify the presentation, let us assume that only two goods are produced: iron and wheat. There is only one activity producing iron, which is the sole basic good: by using one unit of labour and a_{11} of iron, we obtain a certain quantity of iron that we set equal to unity. To produce wheat there are h methods of production available (one per plot); on the ith, by using one unit of labour,[14] a_{b1}^i of iron and a_{bb}^i of wheat on an area t^i, we obtain an output of wheat b^i.

In a golden rule situation $(r=g)$, $\pi_i = (b^i - (1+g)a_{bb}^i)/t^i$ represents the net g-surplus per acre of the ith method, or in short the net g-return (of the method). The available area of each plot written T_i being by assumption known, we can distinguish two cases:

1st case
The final demand for wheat is low: $D_b < \min(\pi_i T_i)$.

It stems from this that, taking into account the cultivation methods, the demand for wheat can be satisfied by any one of the plots. At $r=g$ given, and owing to the cost minimisation rule, demand can be satisfied by using the least expensive method. By writing the normalisation condition $p_1 = 1$, and if the least expensive method of production of wheat is the eth, the complete production system then writes

$$\begin{cases} (1+r)a_{11} + w = 1 \\ (1+r)(a_{b1}^e + a_{bb}^e p_b) + w + \rho t^e = b^e p_b \end{cases}$$

Then there is only one method of production of wheat and since, by assumption, the land on which that method is applied is not fully used, its price and the rent springing from it are zeros, $\rho_e = 0$; hence the following system

$$\begin{cases} (1+r)a_{11} + w = 1 \\ (1+r)(a_{b1}^e + a_{bb}^e p_b) + w = b^e p_b \end{cases}$$

This notation does not mean that wheat does not use land, but that the *rent* of the overabundant resource perceived by the landlord is *zero*. As a consequence, the price of wheat is fixed by the cultivation conditions of the eth cultivation method, that is to say

$$p_b^e = \frac{(1+r)a_{b1}^e + 1 - (1+r)a_{11}}{b^e - (1+r)a_{bb}^e}$$

Thus, let us assume that the demand for wheat is low (in the sense defined above); or the basis of the production cost minimising condition, we can now determine which is the only cultivated land. Then a *fertility order* is defined ordering the cultivation of land. *The concept of fertility does not appear as a natural property, but as a purely agronomic one.*

The fertility order is not unchanging natural data; it depends first on the method of production used since the choice of land, the fertility order, is defined on the basis of the minimisation of costs, and therefore uses the same logic as the one used in the choice of techniques (chapter 7). But for this reason, and assuming that the state of the technique remains unchanged, that there are no technical improvements, *the fertility order depends on distribution.*[15]

This is quite easy to understand: indeed, the production of wheat on each plot requires intermediate consumption and uses direct labour. At different levels of distribution, the production prices of the various goods are of course altered. It is therefore quite possible that, at a given value of the rate of profit, it becomes more profitable to cultivate land (e), while at another value of r, it would be more profitable to cultivate land (f) or (d). Note that such a modification[16] happens at a given level of final demand for wheat. Changes in the latter present another problem that we shall now address.

2nd case

Demand for wheat cannot be satisfied by the first cultivated land: $D_b > \min \pi_i T_i$, i.e., since according to our assumption land (e) appeared as the 'best', the 'most fertile', we have $\cdot D_b > \pi_e T_e$. Land (e) is thus totally used: it will therefore have a positive price and its owners will perceive a rent, the level of which will be specified.

Thus, to satisfy demand, it is necessary to cultivate at least another plot of land which will have to be chosen among the $(h-1)$ plots still available; here again the choice will be based on the minimisation of costs, which will lead to land (f). For simplicity's sake, we shall temporarily assume that only one part of land (f) needs to be cultivated to satisfy demand, while land (e) is fully used.

Wheat is thus produced on two plots of land, two methods of cultivation. Then the production system writes

$$\begin{cases} (1+r)a_{11} & +w & =1 \\ (1+r)(a_{b1}^e + a_{bb}^e p_b) + w + \rho^e t^e = b^e p_b \\ (1+r)(a_{b1}^f + a_{bb}^f p_b) + w + \rho^f t^f = b^f p_b \end{cases}$$

Since the fth land is not fully used, we have, by the rule of free goods

$$\begin{cases} (1+r)a_{11} & +w & =1 \\ (1+r)(a_{b1}^e + a_{bb}^e p_b) + w + \rho^e t^e = b^e p_b \\ (1+r)(a_{b1}^f + a_{bb}^f p_b) + w & = b^f p_b \end{cases}$$

The *marginal land* is the land that is not fully used and which is therefore rentless: it is here land (f). It forms with the 'industrial' sector of the first $(k-1)$ equations the system which allows the calculation of, at a given rate of profit r exogenously given, the wage and production prices of the whole system, and more particularly the price of wheat. The price of wheat is here denoted by p_b^f, since it is fixed on the basis of the most expensive production conditions.

The differential rent perceived by the owner of the most fertile land is obtained by using the values of wage and production prices in the equation corresponding to that land, and since it is land (e), we have

$$b^e p_b^f = (1+r)(a_{b1}^e + a_{bb}^e p_b^f) + 1 - (1+r) + a_{11} + \rho^e t^e$$

$$p_b^f = \frac{(1+r)a_{b1}^e + 1 - (1+r) + a_{11}}{b^e - (1+r)a_{bb}^e} + \frac{\rho^e t^e}{b^e - (1+r)a_{bb}^e}$$

And, owing to the previous definitions of the net g-return π^e and p_b^e

$$p_b^f = p_b^e + \frac{\rho_e}{\pi_e} \Rightarrow \rho^e = \pi_e(p_b^f - p_b^e)$$

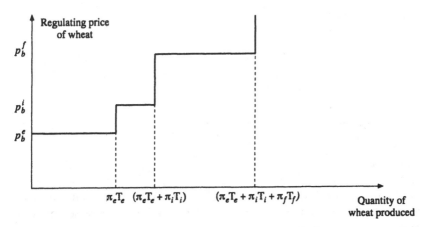

Figure 8.5

The differential rent thus emerges from the difference between the production conditions on the marginal land and the land in question. It is clear that the level of rent depends on distribution.

Generalisation

Let us assume that the demand for wheat has increased, and, to meet wants, a greater number of land (g) among the (h) available, had to be taken under cultivation. The previous demonstration can be specified and generalised; let p_f^i be the differential rent per acre for the ith land when the marginal land is the fth, p_b^f being the production price of wheat on the marginal land, p_b^i being the production price of wheat when the marginal land is the ith, and π_i the net g-return of the ith land, we have

$$p_f^i = \pi_i(p_b^f - p_b^i) \text{ for } i = 1, 2, \ldots, g \leq h \text{ with } \rho_i^i = 0$$

Therefore, *the rent yielded by the land* used to cultivate wheat depends, at r given, *on its production conditions* (more precisely on p_b^i and π_i) and the *marginal land's* (where the 'regulating price' p_b^f is fixed) (see figure 8.5).

In the absence of technical progress, thus assuming that the cultivation methods are given, and no changes or innovations are introduced, the accumulation process which develops at a rhythm g, taken to be exogenous and constant, will necessarily face the exhaustion of natural resources or scarcity of fertile land at the end of a certain number of periods (owing to the cultivation methods). Even if every method, each production process, has been assumed to have constant returns to scale, the increase in demand, the development of accumulation, explain the appearance of diminishing returns; to satisfy demand (at a given $r = g$) producers have to start inferior

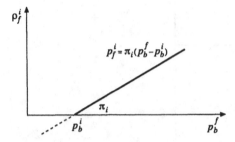

Figure 8.6

production processes, to cultivate less 'fertile' land. As a result the 'best' land yields differential rents (relative), prices of wheat increase and at a given r, wages decrease.

8.2.3 Fertility order and profitability order

The most profitable plots are obviously those yielding the highest rent per acre. The most fertile are the first that have been taken under cultivation (owing to the cultivation methods and the going rate of profit).

It is clear that when there are only two plots, the most profitable is the one which has been cultivated the first. Thus, a rent is yielded by the land which is both the most profitable *and* the most fertile; the marginal land, which is the second taken under cultivation, is rentless.

Such an equivalence of the fertility order and the profitability order always exists in the simple case with two plots being cultivated. It does not hold when more than two are cultivated.

To analyse the problem, let us revert to the formula of the differential rent given previously, illustrated by figure 8.6.

$$\rho i_f = \pi_i (p_b^f - p_b^i)$$

The differential rent per acre is an increasing function of the regulating price of wheat; the relation is linear. The line which links the level of the rent to the regulating price of wheat crosses point $(p_b^i, 0)$ and has a slope π_i.

Let us now assume that there are four plots with limited surface areas on which wheat can be grown at different production prices (at a given $r = g$). We can thus determine four linear relations between the differential rents and the regulating price of wheat (one per method) and represent them on the same diagram.

In the first example, the most fertile land, the first to be cultivated is land n°2 which, owing to the methods of cultivation used and the rate of profit, allows to produce wheat at the lowest cost. If demand increases, the same criterion – the minimisation of production costs on all the land not yet cultivated – will lead to successively taking under cultivation land n°1 then land n°3 and finally land n°4. Thus, the fertility order is defined as the order of cultivation of land based on the cost minimisation criterion (at a given $r = g$) owing to the methods of cultivation used. Here we have

$$p_b^2 < p_b^1 < p_b^3 < p_b^4$$

How does the fertility order evolve? If demand is low and only needs land n°2 to be satisfied, the regulating price of wheat amounts to p_b^2 and of course no differential rent is yielded. When demand has increased enough to require the use of land n°1, the regulating price of wheat climbs to p_b^1 and land n°2 yields a rent ρ_1^2 which reads on the diagram just at the vertical of p_b^1 located on the horizontal axis. The most profitable land (the only profitable land in this case) is land n°2 which was the first cultivated; here the fertility order coincides with the profitability order.

When demand increases again and requires the use of land n°3, the regulating price of wheat also increases ($p_b^3 > p_b^1$) and land n°1 is differential rent bearing; here we have $\rho_3^2 > \rho_3^1$. The profitability order here again coincides with the fertility order: $p_b^2 < p_b^1$. As for land n°3, which is the last to be cultivated, it is also the least profitable since it is zero rent bearing.

It is when the demand for wheat requires the use of land n°4 that a paradox appears in the example contemplated. Indeed, when the regulating price of wheat increases again and moves to p_b^4, the profitability order of the first two plots of land differs from their fertility order. We have indeed

$$\rho_4^1 > \rho_4^2 > r_4^3 > \rho_4^4 = 0$$

(see figure 8.7).

The paradox is explained in the mere formula of the determination of the differential rent; recall that at a given r, we have

$$\rho_f^i = \pi_i(p_b^f - p_b^i) \quad \forall i$$

The profitability order is therefore *determined* by the order of the ρ_i^fs and thus, at a given p_b^1 (the rate of profit of the marginal land is taken to be given) *simultaneously by the production price of wheat* (p_b^1) *and the net g-return per acre* (π_i) on each piece of land considered. As for *the fertility order* it is *determined only on the basis of the production price of wheat* (p_b^1) which has to be minimised, while the return per acre is not taken into account at this stage.

Several remarks will complete the analysis:
(a) *the fertility order always coincides with the profitability order for the marginal land*; the last plot taken under cultivation, which conse-

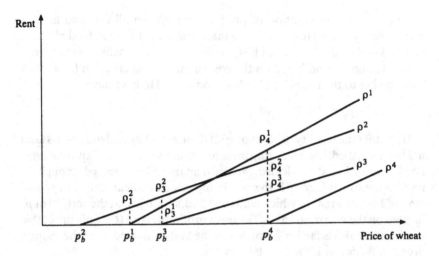

Figure 8.7

quently is the least fertile, is necessarily the least profitable since it yields a zero rent, as by assumption, the marginal land is not fully used

$$p_b^f = p_b^i \Rightarrow \rho^i = 0$$

(b) *The fertility order also coincides with the profitability order when,* as already said, *only two plots are used.*

(c) *The profitability order depends on the last land taken under cultivation* since the differential rent of land depends on the regulating price of wheat p_b^f, which is a function of the production conditions on the marginal land.

Thus, if the extension of cultivation is altered, the differential rents yielded by the various plots will also change and this might disrupt the profitability order. In the example contemplated above we wrote

$$\rho_4^1 > \rho_4^2$$

while we had

$$\rho_3^2 > \rho_3^1$$

Thus, the differential rent yielded by land n°2 is higher than the one yielded by land n°1 when the marginal land is n°3. The profitability order is reversed when land n°4 is taken under cultivation. Then, *the profitability order does depend on the extension of cultivation.*

(d) Finally, it goes without saying that *the fertility and profitability orders could be totally different at other levels of the rate of profit.*

8.2.4 Different returns per acre but identical unit costs

In the previous developments, the differential rents were due to the cultivation methods rather than strictly rents yielded by natural resources or land. The fertility order, the cultivation of land, was determined by the comparison of production costs. The differential rent emerged from the difference between production costs. The rents were as much or even more due to the method used than to the land itself.

To clarify the problem, let us now contemplate a specific case where the same methods of cultivation are used on different plots with the unit production cost being the same for all of them at the considered rate of profit; in such a limit case, the different methods of production only differ in that they result in different yields per acre. In a way, we have here 'purely land rents', and, in this connection, two cases have to be distinguished:

1st case

All the methods of production used have, at the considered rate of profit, *identical production prices*, i.e., $p_b^i(r) = \text{cst} \, \forall i$. In these conditions, it is clear that no land can be preferred to another one since the production costs of wheat are the same (even though the yields per acre are different). Whatever the demand for wheat (provided it does not require the use of all the land available[17]), none of the plots of land may yield differential rents; *all the plots are marginal, and rentless*.

2nd case

Among the methods used on the various plots, *only n of them have identical production costs* (with $n < h$).

We have to distinguish:

(a) If the n methods of production have the lowest costs of production, the n plots simultaneously yield a zero rent when the demand for wheat requires the cultivation of an area that is less than the n plots.

(b) If the n methods of production are not (or any more) those which determine the regulating price, the differential rents perceived by the landlords are not equal, but proportional to the yields per acre.

Let $n = 2$ (this can be easily generalised to any n); if the two methods of cultivation are the ith and the jth, at the considered rate of profit, we have by assumption

$$p_b^i = p_b^1$$

If the marginal land is the fth, the differential rents are then

$$\rho_f^i = \rho_i(p_b^f - p_b^i) \text{ and } \rho_f^j = \rho_j(p_b^f - p_b^j) \text{ with } p_b^i = p_b^j$$

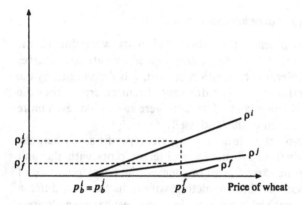

Figure 8.8

hence

$$\frac{\rho_f^i}{\rho_f^j} = \frac{\pi_I}{\rho_j}$$

Thus, the differential rents of two plots on which, at the considered rate of profit r, wheat is grown at the same cost but with different returns per acre, are identical if they are zero (both plots are simultaneously marginal). When they are positive, they are *proportional* to the return per acre they allow: if the ith land yields twice as much as the jth, then its rent is twice as high (see figure 8.8).

8.2.5 Exhaustion and improvement of land

We have already emphasised that under joint production, each method of cultivation simultaneously produces wheat and land. But if land is considered as the same good at the beginning and the end of the process in question, this springs from a very strong hypothesis according to which land remains absolutely unchanged and identical to itself.

The analysis could be elaborated by contemplating the case where the natural resource is progressively exhausting (as machines) and its price steadily decreasing until it becomes negative. As a result the method would be abandoned as well as the good it produced. We may as well contemplate the case when soils are improved and given a better quality with a higher price.

Note

When wheat is a basic good and enters the production of iron the previous developments still hold. The only change consists in defining the *net g-return of the system*

$$\tilde{\pi}_i = \frac{b^i - (1+g)a_{bb}^i + (1+g)a_{1b}}{t^i}$$

where a_{1b} represents the quantity of wheat consumed by the activity to produce iron. Then the production price system writes (with the usual notations)

$$\begin{cases} (1+r)(a_{11} + a_{1b}p_b^f) + w = 1 \\ (1+r)(a_{b1}^i + a_{bb}^i p_b^f) + w + \rho^i t^i = b^i p_b^f \end{cases}$$

From which we obtain $p_b^f = p_b^i + \dfrac{\rho_f^i}{\tilde{\pi}_i}$ and thus $\rho_f^i = \tilde{\pi}_i(p_b^f - p_b^i)$

8.2.6 Changes in the production conditions

The increasing difficulties in production that we have contemplated above, stem from the scarcity of natural resources; an increase in the level of demand caused by accumulation inescapably leads, under the indicated assumptions, to diminishing returns. Such assumptions may be questioned because, on the one hand, the structure of demand can be modified, and, on the other hand, new methods of production could be introduced.

A more than proportional increase in the demand for wheat will obviously entail a change in the activity levels and a quicker appearance of diminishing returns. If the production of wheat requires the use of tractors, an increase in the demand for wheat will translate into the production of new machines. Conversely, if the demand for wheat has a slower increase (or even decreases), symmetrical changes would appear in the activity levels; if changes are important and sudden, phenomena of excess capacity may happen in some sectors; it is only when they are solved that a permanent regime of growth may prevail again and that the price system recovers a uniform rate of profit.

We may also contemplate the consequences of the appearance and application of new methods of production. We face here a problem that is totally different from the one addressed previously (chapter 7) dealing with the choice of methods of production in a known set. Here, it is the outlines of the set which change.[18]

Let us now assume that a new method of production, up to now unknown, allowing to produce the kth good in less costly conditions, has appeared in the economy where, by assumption, a permanent regime prevails in a golden rule situation (given $r = g$). Owing to various types of constraints (technical, financial and social) it is quite unlikely that the new process is immediately spread in the economy in order to totally satisfy demand for the good in question. Consequently, a transitory regime will prevail with the good in question being simultaneously produced by (at least) two methods of production during a series of periods of time. During that stage, that is to say, as long as the former method of production, which is more costly, is used, the production price of the good in question will be determined by the worst production conditions; thus 'quasi-rent' appears, an excess profit yielded by the new method of production that is less costly; indeed, there cannot be two prices for the same good.

The activities used are fixed by the level of demand to be satisfied. The regulating price of the good is the production price determined on the basis of the less efficient activity used. We could call the regulating price the market price for it is determined at least indirectly by demand.

Then capital will progressively be (more or less quickly) used for the production of the kth good through the new process which is the most profitable; in such conditions, good k will sooner or later be produced in excess and its producers will have to decrease its price without it being an equilibrium price; while the producers of good k see their excess profit decrease, other industry producers benefit from the decrease in the price of good k and enjoy an excess profit; the rate of profit is not uniform any more, since the industries using good k enjoy a greater profitability. As a result the adjustment process will continue: capital will flow towards the industries having a higher profitability, then there will be an excess production of goods which will lead to a decrease in their prices until the rate of profit becomes identical in all the industries though greater than the initial level.

This does not mean that capital is flexible. It is indeed the profits of the processes used which will be invested in the most profitable processes and contribute to their extension. As a matter of fact, the adjustment conditions and the agents' behaviour should be developed since the stability of the equilibrium is not ensured at all.

Let us consider a model with circulating capital, no barriers to entry and perfectly 'short-sighted' entrepreneurs; any improvement, as little as it might be, in the conditions of production of a good must then lead to an immediate flow of the whole new capital available towards the production of that good. This ends up creating shortages of other goods and an excess production of the good in question; in other words, rapid fluctuations in the quantities and prices of all the goods. Then it would be proper to introduce adjustment conditions taking into account producers' learning procedures and their abilities to forecast.

It is worth noting that instability may be significantly reduced when the new process requires the use of machines or fixed capital which take time to be produced in sufficient quantities and to satisfy requirements. Because of this, activities may coexist during quite a long period of time with differentiated rates of profit, and adjustment could be carried out progressively; but this may result in excess capacities which are slow to solve and could consequently hamper the recovery of the uniform rate of profit.

8.3 Intensified use of natural resources

We have seen that, with no technical change, the development of the accumulation process may lead to the exploitation of less and less profitable natural resources or land: wheat, and more generally all goods using 'land', are produced in increasingly costly conditions and more profitable land yields differential rents (at the considered rate of profit). The method of cultivation determining the regulating price of wheat is applied on the last plot taken under cultivation, which is both the less fertile and the less profitable. Up to now, we have assumed that this 'marginal' land was not fully used: its price and the rent per acre are thus zero. Such an hypothesis is not always acceptable; there is not necessarily available land. But if the marginal land has a positive price, what is the determination process of that price and therefore of the rent springing from it? This could be explained by landowners' monopolistic behaviour. However, this is not the only explanation nor is it necessary as indicated in the note by Engels in *Capital*: 'this illustration shows how, by means of *differential rent II*, better soil, already yielding rent, may regulate the price and thus transform all soil, even hitherto rentless, into rent-bearing soil'.[19]

We shall first contemplate the determination of rent on land of uniform quality and with a limited surface area. In the few lines devoted to the problem of intensive rent, Sraffa (P.S. chapter 11, *Production of Commodities*) addresses the problem in the same terms. In what follows, we shall follow the same approach by using the same tools of analysis that we have used several times earlier. This will allow a simplified presentation of the problem that was widely developed in the past (notably Montani, 1972 and 1975; Kurz, 1978; Abraham-Frois and Berrebi, 1980; Bidard, 1987). We shall indeed contemplate an extremely simple model where wheat is produced by means of wheat and labour on land of uniform quality and with a limited surface area; the rate of profit is exogenously given (and equal to the rate of growth).

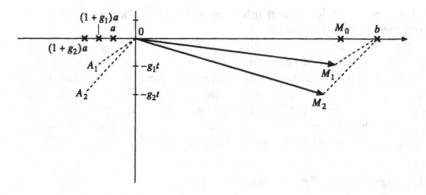

Figure 8.9

8.3.1 Only one method of cultivation of wheat on a limited homogeneous plot of land

Assume that wheat is produced on homogeneous land only by means of wheat and labour. Since the system of production in question consists in, apart from land, only one commodity (wheat), we can simplify the notation: let a and b denote the quantities of wheat respectively used and produced by the unique process considered, t the surface area used, while the quantity of labour used equals unity. Figure 8.9 represents the net g-returns of the different rhythms of accumulation, with the quantities of wheat on the vertical axis and land on the horizontal axis (by assumption there cannot be a net production of land).

At a given g, assuming that wheat and land are jointly produced, the vector of net g-products $\overrightarrow{0M(g)}$ has $[b - (1+g)a]$ and $[t - (1+g)t] = -gt$ as components. At $g = 0$ of course $gt = 0$ and point M_0 has a zero ordinate, with its abscissa being $[b - a]$. At $g > 0$ the vector of net g-products constructed on the basis of the usual rule (see chapter 1) $\overrightarrow{0M(g)} = \overrightarrow{0b} + \overrightarrow{0A(g)}$ moves as indicated on figure 8.9, in the same direction as the origin line M_0 and with a slope

$$\frac{-t(g_1 - g_2)}{b - (1+g_1)a - [b - (1+g_2)a]} = \frac{-t(g_1 - g_2)}{a(g_2 - g_1)} = \frac{t}{a} \; \forall g > 0$$

Let us now assume that g is known and exogenously fixed; if (see figure 8.9) the quantity of land is limited, to satisfy the demand for wheat which is also taken to be known and fixed at level D, we would only need to alter the level of use of the cultivation method in question, i.e., hire the exact number of workers sufficient to produce D; the activity's net surplus of wheat is

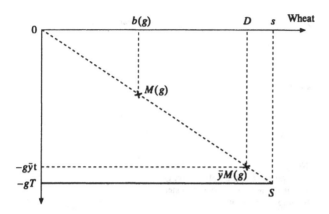

Figure 8.10

given by the abscissa of $M(g)$, that is to say $b(g)$, when the activity is used at the unit level, the activity level sufficient to satisfy demand D is $\bar{y}= D/b(g)$. Since returns to scale are taken to be constant, the development of the activity entails an increased use of the land. When the surface area is limited to T acres, it is clear that the development of the method will be limited, hence the constraint

$$yt \leq T$$

At $g > 0$ we have

$$gyt \leq gT \text{ hence also } -gT \leq -gyt$$

It is this formulation which is used in figure 8.10, where it appears that, in this case, land is not saturated at the level of demand of wheat contemplated and the resulting level of activity $\bar{y}$.

It is quite easy to show the opposite case when the demand for wheat is not satisfied by the method in question.

Let S be the intersection point between $0M(g)$ and $(-gT)$: the abscissa of S, i.e., s, defines the maximum net product of wheat which can be obtained using the activity in question at the rhythm of accumulation g and the surface area T.

8.3.2 Several methods of production available

When at a given g, several methods of production $M_1, M_2, M_3...$ are available to cultivate a uniform and limited plot of land, two cases have to be distinguished.

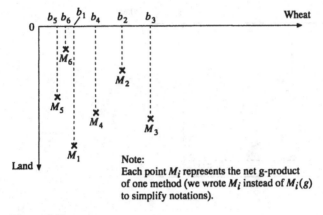

Figure 8.11

1st case

When the land is over abundant, in that the demand for wheat can be staisfied by any method, the usual rule of choice based on the minimisation of costs applies. Since land is not a scarce resource, it is rentless: at a given $r = g$ and as every method uses the same quantity of labour $l_i = 1$, the method providing the greatest net g-surplus of wheat is also the less costly (see chapter 7). Thus, in the example contemplated above, it is method n°3 which, at a given $r = g$, is the less costly; it is therefore the one that will be used if land is over abundant (the other methods are obviously less profitable, the most expensive being method n°5 which has the lowest abscissa). Recall that this order holds only at the considered rate of profit, and there is no reason for it to be the same if distribution changes.

The other component of the net g-product, i.e., land consumption, is not taken into account in this example since land is over abundant. The situation is quite different in the second example contemplated in figure 8.11.

Note   Each point M_i represents the net g-product of a method (we have used M_i for $M_i(g)$ in order to simplify the presentation).

2nd case

When land is scarce, in that the demand for wheat cannot be satisfied by any method, the usual choice criterion is not relevant any more. Let us assume that using the least expensive method does not allow to satisfy demand: the capitalist farmers will however be able to increase their aggregate profit (recall that the rate of profit is given, but not the aggregate rate of profit) by using more costly methods to produce more wheat.

Let us first recall that the ordinate of the representative point $M_i(g)$ of the net g-product of the activity is $(-gt_i)$: as a result, at a given g, the consumption of land is all the more important in that the (negative) ordinate is low; as the yield per acre π_i is the inverse of the consumption of land per produced unit $(\pi_i = l/t_i)$, the yield per acre is greater because the method is represented high in the diagram of the net g-products. In the example contemplated above (figure 8.12) method n°1 has the lowest yield per acre and method n°6 has the greatest.

The choice among the six methods can be limited: methods M_1, M_4 and M_5 are (at the considered rhythm of accumulation) dominated by at least one of the other three methods. Then, the choice will be reduced to M_3, M_2 and M_6; as in the case of choice of techniques (chapter 7) here we take into account the outside envelope of the different methods' net g-products: it defines, at the considered rate of profit, the efficiency frontier of the system.

In figure 8.12, we have limited the choice to the three methods in question and, by using the method specified in figure 8.11, we have denoted the land constraint by $(-gT)$ and the exogenous level of demand for wheat by (D).

Using the least costly method (M_3) would only allow, owing to the available surface area, to produce s_3 units of wheat and would not satisfy demand D; then it would be necessary to start using another method.

Among the available methods, it is method M_2 which will be selected: though its production cost is higher than M_3's (its abscissa is lower) its yield per acre is greater (M_2 is located higher than M_3 on the diagram); as for methods M_1, M_4 and M_5 we have seen that they are dominated by combination M_3M_2 and method M_6, which is more costly than M_2, is not to be used at all. It appears here that the substitution of method (2) for method 1 is not total but partial: since method n°2 is more costly than method n°3, it will be used only in a part of the available surface area, while the least expensive method is used in the other part. Competion among capitalist farmers ensures the use of the least costly method but the need to satisfy demand leads to a parallel use of the method with the greatest yield per acre.

In what proportions will the available surface area T divide between the two methods? We know that when both methods are used at the unit level (i.e., using one unit of labour) they produce net g-products respectively represented by points M_2 and M_3. Of course, any linear combination of these two methods is possible and all points n of M_2M_3 represent a linear combination of these activities using one unit of labour. Changing the level of use of this 'mixture of activities' allows to increase output until the land constraint is saturated.

The previous approach then consists in using a given combination of activities to deduce the production of wheat that can be obtained on the available surface area. Conversely, it is possible to determine the linear

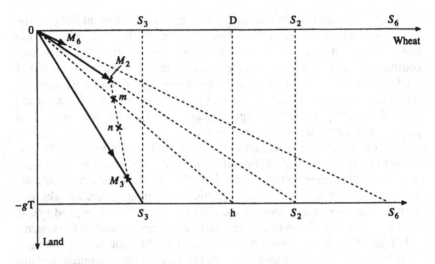

Figure 8.12

combination from the demand for wheat that has to be satisfied. We can see on figure 8.12 that from D we determine point h then point m which is the intersection point of $0h$ and M_2M_3. While the ratio mM_2/mM_3 determines the utilisation ratio of one unit of labour between the two methods, the ratio hS_2/hS_3 determines the ratio of utilisation of a given surface area (T) between the two methods.

We find here the same reasoning as the one used in a different context. We have seen earlier (chapter 1) that in a golden rule situation, the prices of both goods could not be positive unless the slope of the efficiency frontier is negative. This holds here also: the prices of wheat and land, thus the rent, are positive when methods n°2 and 3 are used simultaneously which means that we are on point M_3M_2 of the efficiency frontier which has indeed a negative slope.

Since land is fully used, it is an economic good whose price is determined in conformity with the general theory of production prices; the rent can be easily deduced from the price of land. But, as we have seen, *the rent is positive only because two methods of production are simultaneously used, with the most productive* (defined as the one having the highest yield per acre) *also being the most costly*, which agrees with Sraffa's proposition:

While the scarcity of land thus provides the background from which rent arises, the only evidence of this scarcity to be found in the process of production is the duality of methods: if there were no scarcity, only one method, the cheapest, would be used on the land and there could be no rent. (P.S. 88)

Therefore, the simultaneous use of methods n°2 and n°3 allows to satisfy the demand for wheat when it is included between s_3 and s_2 (see figure 8.12). When demand D is less than s_3, it goes without saying that only one method should be used, the least costly (here n°3): the land is then rentless since it is not fully used. If the demand for wheat lies between s_2 and s_6, then method 3 is totally abandoned: methods n°2 and n°6 are simultaneously used to satisfy demand, and they share the available surface area. The rent is positive, since the slope of the efficiency frontier M_2M_6 is always negative; further, this uniform rent per acre which springs from the simultaneous use of these two methods and consequently denoted by ρ^{26}, is greater than ρ^{32}, which was obtained through the simultaneous use of methods n°3 and 2: we know (chapter 1) that the absolute value of the slope of the efficiency frontier represents the ratio of the price of wheat to the price of land thus, at a given $r = g$, the ratio of the price of wheat to the uniform rent; since |slope M_2M_6| < |slope M_3M_2|, then $\rho^{26} > \rho^{32}$.

Hence the following possibilities:

$D \in [0, s_3]$	overabundant land	$\rho = 0$
$D \in [s_3, s_2]$	fully used land	$\rho = \rho^{32} > 0$
$D \in [s_2, s_6]$	fully used land	$\rho = \rho^{26} > \rho^{32} > 0$

When $D > s_6$ figure 8.12 does not show the additional possibilities of production using both more productive and more costly methods.

Specific cases of indetermination

If $D = s_3$, demand can be satisfied in two different ways. Either method n°3 is used on the whole surface area; then the rent is zero since there is no land constraint hampering the satisfaction of demand using the least expensive method. Or methods n°2 and 3 are simultaneously used on the whole available surface area and $\rho = \rho^{32} > 0$. Consequently, if $D = s_3$, the rent is indeterminate: $\rho \in [0 \quad \rho^{32}]$ which appears clearly on figure 8.12 where the efficiency frontier is broken at M_3. In such a situation, the rent may be fixed *exogenously*[20] between two limits, 0 and ρ^{32}.

If $D = s_2$, the rent is indeterminate and can be fixed exogenously between two limits: ρ^{32} and ρ^{26}. Demand can of course be satisfied by using method n°2 only. But then, the rent cannot be zero for the availability of lands plays as a constraint prohibiting the use of only the least expensive method, i.e., method n°3. The rent is thus positive but indeterminate between the indicated limits.

If $D = s_6$, the situation is similar, with the lower limit being ρ^{26}. As for the higher limit, it cannot be shown on figure 8.12 since it depends on the (unspecified) characteristics of an even more productive and costly method.

8.3.3 Intensification process

Sraffa notes: 'From this standpoint the existence side by side of two methods can be regarded as a phase in the course of a progressive increase of production on the land' (P.S. 88).

In this connection, we need to revert to figure 8.12 and the previous table, where, at a given g, the demand for wheat is low ($D < s_3$), and land is a free good; owing to the accumulation process, the demand for wheat grows as time goes by and, with unchanged methods of production, leads to full exploitation of the land by the least expensive method.

A further increase in the production of wheat becomes possible thanks to a progressive extension of the method producing wheat at a higher unit cost: the duality of the methods of cultivation is evidence of the scarcity of land which yields a positive uniform rent per acre the level of which depends on the characteristics of the two methods. The increase in the production of wheat is possible only if a new method allowing a better yield per acre is introduced at a proper time; since this new method is more costly than the previous one (otherwise it would have been introduced earlier) the rent is positive and increases: 'In this way the output may increase continuously, although the methods of production are changed spasmodically' (P.S. 88).

The intensification process does describe a progressive change as time goes by, but a technical improvement is, by assumption, excluded. Thus, the process describes a rather catastrophic successsion of increasingly costly methods of production. There is indeed a choice of techniques, of processes of intensification; however, the range of techniques, the set of activities, is taken to be known from the very beginning. The historical evolution will in fact be much more complex and more interesting than the logical evolution described above: the appearance of new methods of production which are more productive (per acre) and less costly is not excluded, which will allow an increase in the output with a decrease in the price of wheat and in the rent.

8.3.4 Variations in the price of wheat and in the rent

Let us revert to the simplified economic example with only one basic good, iron, produced by a unique method of production, and one agricultural good, wheat, the demand for which is such that it requires the use of two methods of cultivation on the available surface area, which is taken to be fully exploited. Owing to the hypothesis of a uniform rent for both methods and using the notation already used in the analysis of the differential rent, the price equations are

$$\begin{cases} (1+r)a_{11} & +w & =1 \\ (1+r)(a_{b1}^1 + a_{bb}^1 p_b^{21}) + w + \rho^{21} t^1 = b^1 p_b^{21} \\ (1+r)(a_{b1}^2 + a_{bb}^2 p_b^{21}) + w + \rho^{21} t^2 = b^2 p_b^{21} \end{cases}$$

Both the price of wheat and the ground rent bear the index $(^{21})$ in order to show explicitly the assumption according to which two methods (1 and 2) are *simultaneously used on the same land* to produce wheat. By substitution, we obtain

$$\begin{cases} p_b^{21} = \dfrac{(1+r)a_{b1}^1 + 1 - (1+r)a_{11}}{b^1 - (1+r)a_{bb}^1} + \rho^{21} \dfrac{t^1}{b^1 - (1+r)a_{bb}^1} \\ p_b^{21} = \dfrac{(1+r)a_{b1}^2 + 1 - (1+r)a_{11}}{b^2 - (1+r)a_{bb}^2} + \rho^{21} \dfrac{t^2}{b^2 - (1+r)a_{bb}^2} \end{cases}$$

And by writing p_b^i the production price of wheat which would spring from the use of only one of the two methods of production and π_i the net g-return of each of the methods, we obtain, as shown in section 8.2.2.

$$\begin{cases} p_b^{21} = p_b^1 + \dfrac{\rho^{21}}{\pi_1} \\ p_b^{21} = p_b^2 + \dfrac{\rho^{21}}{\pi_2} \end{cases}$$

with

$$p_b^i = \frac{(1+r)a_{b1}^i + 1 - (1+r)a_{11}}{b^i - (1+r)a_{bb}^i}$$

and

$$\pi^i = \frac{b^i - (1+r)a_{bb}^i}{t^i}) \text{ for } i = 1,2$$

Hence

$$(S) \quad \begin{cases} \rho^{21} = \pi_1(p_b^{21} - p_b^1) \\ \rho^{21} = \pi_2(p_b^{21} - p_b^2) \end{cases}$$

From which we deduce[21] the value of the rent

$$\rho^{21}(r) = \pi_2 \pi_1 \frac{p_b^2 - p_b^1}{\pi_2 - \pi_1}$$

which allows to state the following theorem:

Theorem

If $\pi_2(r) > p_1(r), \rho(r) > 0 \Leftrightarrow p^2{}_b(r) > p_b^1(r)$

Rent $\rho(r)$ is positive if and only if the method with the highest net g-yield of wheat has the highest wheat production price.

Figure 8.13 is drawn on the basis of system (S). Note that, as in the case of differential rent, each of these equations shows that rent is a linear function of the price of wheat. But contrary to the differential rent, *the price of wheat and the (intensive) rent are determined simultaneously* (in the case of differential rent, the price of wheat was determined first by the worst conditions of production; the rent was defined in a residual way).

In figure 8.13 the slopes of each of the lines equal the net g-return per acre and the abscissa at the origin corresponds to the production price of wheat which would appear if the method in question was the only one used. The rent is positive only if the two lines intersect in the positive quadrant of the diagram: which requires $p_b^2 > p_b^1$ since by assumption $\pi_2 > \pi_1$.

When the demand for wheat is low, the least expensive method of production may be used, here it is method n°1. As land is not fully used, its price and rent are zero. The increase in demand for wheat leads to a full use of the land and the impossibility of satisfying demand if only method n°1 is used. Hence its progressive replacement by method n°2, which is more 'productive' ($\pi_2 > \pi_1$) but more costly ($p_b^2 > p_b^1$).

The simultaneous use of these two methods on the fully exploited land leads to *both* an increase in the price of wheat ($p_b^{21} > p_b^1$) but also $p_b^{21} > p_b^2$) and the appearance of a positive uniform rent ρ^{21}. Note that the price of wheat and the ground rent remain at this level as long as both methods are used, in spite of the increase in the demand for wheat (and in its production).

Let us now examine the case when the demand for wheat reaches such a level that the extension of the second method, the most productive (at the considered g) to the whole surface area which can be cultivated, reveals to be insufficient to satisfy wants. A third method necessarily more productive, will have to be introduced, thus such that $\pi_3 > \pi_2 > \pi_1$. The positivity condition of the rent then implies that $p_b^3 > p_b^2 > p_b^1$.

The third method replaces the first and, as a result, owing to the contemplated conditions of cost and of productivity, a new pair, price of wheat p_b^{32} – rent per acre ρ^{32}, appears and will hold until another increase in the demand for wheat leads to a new stage of intensification; the second method has progressively been replaced by method n°3; the latter in turn will have to yield ground (literally) to method n°4; hence a new pair: price of wheat p_b^{43} – rent per acre ρ^{43}.

The increase in the rent and in the prices of wheat are proportional at each stage of intensification, and the relation can be read directly in figure

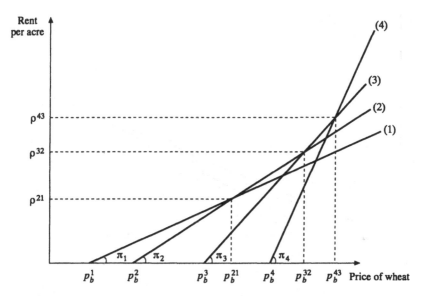

Figure 8.13

8.13. In order to compare ρ^{32} and ρ^{21}, suffice to note that method n°2 is used in both situations; hence

$$\rho^{32} - \rho^{21} = \pi_2(p_b^{32} - p_b^{21})$$

and more generally

$$\rho^{ij} - \rho^{jk} = \rho_j(p_b^{ij} - p_b^{jk})$$

The intensification process explains the fact that only the intersection points of lines $\rho(p_b)$ located on the outside envelope of the set of lines are retained as solutions. The intersection between 1 and 3, in figure 8.13, cannot be considered as relevant since it has been assumed first a progressive substitution of method 1 by method 2, then of method 2 by method 3, with the whole surface area always being fully exploited.

Remark

In the example contemplated below, method n°2, though it is less costly (when used separately) than method n°3, will never be used. When the demand for wheat is low, method n°1 is the only one used since it is the least costly; when the demand for wheat increases, method n°3 is used on one part of the field, for it is more productive than method n°2 and allows a lower price of wheat than the one that would result from the simultaneous use of methods n°2 and n°1 (see figure 8.14).

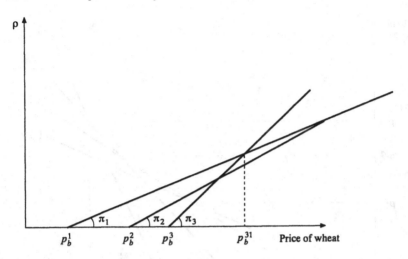

Figure 8.14

8.3.5 The intensive rent: generalisation

The analysis can be generalised from different angles: we may contemplate for instance the example when the intensified use of the scarce resource is indirect or the case when several scarce resources enter the production of a specific good; we could also analyse the case when labour, so far considered as exceeding demand (at least in our analysis) is scarce. These are the topics that we intend to address now. But let us first point out a change of viewpoint: whenever there is a scarcity phenomenon creating an intensive rent, prices cannot be considered as determined as previously; it seems more appropriate to speak of *utilisation prices* rather than *production prices*.

If only one method of production is available to produce wheat on a limited surface area, the intensification may appear indirectly in the use of wheat. Since the production of wheat is fixed, wheat will here play the role of land in the previous analysis: it is indeed quite possible that two methods of production of 'bread' are used simultaneously. We can show that, in such conditions (see Abraham-Frois and Berrebi, 1980, p. 20; also Saucier, 1981–4), the landlord perceives a rent (the land is fully used); such a rent does not result from a duality of the methods of production of wheat, but from a duality of the methods of production of the good ('bread') using wheat. This is in a way a second degree duality: rent is here 'incidental' or 'external', which is passed on to the only scarce resource, land.

Further, Saucier (1984) has shown that when limited primary resources enter the production of several goods, 'it is not in general possible, even at a given rate of profit, to classify lands any more. When demand increases, a

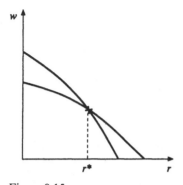

Figure 8.15a

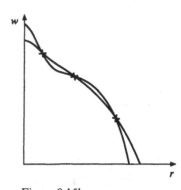

Figure 8.15b

plot of land may be taken under cultivation, then superseded and replaced by another and used again at a higher level of demand'[22] (Saucier, 1984, p. 166).

When one of these resources is fully used, another one has to be introduced. In as much as limited resources are required for the simultaneous prodution of several goods, an increase in demand may lead to sporadic changes in the productive combination every time the expansion limit of a specific productive combination is reached. Hence the important corollary: 'the rent yielded by a land or by another limited primary resource may *decrease*, and even *disappear* when demand increases' (*ibid.*).

Finally, what happens when the development process faces a shortage of labour? Here again, this will lead to the intensified use of the now scarce resource; in other words, in order to satisfy demand, other methods of production will have to be applied, thus saving labour, though their costs will be higher. Consequently the rate of profit cannot be taken as exogenous any more; indeed, the system of production is now composed of $k+1$ methods of production producing the k goods, with one of the goods being simultaneously produced by two methods and one of them is labour saving. Owing to the normalisation condition, we have now $k+2$ equations allowing to define the $k+2$ unknowns, the k prices and the two distributive variables.

If we consider curves $w(r)$, this means that we have two compatible systems and that we are necessarily at an intersection point, or 'switching' point of both curves. It is worth noting that the solution may not be unique: we find here the problem of 'reswitching' contemplated from a different angle (see figure 8.15).

When the labour factor gets scarcer, producers have to introduce other methods of production allowing to save even more labour. Such a

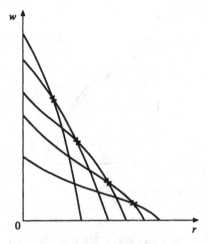

Figure 8.16

substitution results in an increase in wages and a decrease in the rate of profit (see Abraham-Frois 1984). Of course nothing proves that the capitalists will accept the decrease in the rate of profit resulting from the process; beyond a certain threshold, they might stop investing and thus create a crisis due to the insufficient profitability, which will stop the accumulation process (see figure 8.16).[23]

In situations of scarcity, directly or indirectly leading to an intensified use of a resource, the number of methods used is necessarily greater than the number of goods produced; this logic is quite different from that of production prices where there is one degree of freedom. The emergence of scarcity emphasises systems where the set of distributive and price variables is determined endogenously, with no degree of freedom; hence, the concept of *utilisation price* and not of production price any more.

8.3.6 Intensive rent and differential rents

Let us now contemplate the combination of intensive rent and differential rents. We have previously assumed that, when land was of different qualities, the least fertile was not fully used; it was thus rentless. Then, on the basis of that land, more precisely on the method of cultivation used, we have determined the regulating price of wheat p_b^f and the differential rents per acre yielded by the various plots of land:

$$\rho_f^i = \pi_i(p_b^f - p_b^i) \text{ with } i = 1, 2, \ldots, h$$

Now, if we assume that the last plot taken under cultivation is fully used

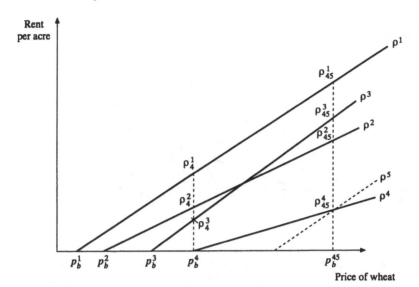

Figure 8.17

by two methods (e) and (f), then it yields a positive intensive rent; consequently, the price of wheat is fixed at a higher level $p_b^{ef} > p_b^f$ and the differential rents of the various plots are now determined by

$$\dot{\rho}_i^{ef} = \pi_i(p_b^{ef} - p_b^i) > \rho_f^i$$

Then *all the plots yield positive rents.* As a matter of fact it is quite possible that *the profitability order of the various plots is altered by the emergence of a positive rent on the marginal land* as shown on figure 8.17; the solid line shows the characteristic price of wheat/rent relations of the four methods of cultivation used on the four plots available. When plot of land n°4 is not fully used, the regulating price of wheat is then determined by p_b^4 and the order of the differential rents reads on the vertical of that point; we have $\rho_4^1 > \rho_4^2 > \rho_4^3 > \rho_4^4 = 0$.

If the increase in demand for wheat causes an intensified use of land n°4, then a new method of production (n°5 for short) characterised by a relation $\rho^5(p_b)$ (broken line in figure 8.17) has to be introduced. The intersection between ρ^5 and ρ^4 determines both the new regulating price of wheat p_b^{45} and the intensive rent yielded by land n°4 which is now fully used. The order of the differential rents of lands n°2 and n°3 has changed, since, by writing p_{45}^i the rent per acre yielded by each land, with $i = 1,2,3,4$, we have

$$\rho_{45}^1 > \rho_{45}^3 > \rho_{45}^2 > \rho_{45}^4 > 0$$

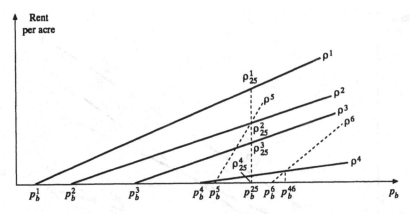

Figure 8.18

It is worth noting that intensification does not have to take place on the marginal land. When the demand for wheat increases and the marginal land is fully used, it is sometimes possible (and may be less costly) to intensify cultivation on land that is already fully used and whose owner already perceives a differential rent.

In the example contemplated in figure 8.18, it is assumed that method n°5 could be substituted for the method of cultivation used on land n°2. As foreseen by Marx and Engels in the quotations drawn from *Capital*, the regulating price of wheat is then fixed by the 'better soil' then yielding a differential rent, and now an intensive rent. Since all the other land is fully used, the owners perceive differential rents; the amount of the latter depends of course upon the characteristics of the method of production contemplated, but also on the new regulating price of wheat determined by the land on which cultivation is intensified. Note that in that example it could have been possible, though more costly, to intensify cultivation on land n°4 with method n°6 (broken line).

Thus, *intensification does not necessarily take place on the last land taken under cultivation*. Let us note also that *intensification does not necessarily happen after cultivation has been extended*. At each level of demand, and taking into account the rate of profit, the method of cultivation used is the one allowing to satisfy demand at the lowest production price. If the cultivated soil is fully used, generally the producer may choose between intensifying cultivation or extending it to other soils. He will, however, have to solve the problem of choosing a method of cultivation allowing a low production cost. The simplified assumption according to which one method of production is available for each type of soil has to be relaxed; or rather, it is the expression, the final result of a choice among more or less costly methods of cultivation. And sometimes, owing to the level of demand, it will be better to increase the output of the considered soil by using a more costly method of production than extending cultivation to other soils; intensification is not (necessarily) the consequence of a physical constraint (the impossibility of producing more), but the evidence of an economic constraint: the minimisation of production costs under the constraint of satisfying a determined demand.

The analysis of rent, either it is intensive or differential, allows to go beyond the analysis of permanent regimes. When the process is dynamic, it is of course quite impossible to address the problem of distribution independently of the problems induced by accumulation. The efficiency of the choice of technique is ensured by the golden rule hypothesis, the equality of the rate of profit and the rate of growth. Regulating prices are production prices defined on the basis of the conditions of production resulting from the available methods of production, demand and the rhythm of accumulation.

8.4 Technical improvement and distortion of the system of prices

The way an increase in profitability obtained by a company, an industry or an economy, are spread can be specified by using the formulation suggested by Jorgenson and Griliches (1967) and Vincent (1968) in a simplified framework with only two factors of production, labour and capital, both taken to be homogeneous. Let Q, L and K be the quantities of output, labour and capital respectively, p the price of one unit of final product, w the wage, p_k the price of one unit of capital good.

We have the accounting identity

$$pQ = wL + p_k K$$

By differentiating the previous relation with respect to time and by writing the derivative of a variable x in relation to time by

$$x' = \frac{dx}{dt}$$

we obtain

$$PQ' + QP' = wL' + w'L + p_k K' + p_k' K$$

$$pQ \left[\frac{Q'}{Q} + \frac{p'}{p} \right] = wL \left[\frac{L'}{L} + \frac{w'}{w} \right] + p_k K \left[\frac{K'}{K} + \frac{p_k'}{p_k} \right]$$

By dividing both members of the equality by pQ and by writing $\alpha = \dfrac{wL}{pQ}$ and

$\beta = \dfrac{p_k K}{pQ}$ respectively the income shares of labour and capital in the total income, we obtain

$$\hat{Q} + \hat{p} = \alpha \hat{L} + \alpha \hat{w} + \beta \hat{K} + \beta \hat{p}_k$$

where $\hat{Q}, \hat{p}, \hat{L}$ respectively represent the growth rates of production, of the final product price, of the quantity of labour used, etc.

We deduce from this

$$\hat{Q} - (\alpha \hat{L} + \beta \hat{K}) = \mu = \alpha \hat{w} + \beta \hat{p}_k - \hat{p}$$

The left-hand side of the expression shows the productivity surplus (denoted by μ) defined as the variation in the volume of production less the variation in the volumes of the production factors used, respectively weighted by α and β.

Note that if the context is a domestic economy, this can be considered as the representation of a 'technical improvement', or 'residual' or 'third factor' in Solow, Meade and Denison's sense.

As for the right-hand side of the expression it can be considered as the representation of how the productivity surplus divides up into an increase in wage, an increase in the price of capital and a decrease in the price of the final product; these variations are respectively profitable for workers, the owners of the means of production and for the final consumers.

Let us now use that method in a disaggregated model with two basic goods (denoted by i and j) and a non-basic good (denoted by c)

$$A = \begin{bmatrix} a_{ii} & a_{ij} & 0 \\ a_{ji} & a_{jj} & 0 \\ a_{ci} & a_{cj} & a_{cc} \end{bmatrix} \qquad L = \begin{bmatrix} l_i \\ l_j \\ l_c \end{bmatrix} \qquad B = \begin{bmatrix} b_i & 0 & 0 \\ 0 & b_j & 0 \\ 0 & 0 & b_c \end{bmatrix}$$

Let p_i, p_j and p_c be the production prices of the three goods, w the wage and r the rate of profit.

For industry (i), we have the following equation

$$b_i p_i = (1 + r)(a_{ii} p_i + a_{ij} p_j) + w l_i$$

and by writing $(1 + r) = \pi$ to simplify notations

$$b_i p_i = \pi (a_{ii} p_i + a_{ij} p_j) + w l_i$$

Assuming a variation in the production conditions of good i, we have, by differentiating the relation above with respect to time and using the notations of the first illustration

$$b_i p_i' + p_i b_i' = \pi a_{ii} p_i' + \pi a_{ii}' p_i + \pi' a_{ii} p_i + \pi a_{ij} p_j' + \pi a_{ij}' p_j + \pi' a_{ij} p_j + w l_i' + l_i w'$$

that is

$$b_i p_i \left[\frac{p_i'}{p_i} + \frac{b_i'}{b_i} \right] = \pi a_{ii} p_i \left[\frac{p_i'}{p_i} + \frac{a_{ii}'}{a_{ii}} + \frac{\pi'}{\pi} \right] + \pi a_{ij} p_j \left[\frac{p_j'}{p_j} + \frac{a_{ij}'}{a_{ij}} + \frac{\pi'}{\pi} \right]$$
$$+ w l_i \left[\frac{l_i'}{l_i} + \frac{w'}{w} \right]$$

We define

$$\alpha_i = \frac{w l_i}{b_i p_i} \qquad \beta_{ii} = \frac{\pi a_{ii} p_i}{b_i p_i} \qquad \beta_{ij} = \frac{\pi a_{ij} p_j}{b_i p_i}$$

and by denoting the growth rates of the various variables by

$$\hat{x} = \frac{x'}{x}$$

we have

$$\hat{p}_i + \hat{b}_i = \beta_{ii}(\hat{p}_i + \hat{a}_{ii} + \hat{\pi}) + \beta_{ij}(\hat{p}_j + \hat{a}_{ij} + \hat{\pi}) + \alpha_i(\hat{l}_i + \hat{w})$$

By denoting the productivity surplus in industry i by μ_i we have:

$$\hat{b}_i - (\beta_{ii}\hat{a}_{ii} + \beta_{ij}\hat{a}_{ij} + a_i\hat{l}_i) = \mu_i$$

Hence by setting $\beta_i = \beta_{ii} + \beta_{ij}$

$$\mu_i = \alpha_i \hat{w} + \beta_i \hat{\pi} + \beta_{ii}\hat{p}_i + \beta_{ij}\hat{p}_j - \hat{p}_i$$

as far as the other industries are concerned, we would have

$$\mu_j = \alpha_j \hat{w} + \beta_j \hat{\pi} + \beta_{ji}\hat{p}_i + \beta_{jj}\hat{p}_j - \hat{p}_j$$
$$\mu_c = \alpha_c \hat{w} + \beta_c \hat{\pi} + \beta_{ci}\hat{p}_i + \beta_{cj}\hat{p}_j + \beta_{cc}\hat{p}_c - \hat{p}_c$$

that is

$$\begin{bmatrix} (1-\beta_{ii}) & -\beta_{ij} & 0 \\ -\beta_{ij} & (1-\beta_{jj}) & 0 \\ -\beta_{ci} & -\beta_{cj} & (1-\beta_{cc}) \end{bmatrix} \begin{bmatrix} \hat{p}_i \\ \hat{p}_j \\ \hat{p}_c \end{bmatrix} = \begin{bmatrix} \alpha_i & \beta_i \\ \alpha_j & \beta_j \\ \alpha_c & \beta_c \end{bmatrix} \begin{bmatrix} \hat{w} \\ \hat{\pi} \end{bmatrix} - \begin{bmatrix} \mu_i \\ \mu_j \\ \mu_c \end{bmatrix}$$

or also in compact notations, with $\hat{p}$ as the vector of changes in production prices, β the semi-positive square matrix of the β_{ij}s, T the vector representing the first part of the line of the previous expression, and μ the surplus vector achieved in each industry

$$(I - \beta)\hat{p} = T - \mu$$

We can then calculate vector $\hat{p}$, with matrix $(I - \beta)$ normally having an inverse, and determinate the variation in production prices[24] for any variation μ_i, μ_j or μ_c in the productivity surplus.

Note that when surplus emerges in the sector of consumption goods, it

affects the price of the (non-basic) consumption good, but has no consequences on the prices of the basic goods i and j. Conversely, any surplus
emerging in the basic sector alters all the prices. This way we can measure
the magnitude of the 'increase in productivity' of the basic sector.

It is clear that this formulation is linked to the neo-Ricardian tradition as
shown in the following passage by Sraffa:

> If an invention were to reduce by half the quantity of each of the means of
> production which are required to produce a unit of a 'luxury' commodity of this
> type, the commodity itself would be halved in price, but there would be no further
> consequences; the price-relations of the other products and the rate of profits would
> remain unaffected. But if such a change occurred in the production of a commodity
> of the opposite type, which *does* enter the means of production, all prices would be
> affected and the rate of profits would be changed. (P.S. 6)

If the nominal wage and the rate of profit are fixed, i.e., $\hat{w} = 0$ and $\hat{r} = 0$,
the distortions in the system of prices directly and totally reflect the
variations in the surplus of each industry. We may of course suppose
that only the wage or the rate of profit remains fixed; such limit cases
could be interesting.

Note that even if the surplus prevailing in each industry is equal, this
would not mean that prices are constant or that they vary in the same
proportions. The distortion in the level and structure of prices ensures
the redistribution of surplus in the whole economy through the
distortion of a technology matrix from one period of time to another.

The limit case where prices are constant is interesting to analyse

$$\hat{p}_i = \hat{p}_j = \hat{p}_c = 0$$

Each sector is then insulated from the other, and we find here many
aspects of the simplified framework of the one-sector model; the whole
productivity surplus of a given sector divides up between a rise in
wages and an increase in the rate of profit. Note that in general this case
is impossible because there are three equations for two unknowns
namely $\hat{w}$ and $\hat{r}$.

It is worth emphasising another peculiar case which this time springs
from technical characteristics. Suppose that there is no basic sector,
and that for instance the sector of consumption goods uses no
intermediate goods, thus $\beta_{ci} = \beta_{cj} = 0$. The sector in question is related
to the rest of the system only through increases in wages and profits. If
we further assume that the sector is 'non-progressive', namely $\mu_c = 0$,
we find the same results as the model due to Baumol (1967): the price of
the good produced by the 'non-progressive sector' (here, the consumption good) increases provided a productivity increase in the 'progressive sector' is followed by an increase in wages.

Notes

Preface

1 See Nassau Senior's third postulate which reads: 'The powers of Labour, and of the other instruments which produce wealth, may be indefinitely increased by using their products as the means of further Production', quoted by Schumpeter, *History of Economic Analysis*, Allen and Unwin, 1954, p. 638.
2 See common works: Abraham-Frois and Berrebi, *Theory of Value, Prices and Accumulation*, Cambridge University Press, 1979; see also: *Rentes, rarete, surprofits*, Economica, 1980. See also Abraham-Frois (ed), *L'économie classique – nouvelles perspectives*, Economica, 1984 and Abraham-Frois, *Dynamique économique*, Dalloz, 1991, 7th edition.

1 The golden rule of accumulation and prices

1 In the present book, the terms 'method of production' and 'activity' are considered as synonyms. Consequently, we shall use both of them equally.
2 We can get rid of any excess of any good at zero price.
3 Actually, the assumption about the structure of consumption is vital. We are grateful to Bidard for having clarified the topic.
4 More generally, we can show that production prices are positive only for $l_2/l_1 \in [0 \quad 44/90]$ and for $r \in \left[0 \quad \dfrac{0.044 - 0.09 l_2/l_1}{1.1 - l_2/l_1} \right]$.

  If this is not satisfied, only one activity can be used, and, owing to the structure of demand, there is a free good and only one economic good. Thus there is only one activity producing only one economic good. The maximum rate of profit can then be easily determined.
5 This term is due to Schefold (1984).
6 See Schefold (1984), pp. 32–3, for a complete demonstration of the general case.

2 Systems of production prices

1 Reference to Sraffa's (1960) *Production of Commodities by Means of Commodities* are given by the initials P.S. followed by the number of the relevant section.

2 Here, we implicitly assume that all goods are basic goods. Thus all prices are positive. We shall revert to these important problems.

3 P.S. 3, the system of k equations is of rank $(k-1)$.

4 From now on, we have $\sum_{i=1}^{k} a_{ij} \leq 1$ for all j, the inequality being strict for at least one j.

5 Note that according to the Perron-Frobenius theorem, the dominant eigenvalue $1/(1+r)$ is included between 0 and 1 since the sum of every column is included between 0 and 1. As a result, r is positive and finite.

6 Matrix A is obtained by dividing the quantities in the column by the quantities produced.

7 Indeed, we have: $|A - \alpha I| = \alpha^2 - \alpha \left[\dfrac{56}{115} + 0.4 \right] + \dfrac{22.4 - 14.4}{115} = 0$ that is, $\alpha^2 - \dfrac{102}{115}$

$\alpha + \dfrac{8}{115} = 0$ whose discriminate is

$$\Delta = \left(\frac{102}{115} \right)^2 - \frac{4.8}{115} = \frac{6724}{(115)^2} = \left(\frac{82}{115} \right)^2$$

from which, we obtain, $\alpha = \dfrac{102 + 82}{2 \times 115} = \dfrac{92}{115} \Rightarrow r = 25\%$.

Note that in a case of production with a surplus, the dominant eigenvalue $\alpha = 92/115$ is less than 1 while in the case of production for subsistence we had $\alpha = 1$.

8 Here, industries, methods of production and activities are considered as equivalent.

9 If labour is not uniform in quality (for instance, n skills), there are n column vectors of needs in labour, n wages ($w_1, w_2, \ldots, w_n$); then, to solve the system, n distribution variables (and not only one) have to be determined exogenously.

10 See mathematical appendix to chapter 3.

3 Irregular and decomposable systems

1 A permutation of matrix A is the matrix obtained by a permutation of the rows of A combined with the same permutation of the columns. Such a matrix can always be expressed by $\bar{A} = PAP'$ where P is a permutation matrix and P' its transpose. Recall that a permutation matrix P is composed of 0 and 1, each row and each column having *one and only one* 1.

2 We write $|M|$ the determinant of a square matrix M.

3 We assume that for any i, the row $a_i \neq 0$, otherwise there would be no basic commodities. Indeed, if the ith row of A is zero, none of the commodities enters directly or indirectly in the production of good i. But one or several columns a_j of A may be zero in the following analysis.

4 However, we shall see in section 1.1.6 that the maximum rate of profit is not determined by the basic sector.

5 When rank $[A^1, I^1] > k - m$ and A_2^2 is decomposable, there is no rule as far as the existence of basic goods is concerned. Recall that by assumption A_1^1 is indecomposable.

6 The eigenvectors q_i on the left and p_j on the right of a square matrix A and corresponding to eigenvalues α_i and α_j which are different, are necessarily orthogonal, for from the relations $q_i A = \alpha_i q_i$ and $A p_j = \alpha_j p_j$, we deduce $\alpha_i.q_i p_j = \alpha_i q_i.p_j = q_i A.p_j = q_i.\alpha_j p_j = \alpha_j q_i p_j$ that is $(\alpha_i - \alpha_j) q_i p_j = 0$ where $\alpha_i - \alpha_j \neq 0$ hence $q_i p_j = 0$.

7 We assume that for any $i = 1, 2, \ldots, k$ the column $a_i \geq 0$, otherwise there would be no antibasic process. However, if a row a_j of A is zero there may be antibasic processes. But there would be no basic good.

8 See the $(k - n)$ last processes of matrix A.

9 In this configuration and in the following three, we assume that matrices A_1^1, A_2^2 and A_3^3 are indecomposable.

10 When rank $[A^1, I^1] > k - m$ and A_2^2 is decomposable, there is no general rule as far as basic goods are concerned. Recall that by assumption, A_1^1 is indecomposable.

11 We assume that model $[A, I, d]$ is regular; we shall revert to this in the next section. Note that if vector d is the eigenvector on the left of matrix A corresponding to its dominant eigenvelue (d homothetic to q) the curve $c - g$ is linear whatever the numeraire.

12 Suffice to substitute $\bar{p}_2$ and G_2 for $\bar{p}$ and G in the demonstration above.

13 This assumption implies that every row a_i and every column a_j of matrix A has at least one non-zero component.

14 An eigenvalue is said to be semi-simple if it is a simple root of the characteristic equation or a multiple root such that the sub-space corresponding to it is of dimension 1.

15 See mathematical appendix.

16 Indeed, vector y can be broken down into $\sum_{j=1}^{n} \gamma_j dA^j$ as p was broken down into $\sum_{j=1}^{m} \beta_j dA^j L$.

17 See chapter 2, section 5.2.

4 The analysis of joint production

1 P.S. chapters 7, 8, 9.

2 In the simple production context contemplated previously, matrix B was the diagonal unit matrix $B = I$. Therefore, the analysis framework presented here is very general, with simple production being a peculiar aspect of joint production: $Ap(1 + r) + Lw = Bp = Ip = p$.

3 We will present in the mathematical appendix two requirements that are equivalent to condition (N3).

4 Note first that we are speaking here of an indecomposable *system* and not of an indecomposable *matrix*, and second that in the case of simple production there is

an equivalence between a basic system and an indecomposable system. We shall return to these two points below.

5 In case of simple production $B = I$ remains invariant whatever the permutation of the rows and columns since I is a diagonal matrix and this implies that a simple production system $[A, I]$ is decomposable if, and only if, A is a decomposable matrix.

6 Obviously the system composed of the A and B matrices is indecomposable if there are no such permutations. Similarly, a simple production system (A, I) is indecomposable if, and only if, A is an indecomposable matrix.

7 Refer to Manara (1968).

8 This relation means that the rank of matrix $[A^2, B^2] = \begin{bmatrix} a_{12} & b_{12} \\ a_{22} & b_{22} \end{bmatrix} = \begin{bmatrix} \beta a_{22} & \beta b_{22} \\ a_{22} & b_{22} \end{bmatrix}$ is

equal to one (there is only one independent row vector).

9 Refer to Manara (1968).

10 Recall that this means that rank $[A^2, B^2] = 1$. In other words the rank of the matrix composed of the last columns of A and B (and thus of dimension (2×2)) is equal to 1.

11 Many authors became interested in this topic, among them Manara (1968), Pasinetti (1980a), Steedman (1980–4), St Burnell (1982), Bidard (1984).

12 Sraffa wrote 'at most of rank m' (P.S. 60). But we have to exclude the case when the rank of $[A^2, B^2]$ is less than m since condition (N3) would not be satisfied (see the mathematical appendix).

13 In the preceding example $k = 2$, $m = 1$, the dimension of matrix $H(k - m, 1)$ is reduced to 1×1, i.e., a scalar. Matrix $[A^2, B^2]$ of dimension $(k, 2m) = (2,2)$ is of rank $m = 1$.

14 We assume that $X^{-1}A = \begin{bmatrix} Z_1^1 & 0 \\ Z_2^1 & Z_2^2 \end{bmatrix} \begin{matrix} {\scriptstyle k-m} \\ {\scriptstyle m} \end{matrix}$ $Z_2^1 \neq 0$, Z_1^1 and Z_2^2 indecomposable

15 We assume that $X^{-1}A = \begin{bmatrix} Z_1^1 & 0 \\ 0 & Z_2^2 \end{bmatrix} \begin{matrix} {\scriptstyle k-m} \\ {\scriptstyle m} \end{matrix}$

16 We assume that matrix $AX^{-1} = \begin{bmatrix} Z_1^1 & 0 \\ Z_2^1 & Z_2^2 \end{bmatrix} \begin{matrix} {\scriptstyle n} \\ {\scriptstyle k-n} \end{matrix}$ where $Z_2^1 \neq 0$, Z_1^1 and Z_2^2 are indecomposable

17 We assume that matrix $AX^{-1} = \begin{bmatrix} Z_1^1 & 0 \\ 0 & Z_2^2 \end{bmatrix} \begin{matrix} {\scriptstyle n} \\ {\scriptstyle k-n} \end{matrix}$

18 This theorem is demonstrated in an article by Schefold (1978a). Note that the terms are slightly different.

5 Standards and blocking goods

1 Here, we assume that the system is regular, i.e., the labour profile matrix

$K=[L, AL, ..., A^{k-1}L]$ is of full rank, which ensures the uniqueness of the standard. Irregular systems are contemplated in section 3.

2 See chapter 3, section 1.1.5.

3 We can even say that the standard does not include the basic goods and the beans, but ... the beans and the basic goods.

4 At the end of the present chapter, we write $\overline{d}$ the demand vector in order to avoid any confusion with the 'differential' operator d.

5 A model is d-regular if the square matrix $(d, dA, dA^2, ..., dA^{n-1})$ is regular.

6 Labour values and the problem of transformation

1 In this chapter quotations from *Capital* are generally drawn from the unabridged edition, published by International Publishers. Roman numerals correspond to the volume and Arab numerals stand for page numbers.

2 We have already noted the equality of labour values and wage prices at $r=0$: $\Lambda \equiv p(0)/w$ (see chapter 2).

3 Referred to as the Marx–von Neumann regime in Abraham-Frois and Berrebi (1979, chapter 6).

4 See Abraham-Frois and Berrebi (1984a).

5 See Parys, 1982.

6 It seems that the first demonstration was due to Okishio, *On Marx's Production Prices* (in Japanese), Keizaigaku Kenkyu, 1972; A. Shaikh stated the procedure in a paper presented at Yale University in Feb. 1973 and included in 'Marx's theory of value and the transformation problem' published in *The Subtle Anatomy of Capitalism*, J. Schwartz edn., Goodyear Publishing Cy, 1977.

7 See chapter 1.

8 This comes down to saying that by producing one more unit of good i with a negative value, less labour would be consumed. Indeed, values Λ in the model $[A, B, L]$ write $B\Lambda = A\Lambda + L$ that is, $\Lambda = (B-A)^{-1}L$, assuming that $(B-A)$ has an inverse. Further, in order to obtain a final production z, activity levels y must establish $yB = yA + z$. The aggregate labour in the system is thus $yL = z(B-A)^{-1}L = z\Lambda$ since $y(B-A) = z$ that is, $y = z(B-A)^{-1}$. When one more unit of good i is produced, we have $z = (0, 0, ..., 1, 0, ..., 0)$ and by assumption $yL = z\Lambda = \lambda_i < 0$.

9 The figures given here are different from those given by I. Steedman, for he, as well as Sraffa, but contrary to Marx, considers that wages are paid on surplus and not 'advanced'. Also see Morishima and Catephores for similar results, 1978, p. 29.

10 See Morishima, 'Marx in the light of modern economic theory', *Econometrica*, July, 1974 and 'Positive profits with negative surplus value: a comment', *Economic Journal*, December, 1976; Morishima and Catephores, *Values, Exploitation and Growth*, 1978.

11 We made the same criticism of Morishima and Catephores in a previous work (Abraham Frois, 1981, foreword). Also see Fujimori, *Modern Analysis of Value Theory*, 1982, p. 73; P. Flaschel: 'Actual labor values in a general model of production', *Econometrica*, March, 1983, p. 440.

12 For a more general treatment of inefficiencies and outclassing appearing in such a case, see Dumenil and Levy, 1982 and 1984, Fujimori, 1982.

13 The extension of such treatments to separately reproducible joint products is immediate.

7 Switch in methods of production

1 Our italics.

2 Though Sraffa does not provide us with the demonstration.

3 Sraffa specifies that 'the rate of profit is taken as the independent variable in this connection; but the argument would not be affected if the wage, expressed in any given commodity or composite commodity, were taken instead' (footnote 1, section 92).

4 In this context, this does not mean a zero profitability, a zero rate of profit, but a profit rate that is not greater than the uniform interest rate.

5 Also see Brody (1970), pp. 73–4.

6 See Bidard (1984), Salvadori (1982, 1984).

7 It is worth emphasising that since systems (h) and (k) differ only by one activity, one of them necessarily dominates the other.

8 Provided we choose the final consumption vector d as numeraire for prices.

9 If $u = 0$, 'wheat' is chosen as a numeraire and its price is by definition constant.

10 We can see in the formulas that at a given w, p_b is a decreasing function of r and p is an increasing function of r if $u = (u\ u_b) > 0$.

11 Example inspired by Bidard (1984), p. 189.

12 See footnote 1 of section 96 in *Production of Commodities by Means of Commodities*.

13 Sraffa assumes that a machine works with constant efficiency throughout its life, which allows an additional simplification of notations; but such a restrictive hypothesis is not necessary at all.

14 See for example Schefold (1978b) and Baldone (1974).

15 For more details refer to Schefold (1971–1978), Baldone (1974) and Roncaglia (1971), X. Galiègue (1985).

16 See Baldone (1974) and Schefold (1978b).

17 An extreme case is when the net return of a machine F_h is constant from its first day of use until the end of time. In such a case we would have

$$p_0^m = \sum_{t=1}^{\infty} \frac{F_t}{(1+r)^t} = p_h^m \ \forall h \text{ and } p_0^m = p_h^m = \frac{F_h}{r}$$

The machine is not only everlasting but its price is also constant whatever the period of use.

18 In a von Neumann model with more than two goods several algorithms can be used to find the solution (see for example Morgenstern and Thompson, *Mathematical Theory of Expanding and Contracting Economics*, D.H. Heath, Lexington, Mass., 1976; also see Afriat, 'Von Neumann's economic model' in M. Dore, S. Chakravarty and R. Goodwin (eds), *John Von Neumann and Modern Economics*, Clarendon Press, Oxford, 1989).

8 The dynamic evolution

1 The following developments can easily be generalised to the case of joint production satisfying demand in a context of g-efficiency. However, we have chosen to keep the simplest presentation.

2 For further information about the stability of the system, refer to Solow and Samuelson: 'Balanced growth under constant returns to scale', *Econometrica*, 21, July 1953.

3 Called 'discounted prices' by Malinvaud (1982, chapter 10). Also see Bliss (1975), Burmeister (1980), d'Autume (1982).

4 Our translation from French.

5 For simplicity's sake, we assume that the rate of profit demanded by the capitalists in the different activities is uniform. The following results can be applied to the case of differentiated rates of profit: see, Catz and Laganier (1984).

6 For a more general treatment see Catz and Laganier (1984).

7 Note that this can be obtained by applying to prices the results obtained by Solow and Samuelson (1953) concerning balanced growth.

8 For further information see d'Autume (1985), Schefold (1985a and b).

9 This assumption is temporary and will be relaxed later on, see section 8.3.

10 The following developments owe a lot to Bidard's work (1987), as well as to those due to Kurz (1978), Montani (1972 and 1975), Guadrio Curzio (1980), Saucier (1981), and Schefold. Also see Abraham-Frois and Berrebi (1980).

11 This analysis also holds with 'advanced' wages, and the rate of profit also applies to the wages paid.

12 E. Lecouteux, 'Principes économiques de la culture améliorante', quoted by Barthélemy, *Economica*, 1982, p. 63 (our translation).

13 This was well enhanced by Vidonne (1982) and Regnault (1984) among others.

14 Let $l^i = 1 \ \forall i$.

15 The fertility order of two methods of cultivation is independent of distribution in the specific case when each of the input and labour coefficients used on land A is less than or equal to the corresponding coefficient of land B (with a strict inequality for at least one of the coefficients). We find here (by generalising them) the results of the Ricardian analysis. For further information see Boudhiaf (1985).

16 For an arithmetical example, see Abraham-Frois and Berrebi, 1980, pp. 40–2.

17 We make here the same assumption, that we shall relax later on, as in the previous developments (unsaturated land).

18 The reasons behind the appearance of that new method of production are not analysed here; they would require specific developments. We could suppose that it is due to an 'exogenous' technical improvement (an innovation in Schumpeter's sense) or we may as well assume that it is due to the conditions of production, distribution or the social characteristics of the system.

19 *Capital*, volume III, p. 740. Our italics.

20 About this problem, see Abraham-Frois and Berrebi, 1980, pp. 27–30.

21 If wheat, basic, enters the production of iron, the previous formulation still holds provided $\tilde{\pi}_i = [b^i(1+r)a_{bb}^i + (1+r)a_{1b}]/t^i$ with $i = 1,2$ and a_{1b} being the quantity of wheat required for the production of one unit of iron.

22 Our translation from French.
23 This looks like the overaccumulation crisis described by Marx; for a presentation and reinterpretation see Abraham-Frois and Berrebi, 1976, pp. 391–2 and Abraham-Frois, 1984, pp. 187–93.
24 Assuming of course a uniform rate of profit and wage.

References

Abraham-Frois, G. (ed.) (1984) *L'économie classique – nouvelles perspectives*, Economica.

(1991) *Dynamique économique*, Dalloz, 7th edition.

Abraham-Frois, G. and Berrebi, E. (1976) *Theorie de la valeur, des prix et de l'accumulation*, Economica.

(1978) 'Pluralité des marchandises-étalon existence et construction', *Revue d'Economie Politique*, September.

(1979) *Theory of Value, Prices and Accumulation*, Cambridge University Press.

(1980) *Rentes, rareté, surprofits*, Economica.

(1981) 'La demande, face cachée de la production jointe', *Revue Economique*, November.

(1984a) 'Le problème de la transformation solution(s)', *Econometrica*, September.

(1984b) 'Taux de profit minimum dans les models de production', in Ch. Bidard (ed.).

(1985) 'L'ambiguité de l'étalon', The Round Table, Latapses, Sophia-Antipolis.

(1989a) 'A la recherche de l'étalon invariable des valeurs', *Revue d'Economie Politique*, 1.

(1989b) 'Biens Bloquants et étalons', *Revue Française d'Economie*, 2.

(1990) 'Dualité et étalon', *Revue Economique*, July.

Afriat, S. (1989) 'Von Neumann's economic model', in M. Dore, S. Chakravarty, and R. Goodwin (eds.), *John Von Neumann and Modern Economics*, Clarendon Press, Oxford.

d'Autume, A. (1982) 'L'introduction du emps dans la théorie de l'équilibre général', *Cahiers d'Economie Politique*, 7.

(1985a) 'Prix, taux de profit et étalons', *Revue d'Economie Politique*, January.

(1985b) 'La production jointe un point de vue néoclassique', contribution to The Round Table 'The influence of the production of commodities by means of commodities in France', Latapses, Sophia-Antipolis, December.

(1988) 'La production jointe: le point de vue de l'équilibre général', *Revue Economique*, March.

Baldone, S. (1974) *Fixed Capital in Sraffa's Theoretical Scheme*, Studi Economici.

Barthélemy, D. (1982) 'Propriété foncière et fonds-entreprise', Economica.

Baumol, W. (1967) 'Macroeconomics of unbalanced growth: the anatomy of urban crisis', American Economic Review, June.

Benzoni, L. (1985) 'Elements pour une théorie des ressources épuisables – contribution à l'analyse du marché du gaz naturel', doctoral thesis, Paris-XIII University, France.

Berrebi, Z.M. (1981) 'Comparaison de techniques et normes de prix', Revue Economique, 09.

Bidard, Ch. (1978) 'Sur le system étalon de Sraffa', Revue d'Economie Politique, September.

(1981) 'Travail et salaire chez Sraffa', Revue Economique, May.

(1982a) 'Technologie et production jointe', mimeo, Paris-X University, France.

(1982b) 'La notion d'indécomposabilité', mimeo, Paris-X University, France.

(1983) 'Sur les systèmes joints non fondamentaux', mimeo, Paris-X University, France.

(1984a) 'The extended Perron-Frobenius theorem and joint production', mimeo, Paris-X University, France.

(1984b) Choix Techniques en production jointe', in La production jointe – Nouveaux débats, Economica.

(1984c) 'Efficience, concurrence et salaire réel', in G. Abraham-Frois (1984).

(1986) 'Is von Neumann square?', Journal of Economics and Zeitschift Für Nationalökonomie, 46, 407–19.

(1987) La rente. Actualité de l'approche classique, Economica.

Bidard, Ch. (ed.) (1984) La production jointe – Nouveaux débats, Economica.

Bliss, C.J. (1975) Capital Theory and Distribution of Income, North Holland.

Bortkiewicz, L. von (1907) 'On the correction of Marx's theoretical construction in the third volume of Capital', in Sweezy, P. (1949).

(1952) 'Value and prices in the Marxian system', International Economic Papers, 2.

Boudhiaf, M. (1985) 'Generalisation des résultats de Ricardo, à biens fondamentaux', mimeo, University of Economic Science and Law at Tunis, Tunisia.

Brody, A. (1970) Proportions, Prices and Planning, North Holland.

Bromek, T. (1974) 'Consumption–investment frontier in von Neumann models', in J. Los and M.W. Los (eds.), Mathematical Models in Economics, North Holland.

Burmeister, E. (1980) Capital Theory and Dynamics, Cambridge University Press.

Burnell, St. (1982) 'Three essays on Sraffa, basic commodities and joint production', discussion paper 19, Victoria University, Wellington, New Zealand.

Cass, D. (1972) 'On capital overaccumulation in the aggregative neo-classical model of economic growth: a complete characterization', Journal of Economic Theory, 4.

Catz, F. and Laganier, J. (1982) 'Un théorème de mathématique pour l'économie suivie de quelques applications à la propagation de l'inflation', Cahiers de la Faculté des Sciences Economiques de Grenoble, 2.

(1984) 'La Gravitation inflationiste autour des prix de production', presentation at a symposium 'Gravitation' organized by R.C.P. 'System of production prices', Paris-X University, France.

Champerowne, D.G. (1945–6) 'A note on J. von Neumann's article on "A model of economic equilibrium"', *Review of Economic Studies*, 8(1), 33.

Dana, R.A., Florenzano M., Le Van, C. and Levy, D. (1984) 'Production prices and general equilibrium prices', document 8422, CEPREMAP.

Dana, R.A. and Levy, D. (1984) 'Comportement asymptotique de l'équilibre général', document 8423, CEPREMAP.

Dumenil, G. and Levy, D. (1982) 'Valeur et prix de production le cas des productions jointes', *Revue Economique*, January.

(1983) 'Classiques et néo-classiques', document 8325, CEPREMAP.

(1984) 'Une restauration de l'analyse classique de la dynamique concurrentielle', presentation at the symposium 'Gravitation', Paris-X University, France.

Faccarello, G. and Lavergne, Ph. (1977) *Une nouvelle approche en économie politique?* Economica.

Flaschel, P. (1983) 'Actual labour values in general model of production', *Econometrica*, March.

(1986) 'Sraffa's standard commodity no fulfilment of Ricardo's dream of "an invariable measure of value"', *Journal of Institutional and Theoretical Economics*, 142.

Fujimori, Y. (1982) *Modern Analysis of Value Theory*, Springer-Verlag.

Galiegue, X. (1985) 'Le capital fixe dans les models de production', doctoral thesis, Paris-X University, France.

Gantmacher, F.R. (1966) *Theorie des matrices*, Dunod.

Garegnani, P. (1984) 'Value and distribution in the classical economists and Marx', *Oxford Economic Papers*, 36.

Hageman, H. and Kurz, H.D. (1976) 'The return of the same truncation period and reswitching of technique in neo-Austrian and more general models', *Kyklos*, 29, 4.

Hahn, F.H. (1982) 'The neo-Ricardians', *Cambridge Journal of Economics*, December.

Hayek, F.A. von (1935) *Prices and Production*, G. Routledge and Sons Ltd.

Jorgenson, D.W. and Griliches, Z. (1967) 'The explanation of productivity change', *Review of Economic Studies*, July.

Koopmans, T.C. (1951) 'Analysis of production as an efficient combination of activities', in T.C. Koopmans (ed.), *Activity Analysis of Production and Allocation*, J. Wiley and Sons.

Kurz, H.D. (1978) 'Rent theory in a multisectorial model', *Oxford, Economic Papers*, March.

Lacaze, D. (1976a) 'Théorie des prix et décentralisation des décisions par dualité', CNRS.

(1976b) *Croissance et dualité en économie Marxiste*, Economica.

Lecouteux, E. (1982) 'Principes économiques de la culture ameliorante', quoted by D. Barthélemy (1982).

Levy D. (1984) 'Le formalisme unificateur du surclassement', in Ch. Bidard (ed.).

Malinvaud, E. (1981) *Théories Macro-Economiques*, Dunod.

(1982) *Leçon de théorie microéconomique*, Dunod, 4th edition.

Manara, C.F. (1968) 'Il modello di Piero Sraffa per la produzione congiunta di merci a mezzo di merci', *L'industria*, vol. I, pp. 3–18.

Mangasarian, O.L. (1971) 'Perron-Frobenius properties of $Ax-\lambda Bx$', *Journal of Mathematical Analysis and Applications*, 36.

Marx, K. *Collected Works*.

Miyao, Takahiro (1977) 'A generalisation of Sraffa's standard commodity and its complete characterisation', *International Economic Revue*, February.

Montani, G. (1972) 'La théorie ricardienne de la rente', *Industria*, 3–4.

(1975) 'Scarce natural resources and income distribution', *Metroeconomica*, 1.

Morgenstern, O. and Thompson, G.L. (1976) *Mathematical Theory of Expanding and Contracting Economies*, D.C. Heath.

Morishima, M. (1969) *Theory of Economic Growth*, Clarendon Press.

(1973) *Marx's Economics – A Dual Theory of Value and Growth*, Cambridge University Press.

(1974) 'Marx, in the light of modern economic theory', *Econometrica*, July.

(1976) 'Positive profits with negative surplus value; a comment', *Economic Journal*, December.

Morishima, M. and Catephores, G. (1978) *Value, Exploitation and Growth*, McGraw Hill.

Neumann, J. von (1945–6) 'A model of general equilibrium', *Review of Economic Studies*, 13(1), 33.

Newman, P. (1962) 'Production of commodities by means of commodities', *Schweizerische, Zeitschrift für Volkswirtschaf und Statistik*, 98.

Newman, P. and Sraffa, P. (1982) 'Correspondence', reproduced in G. Faccarella and Ph. Lavergn, *Une nouvelle approche en économie politique?* Economica, 1977.

Nikaido, H. and Koyabashi, S. (1978) 'Dynamics of wage-price spiral and stagflation in the Leontief–Sraffa system', *International Economic Review*, February

Okishio, N. (1961) Technical change and the rate of profit, *Kobe University Economic Review*, pp. 86–99.

(1972) 'On Marx's production prices', *Keizaigaku Kenkyu*, 19.

Parys, W. (1982) 'Standard commodities and the transformation problem', mimeo, UFSIA, University of Anvers.

Pasinetti, L. (1977) *Lectures on the Theory of Production*, Columbia University Press.

Pasinetti, L. (ed.) (1980a) *Essays on the Theory of Joint Production*, Macmillan.

(1980b) 'A note on the basics, non basics and joint production', in Pasinetti, 1980a.

Quadrio, Curzio A. (1967) *Rendita e distribuzione in un modello economico plurisettoricale*, Guiffré.

(1980) 'Rent, income distribution and orders of efficiency and rentability' in L. Pasinetti (1980a).

Regnault, H. (1984) 'Fertilité naturelle et révolution agricole d'une évidence ricardienne à l'échec de l'économie Marxienne' doctoral thesis, Paris-I University, France.

Ricardo, D. (1984) *The Principles of Political Economy and Taxation*, Dent.

Rongalia, A. (1978) *Sraffa and the Theory of Prices*, John Wiley and Sons.

Salvadori, N. (1981) 'Falling rate of profit with a constant real wage: an example', *Cambridge Journal of Economics*.

(1982) 'Existence of cost-minimizing systems within the Sraffa framework', *Zeitschrift für Nationalökonomie*, September.

(1984) 'Le choix de techniques chez Sraffa, le cas de la production jointe' in *La Production Jointe*, Economica.

(1985) 'Fixed capital within linear models of production and distribution', mimeo.

Samuelson, P.A. (1971) 'Understanding the Marxian notion of exploitation a summary of the so-called transformation problem between Marxian values and competitive prices', *Journal of Economic Literature*, 9.

Saucier, Ph. (1981) 'Le choix des techniques en situation de limitation de resources', doctoral thesis, Paris-II University, France.

(1984a) 'L'évolution des rentes dans une économie en croissance', in G. Abraham-Frois.

(1984b) 'La production jointe en situation de concurrence', in Ch. Bidard (ed.).

Schefold, B. (1976) 'Relative prices as a function of the rate of profit', *Zeitschrift für–Nationalökonomie*, 36.

(1978a) 'Multiple product techniques with properties of single product systems', *Zeitschrift für Nationalökonomie*, 38, 1–2.

(1978b) 'On counting equations', *Zeitschrift für Nationalökonomie*, 38, 3–4.

(1984) 'Marchandises résiduelles et procès facultatifs', in Ch. Bidard (ed.).

(1985a) 'Sraffa and applied economics joint production', *Political Economy*, 1.

(1985b) 'On changes in the composition of output', Conference on Sraffa's *Production of Commodities*, Florence, August.

(1985c) 'Cambridge price theory special model or general theory of value?', *American Economic Review Papers and Proceedings*, May.

(1986) 'The standard commodity as a tool of economic analysis – a comment on Flaschel', *Journal of Institutional and Theoretical Economics*.

(1989) *Mr. Sraffa on Joint Production and Other Essays*, Unwin Hyman.

Schneider, T. (1985) 'Valeur travail et production jointe', doctoral thesis, Paris-X University, France.

Schumpeter, J. (1954) *History of Economic Analysis*, Allen and Unwin.

Schwartz, J.T. (1961) *Lectures on the Mathematical Method in Analytical Economics*, Gordon and Breach, London.

Shaikh, A. (1977) 'Marx's theory of value and the transformation problem', in *The Subtle Anatomy of Capitalism*, Goodyear Publishing.

Solow, R.M. and Samuelson, P.A. (1953) 'Balanced growth under constant returns to scale', *Econometrica*, July.

Sraffa, P. (1960) *Production of Commodities by Means of Commodities*, Cambridge University Press, 1960.

(1970) *The Works and Correspondence of D. Ricardo*.

Steedman, I. (1975) 'Positive profits with negative surplus value', *Economic Journal*, March.

(1980) 'Basics, non-basics and joint production', in Pasinetti (1980a).

(1984) 'L'importance empirique de la production jointe', in Ch. Bidard (ed.).

Sweezy, P.M. (1942) *The Theory of Capitalist Development*, Oxford University Press.

(1949) *Karl Marx, and the Close of the System*, A.M. Kelley.

Takeda, S. (1983) 'Joint production and a discontinuous switch on the wage–profit frontier', mimeo.

Thompson, G.L and Morgenstern, O. (1976) *Mathematical Theory of Expanding and Contracting Economics*, D.C. Heath.

Vidonne, P. (1982) 'Le paradoxe d'Anderson', *Cahiers d'Economie Politique*, 7.

Vincent, A. (1968) *La mesure de la productivité*, Dunod.

Walsh, V. and Gram, H. (1980) *Classical and New Classical Theories of General Equilibrism*, Oxford University Press.

Zaghini, E. (1967) 'On non-basic commodities', *Schweizerische, Zeitschrift für Volkswirtschaf und Statistik*, 2.

Index

linearisation of, 51–2, 58, 71–4, 84, 138, 202
and standard of value, 134, 135, 138
wages, 150, 153, 166, 167, 173, 230, 234
  advanced, and Marx's analysis, 185–7
  'advanced' and paid 'post factum', 55–8
  and exogenous rate of profit, 212–13
  as exogenous variable, 213–16
  maximisation and cost minimisation, 180–3
  optimisation and production prices, 206, 210–11, 213–16
  and prices, 45
  and productivity surplus, 260–2
  rigidity to decrease, 221–4
  and standard commodity, 134
  and surplus distribution, 43–4, 46
  see also advanced wage; wage prices; wage–profit relation
wants, 150, 178, 187, 198, 213, 222, 225
  see also demand
wheat, 41, 183, 217, 243
  and changes in production conditions, 241
  and classification of goods in decomposable system, 65–6

different returns per acre but identical unit costs, 239–40
exchange values of, 42, 43
fertility order and differential rent, 232–6
fertility order and profitability order, 236–8
and fixed life span of machines, 200–1
intensification process, 250, 258
and intensive and differential rents, 257–8
and machines in joint production, 201–2, 203, 206
one cultivation method on uniform plot of land, 244–5, 254
price of, and cultivation method, 229, 233, 239, 240, 248
several production methods available, 245–50
and standard of value, 132–4
variations in price of, 250–3
workers, 167, 174, 183, 198, 199, 221, 222
  and consumption goods, 166
  and golden rule of prices, 13–14, 158
  surplus distribution to, 45–6
  wages of, 43–4
  wants, 150

Printed in the United States
By Bookmasters